INK! INK!
WHAT DO YOU THINK?

Linnea R. Strand

Copyrighted Material

Ink! Ink! What do you think?
Copyright © 2020 by Linnea R. Strand. All Rights Reserved.
No part of this publication may be reproduced, stored in a retrieval system or transmitted, in any form or by any means - electronic, mechanical, photocopying, recording or otherwise - without prior written permission from the publisher, except for the inclusion of brief quotations in a review.

For information about this title
or to order other books and/or electronic media,
contact the publisher:

Bethel1808 Publishers
Lewisville, TX 75057
www.Bethel1808.com
Info@Bethel1808.com

ISBNs for Ink! Ink! What do you think?
Softcover: 978-1-947201-40-8
eBook:978-1-947201-41-5

Printed in the United States of America

Memories....

This book is a book of memories.
Not just my memories, but yours too.

As I was clearing out a cabinet one day, I came across an old pastebook, we call them scrapbooks today. But this one was different. There were almost no words, but it was full of all the wonderful stories my grandmother and I shared when I was young. As I flipped through the pages of my grandmother's old pastebook, the memories came flooding back. I remembered her words, her smile and her curious view of life through these ink blots.

Grandma and I would make ink blots almost every day. We would spread ink in different fashions all over a piece of paper and then fold it in half. When we would open it, an entirely new world of discovery would open up to us. Maybe you see it too. Maybe you see the faces looking at you on page 6. Maybe you can see the bearded cowboy on page 82. You may need to squint your eyes or even back up five feet away. You may have to turn the page upside down or look at it with a flashlight. Let your mind find the picture that is there just for you.

These pages are filled with the stories that I saw when I was a nine year old girl experiencing life with my grandmother. But even more than that, these pages are filled with the pictures that will inspire memories for you. There are no wrong answers so turn the page and start making your memories.
What do you think?
Linnea Strand

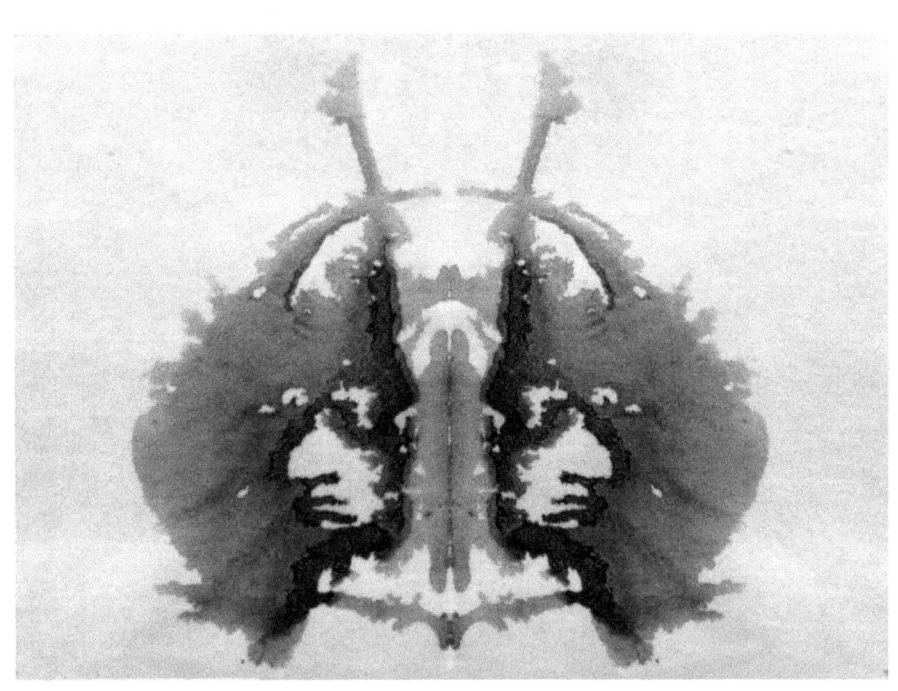

"Where are we going today, grandma?" Grandma humming grabbed the umbrella. "Why do we need that?" Still no answer. Grandma Ellen smiled, and announced we're going to the ocean. Oh boy, the beach!

On the train I realized we didn't bring bathing suits. As we stepped off the train, no beach or sand was in sight, just ugly metal buildings. I followed as we headed towards some fishing boats. Smelly, wiggly fish were everywhere on the dock. Yuk.

Everybody was busy, except two men that were arguing. They were yelling at each other, but I couldn't hear what the fight was about. One pushed and then the other shoved. Now they were rolling on the ground as they punched each other. "Hey watch out!" Splash, they rolled over the edge into the water. All the men on the dock were roaring with laughter.

Grandma opened up her umbrella, held it high above us, and chuckled as we went our way.

What do you think?

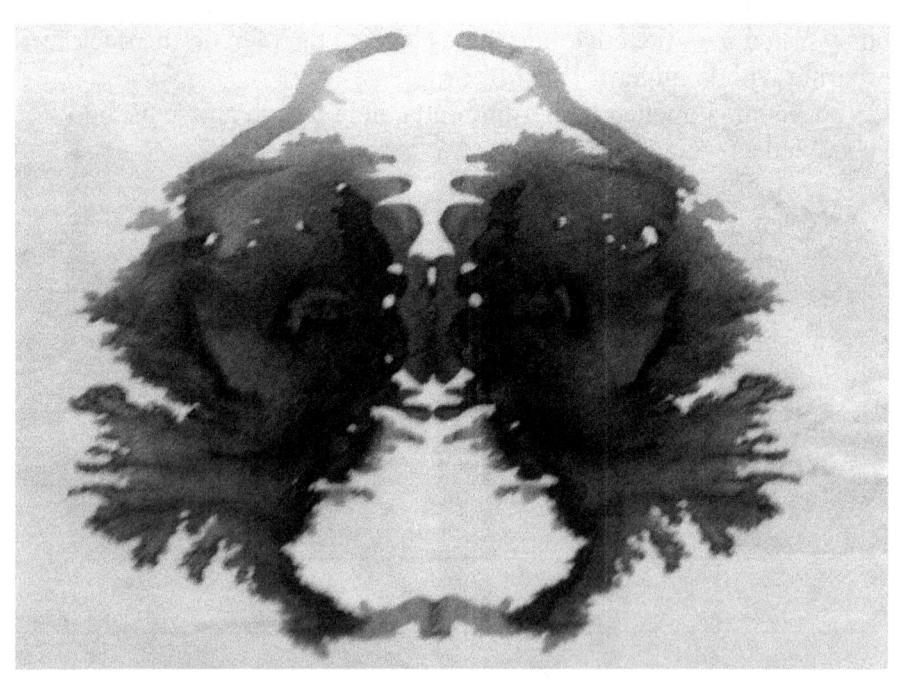

Grandma Ellen's living room hardly ever changed. But this one summer something was different. She had covered her couch with a pretty brown floral print. Seems to me grandma was not afraid to tackle any job. Glancing around the room I spotted some rather peculiar looking rectangular things. I reached for them, but they slipped out of my hand and fell to the floor. "Grandma, what are these?' Grandma just smiled and said they were pillows she had covered to match the couch. "Pillows?" These weren't even soft. They felt strange. "What's this small bump in the middle?" Turned out they were daily newspapers, stacked and tied together with string. The knot was the small bump. Grandma had simply covered the bundle and pronounced it a pillow.

What do you think?

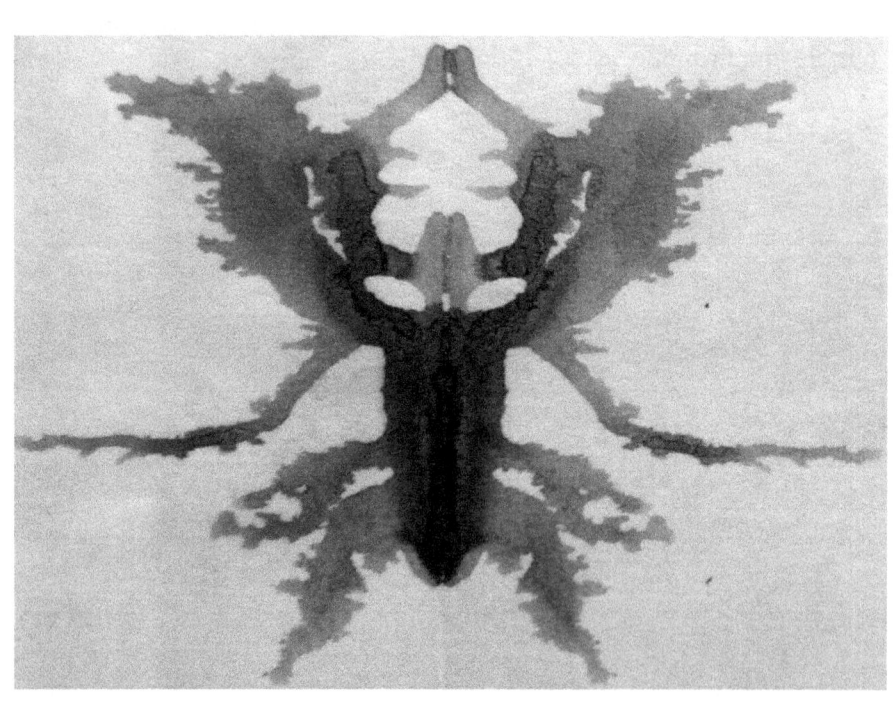

Grandma Ellen walked everywhere. So here we were again, crossing the railroad tracks and walking for blocks and blocks.

"Grandma, my feet hurt."

"You're fine."

"Grandma, look, J C Penny's, maybe I can try on new shoes?"

"No, we are going to take a train ride."

"But, we just crossed the tracks."

"There's another set of up ahead."

If you took the Pacific Electric train south, you, reached the ocean. Boarding the northbound PE took us all the way to the big city. Almost every summer grandma took me to the big city to visit her friends. And they never lived close to the PE tracks. More walking. I don't remember much about the visits, but this is where Grandma expected me to use her coffee drinking rules. She wanted the hostess to know that the coffee was perfect.

"Your first sip of hot coffee should be from the saucer, not the cup, and then you must exclaim: Aahh!"

What do you think?

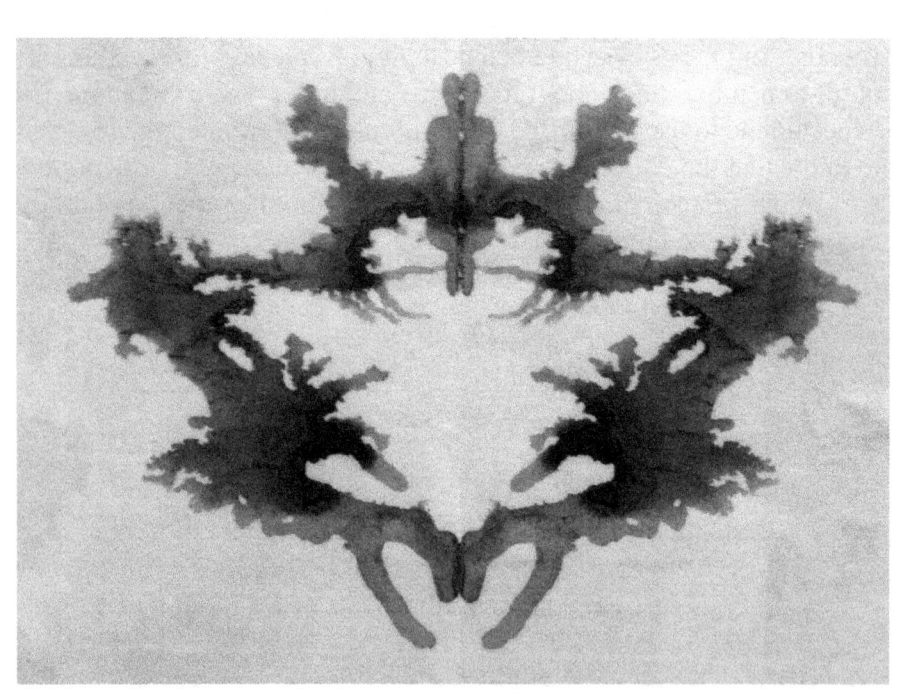

"Let's have a cup of coffee, Linnea."

Afternoons meant I got to drink coffee with grandma and grandpa. Of course, mine was mostly milk. "Here's a match, go light the stove." Oh no, not me! "But grandma I'm scared." The old stove had a mind of its own. Light the match, turn the gas burner on, put the match to it and POUF a flame reached the ceiling or thereabouts.

Grandpa said I did a good job, much better than grandma. It drove him crazy when grandma lit the oven. First grandma would turn on the gas, then she would wander around the kitchen looking for a match. The kitchen would fill with smelly gas. And then there would be a really giant POUF.

What do you think?

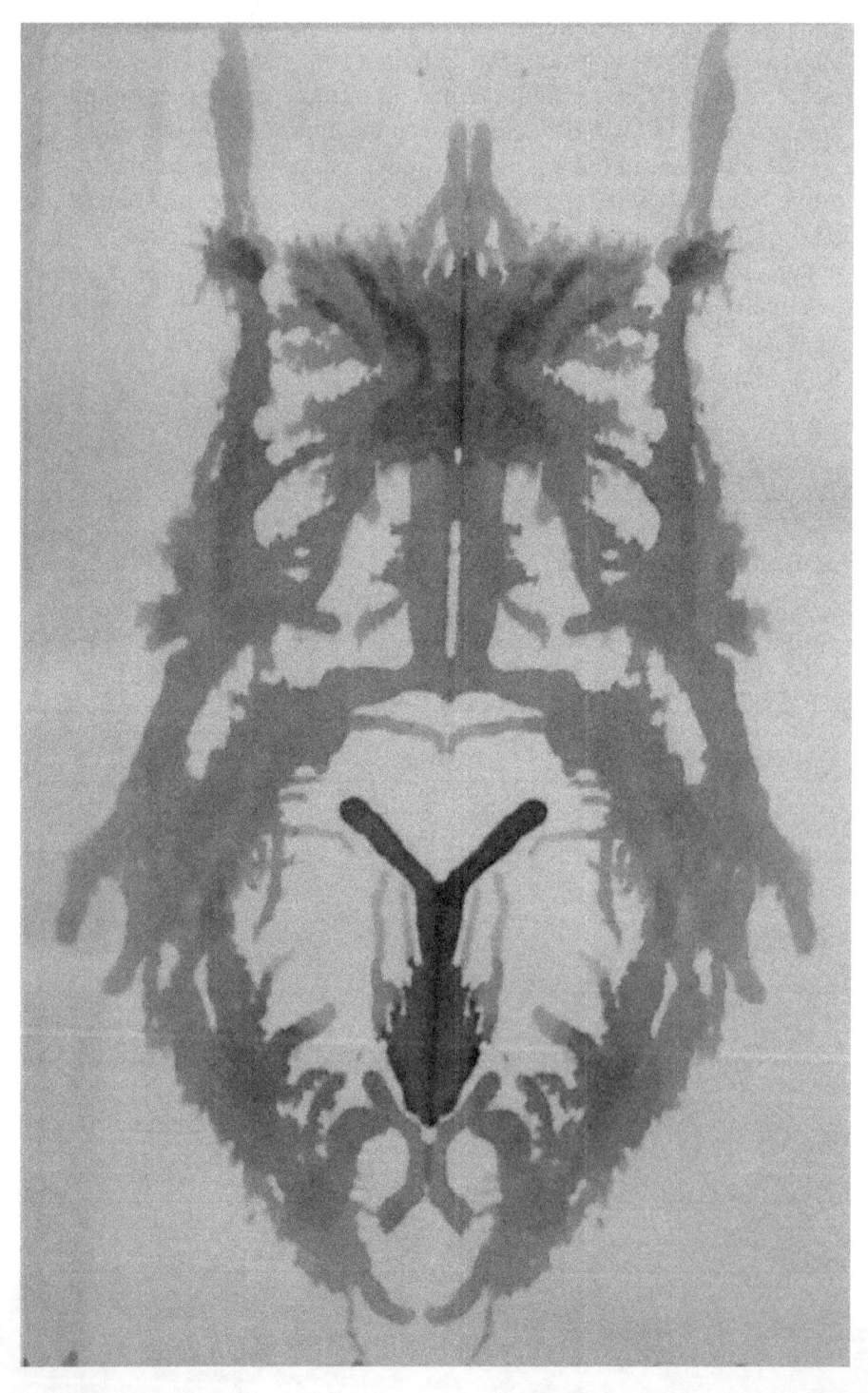

Ink! Ink! What do you think?

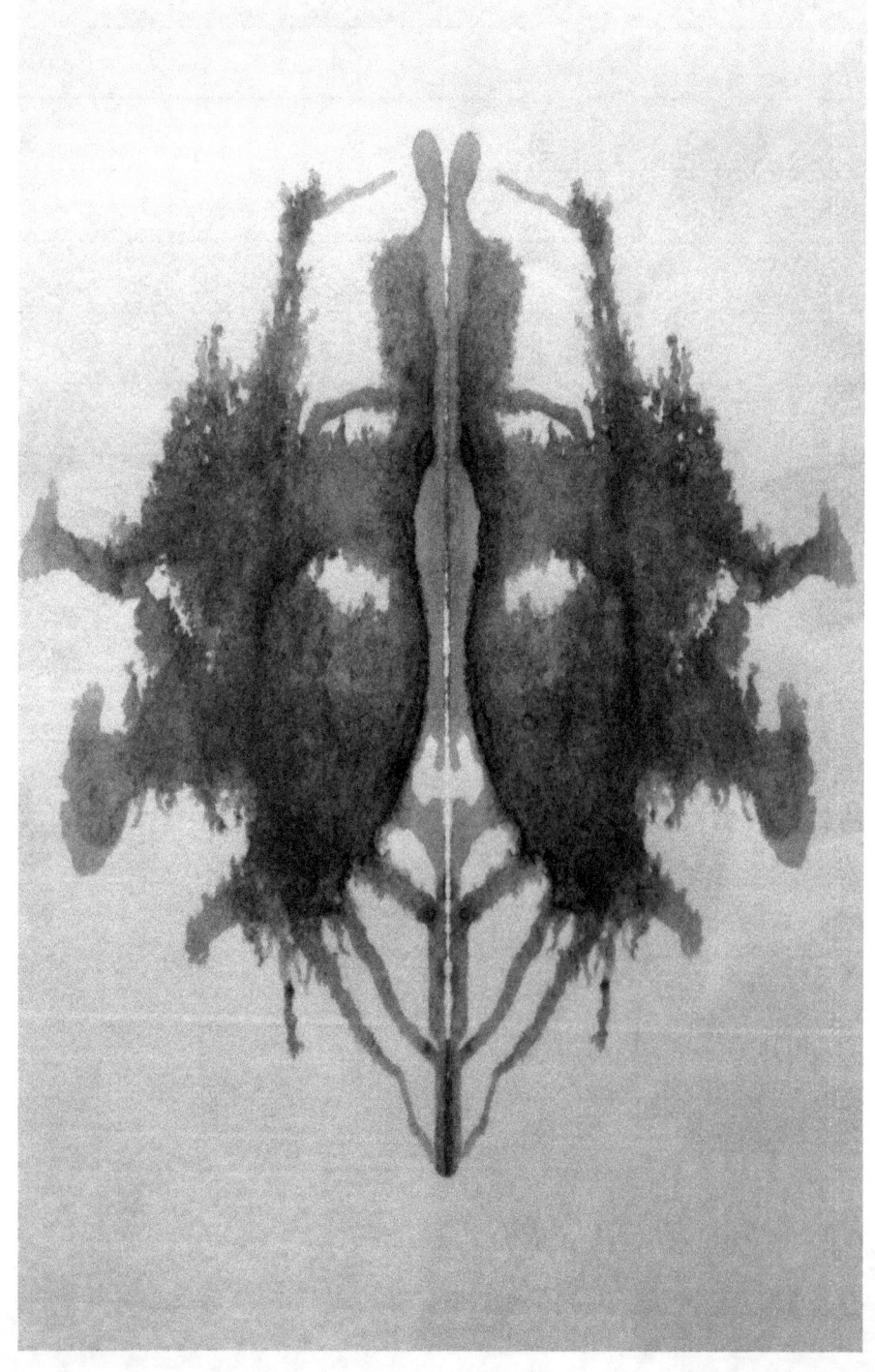

I almost forgot to tell you about the pillow grandma made for daddy at Christmas time. This pillow was something else. Stuffed tightly with so much cotton that it weighed five pounds. It could probably knock someone out in a pillow fight. I think I lost my balance once, just trying to toss it across the room.

It looked harmless as it laid on the couch. It even looked comfortable. But when daddy sat near the pillow, he would move quickly away. He was getting stuck with straight pins that work their way out from their hiding place inside the pillow. Don't remember how many times he pulled out a pin and exclaimed, "Your grandma doesn't like me!"

What do you think?

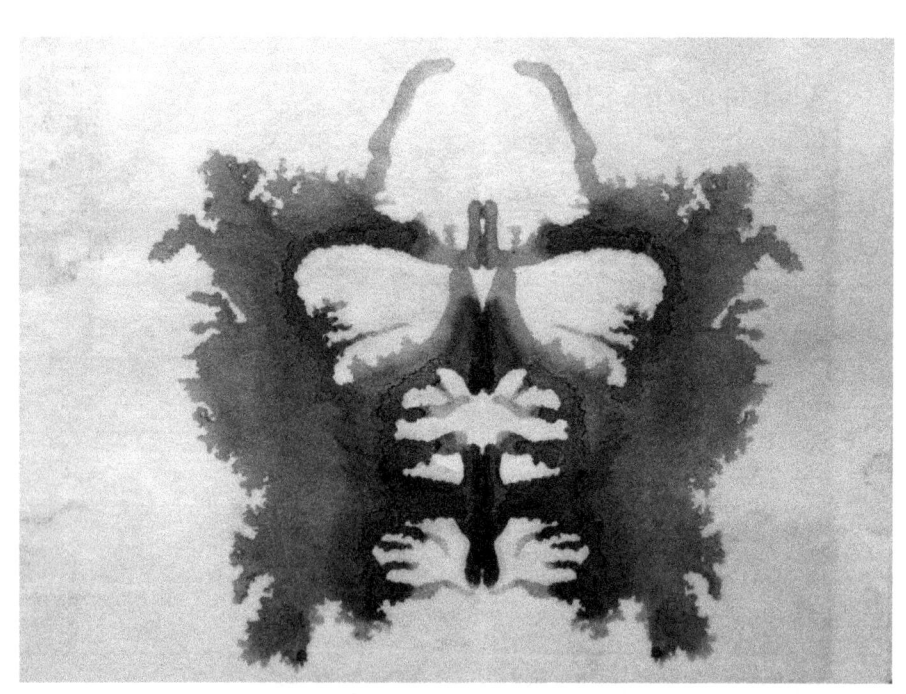

Birch trees were Grandma Ellen's favorite tree. "Every home should have at least three." She had five behind the house. An old metal bed frame created a seating area under those trees where grandma could sit. They were messy trees with lots of dried leaves and peeling bark on the ground. But the sound of a gentle breeze through those five trees was calming and reminded her of growing up in Finland.

It was from these trees that I made a scroll. We peeled off a large section of bark. I wrote a message to my daddy:

"Dear daddy yesterday grandma Ellen and
I made tobacco for your pipe.
Wait 'til you try it.
Grandma said you would certainly enjoy it."
Love Linnea

The "tobacco" I was referring to was dried crushed up Birch leaves. I'm sure he was not anxious to smoke those leaves, but he did put on a happy face and gave me a hug. I don't remember, but I sure hope he didn't really smoke it.

What do you think?

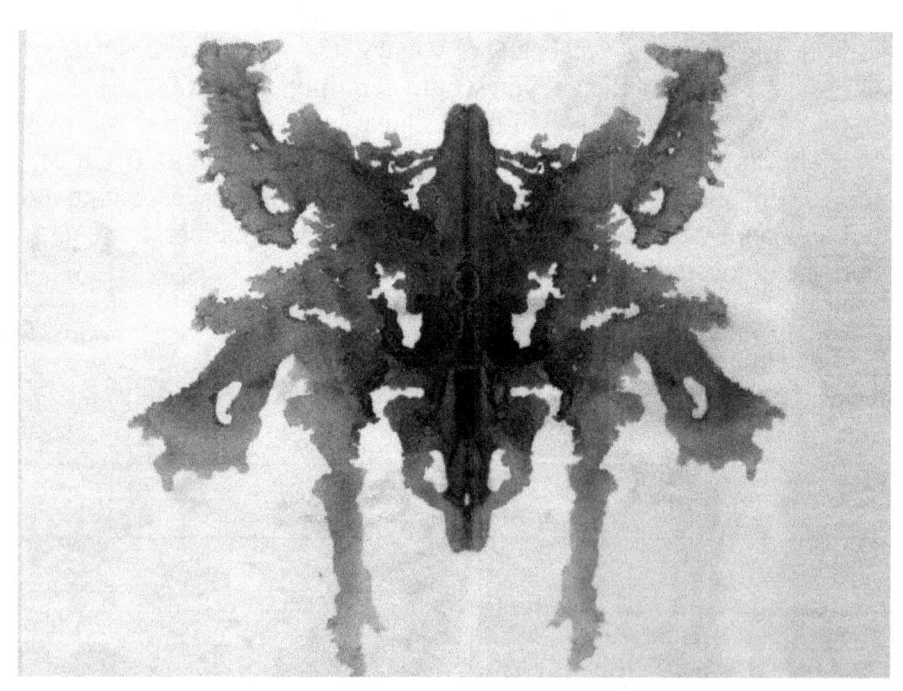

Grandma Ellen and I walked everywhere. This day we were headed to the market across the railroad tracks, dragging an empty two-wheeled cart behind us. We loaded the cart with ice cream, a watermelon, bananas and milk for me.

All of the cashiers and the manager knew my grandma. Each visit she put her grocery receipt in a bucket for the weekly drawing - $5 or $10 free groceries. She won so many times that she would have to remind the cashiers to give her the receipt.

Grandma whispered her winning secret to me and I am going to share it with you right now. Don't tell anybody, let's just keep this between you and me. Instead of letting her receipt float down to the bottom of the bucket to lay flat with the others, she folded it around her thumb, wrinkling it so it would find its way into any hand that was searching for a winner.

What do you think?

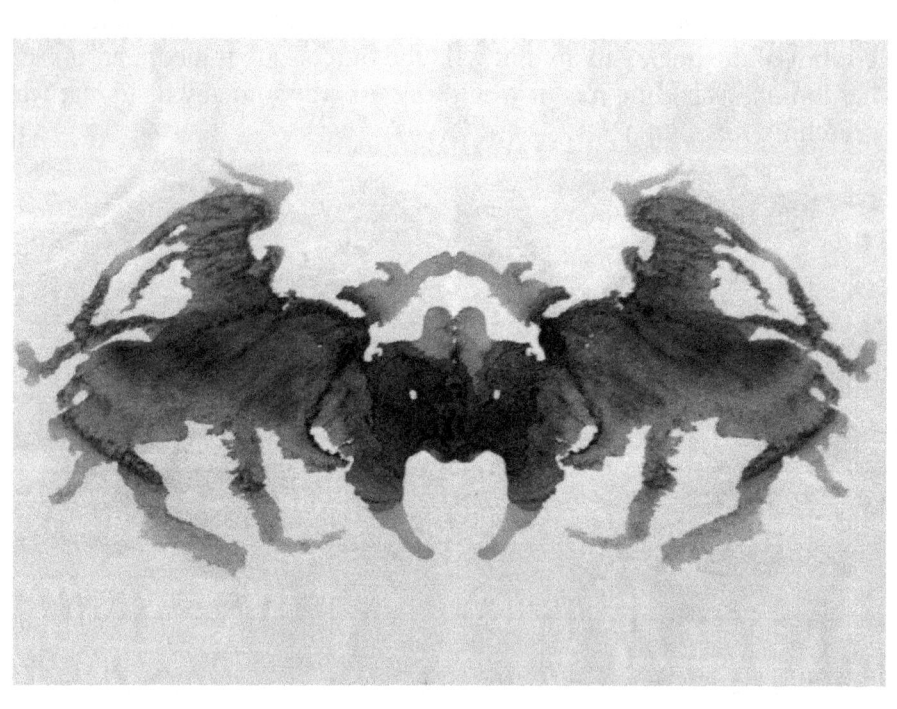

The bull fighter was surprised as he stood in the ring. The crowd of spectators was screaming with laughter. There was no large intimidating bull standing in the center of the ring. It was a buffalo.

What do you think?

If the shoe fits....

What do you think?

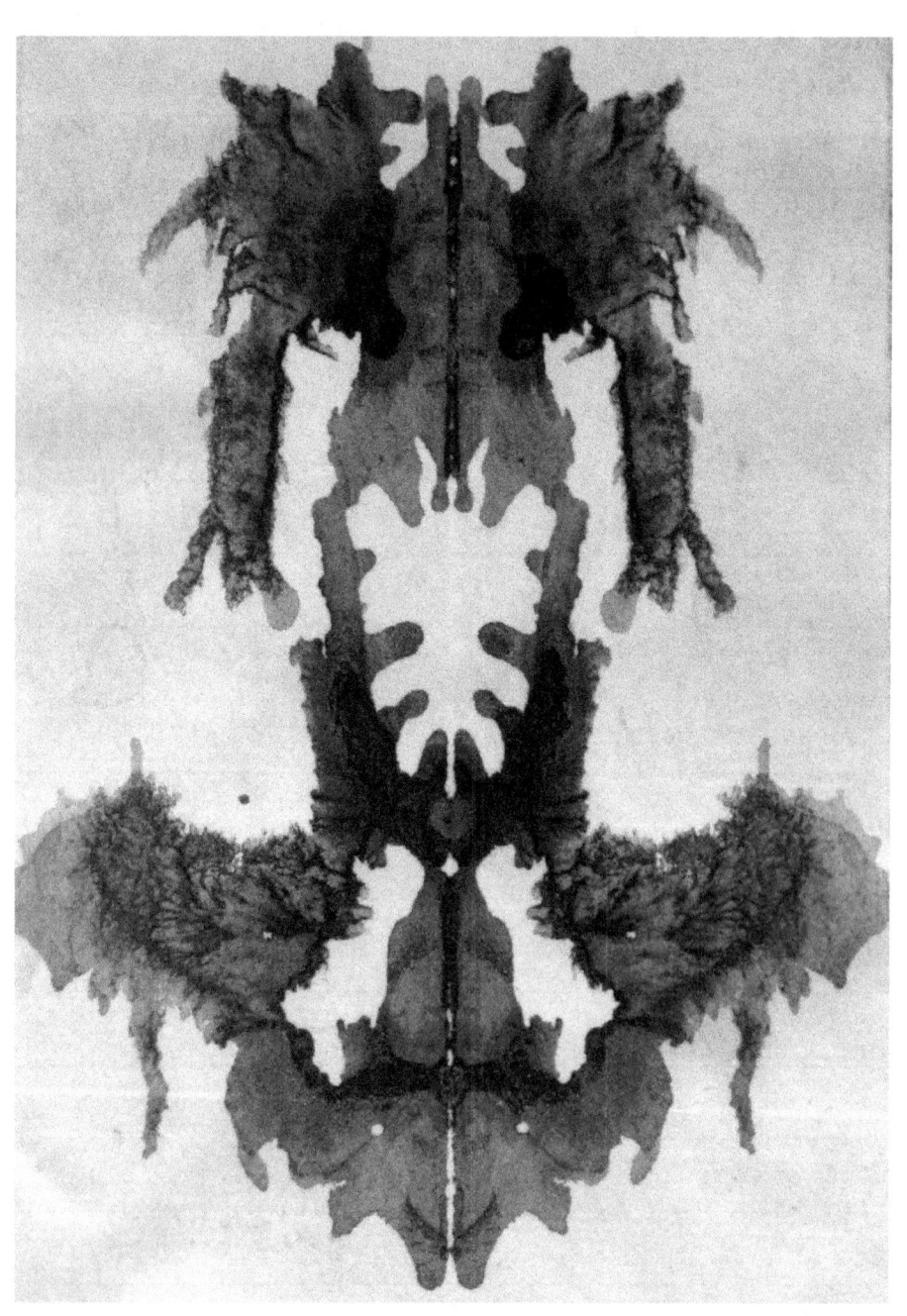

Sometimes Grandpa Swedman would walk me to the market. These trips were usually just to pick up a few items. I loved these trips, because he always put a dime in the store pony ride. It had a real leather saddle (as if I knew what real leather felt like). I sat on the pony until grandpa was ready, or another kid needed a turn.

One time the pony was trotting, no dime necessary. I jumped on it, galloped away into the desert, up the steep mountains, and across the sand dunes. Over to the north I saw a box canyon. The trail was narrow, The dampness of the canyon was cooling. I spotted a small pond. It would be a perfect place to build my hideout.

Suddenly, pony was bucking wildly, up and down and sideways. Then pony froze. What happened? Oh, the ride was over. Grandpa was patiently waiting for me to bring pony back to reality so we could walk home to Rose Ave.

What do you think?

Church service was over and I was suppose to be reading my book while daddy visited with the pastor. My eyes were having a hard time staying focused on my book. Just as my eyelids closed I thought I saw a tiny mouse scurrying by. I could hear mama mouse warning him. "Stay away from there, or you might end up like Cy." Uncle Cy disappeared last year, and all the mice in the field were sure he got lost in the church.

Tommy mouse wasn't afraid. He bragged about going to the patio. Tommy mouse talked about the yummy scraps on the floor. Yummy scraps. Little mouse could only think about yummy scraps. Maybe, just this once.

All the giants left the patio. Little mouse peeked around the corner. "Look at all the crumbs on the floor!" Stuffing his belly paying no attention to his surroundings, he bumped into a giant. Giant screamed, little mouse screamed. "Run,"he told his feet. "Run somewhere, run run run." Everything happened fast, suddenly a door slammed. It was quiet. That's how little mouse became "Church Mouse."

What do you think?

-

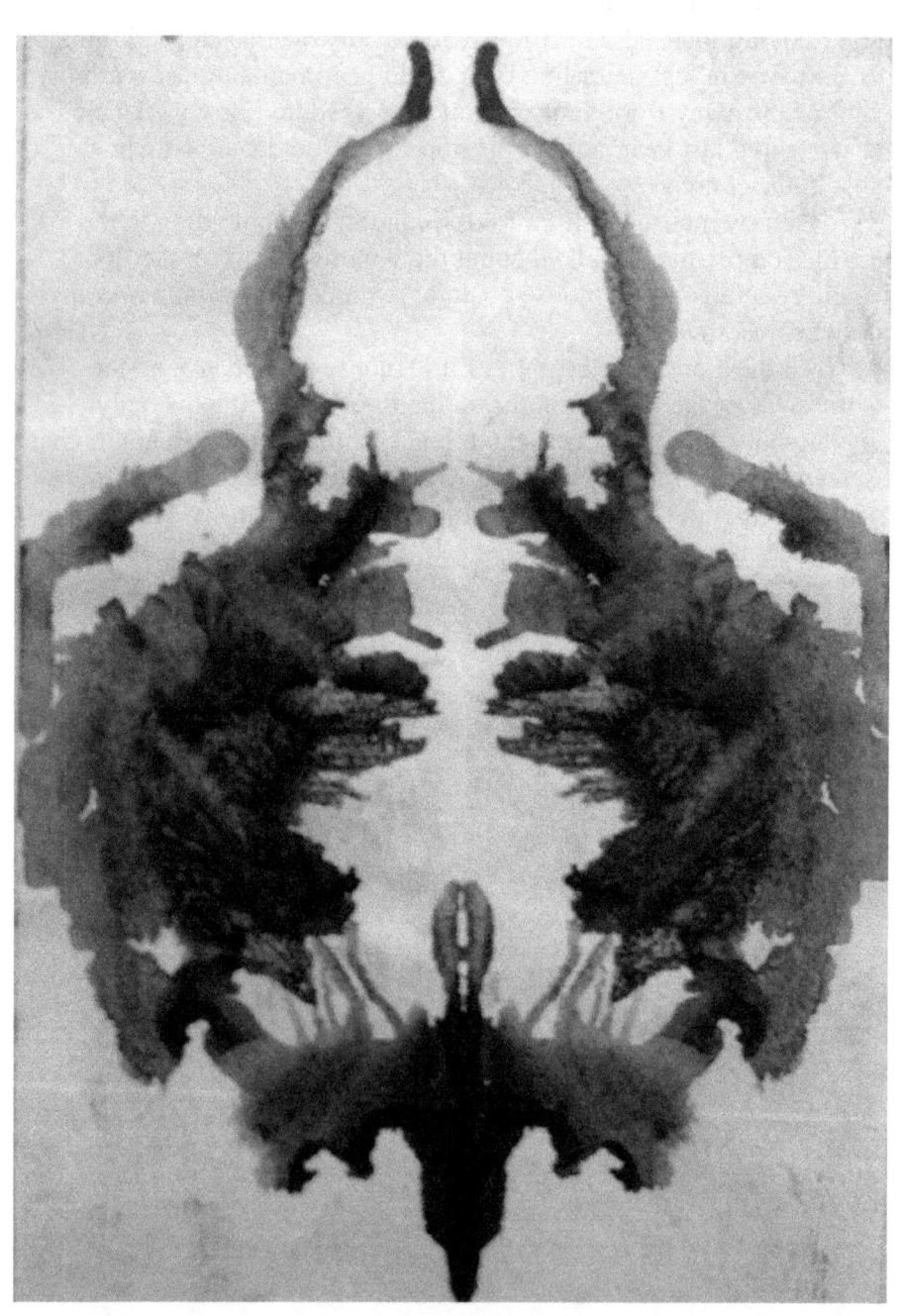

It is such a cute birdhouse. Yellow and green, tin roof, heart shaped doorway, bent spoon on the back for a perch, bent tea strainer at the door and a cake pan for the floor. Did I mention the Texas star placed just above that door?

Many baby birds had called this home. This year it was different. A pair of sparrows appeared happy to have found such a luxurious place. Then one day feathers were filtering out the door.

A single sparrow kept entering the birdhouse carrying out feathers. Many feathers, many trips. This went on all day. I wondered if a blue jay got to the mother? Grandpa said he could get rid of the blue jay. No, I told him. I liked the blue jay too. After all, it's just the "Circle of Life."

Should I open up the birdhouse and check?

What do you think?

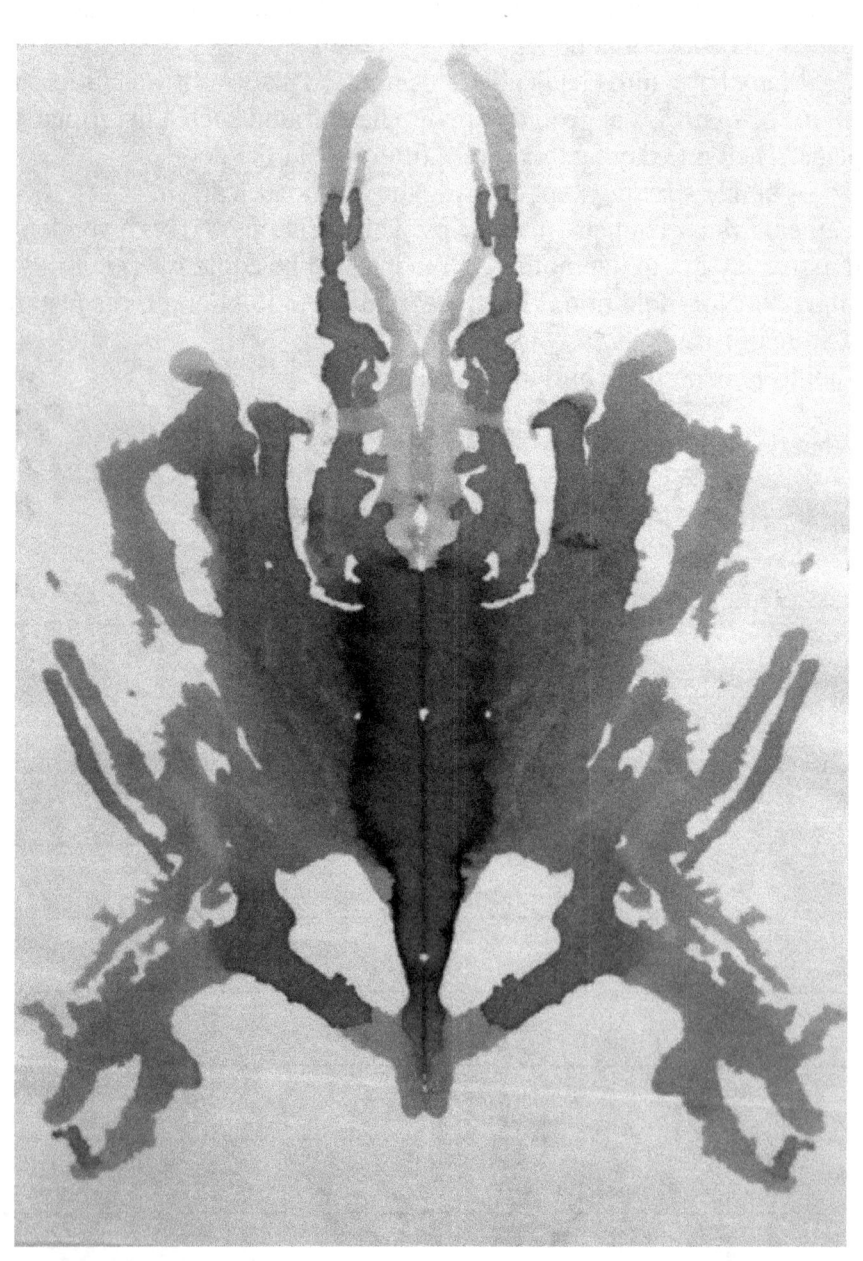

I think letter writing is a thing of the past. It is fun to explore an old trunk and find hand written letters. They can tell you how your family history. A soldier proposes to his gal via the mail. (A future he hopes for). A mother writes to her daughter about her college experiences. (Go to my school, it was great.) A dad leaves a note in his tackle box telling his son how this fish hook caught the biggest fish in the lake. (Here's wishing you good luck in the future).

I have a few bundles of old letters from the 1930's. Grandma Ellen tied them together with old string. Releasing a bundle, began an afternoon of exploring my family history.

I was reading letters that grandma wrote to grandpa many years ago. Grandma had an accident boarding a streetcar that lurched forward when she was halfway aboard. She wore a back brace for months. In several of the letters she mentioned the money she got from the streetcar company. It was enough to move the whole family across the country. I can see by those letters "from" the past how my future was formed.

What do you think?

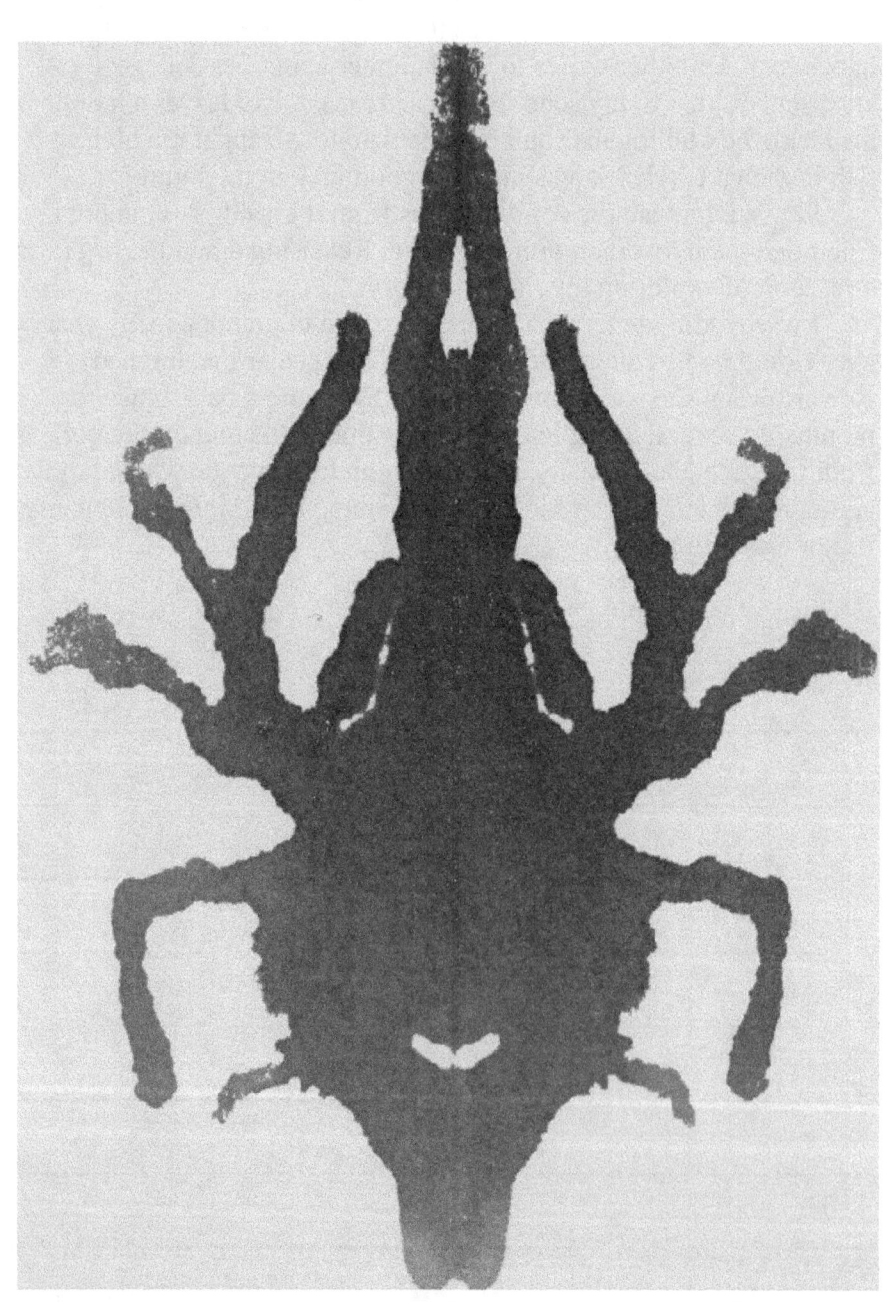

"I'm right!" "No, you're not!" The two doves were arguing again. Papa dove flew in to settle them down. "What's the problem now?" "Oh, papa, Dewy won't leave me alone." "Me? I am trying to keep Lizbird safe." "All Dewy wants to do is argue, argue, argue. He thinks I should be afraid of brown dog, but I'm not." "Lizbird wants to go play in the birdbath, and brown dog could hurt her!"

Papa glanced down at brown dog, who was busy digging a hole. Lizbird and Dewy continued fighting. Dewy was telling her how he had seen brown dog jump higher than the fence, just to see the garbage man. Lizbird said she wasn't a garbage man. Dewy said brown dog runs fast. Lizbird didn't care, she'd been to the bird bath and down to the grass when brown dog was sleeping. Papa knew brown dog rarely chased birds, he'd rather go after squirrels.

"Papa, Dewy always has to be right, even if he is wrong. He won't give up. I get so tired of him never agreeing with me." Papa decided it was time to settle this once and for all. He whispered to Lizbird what she could tell Dewy to make him be quiet. Just say, "you could be right."

What do you think?

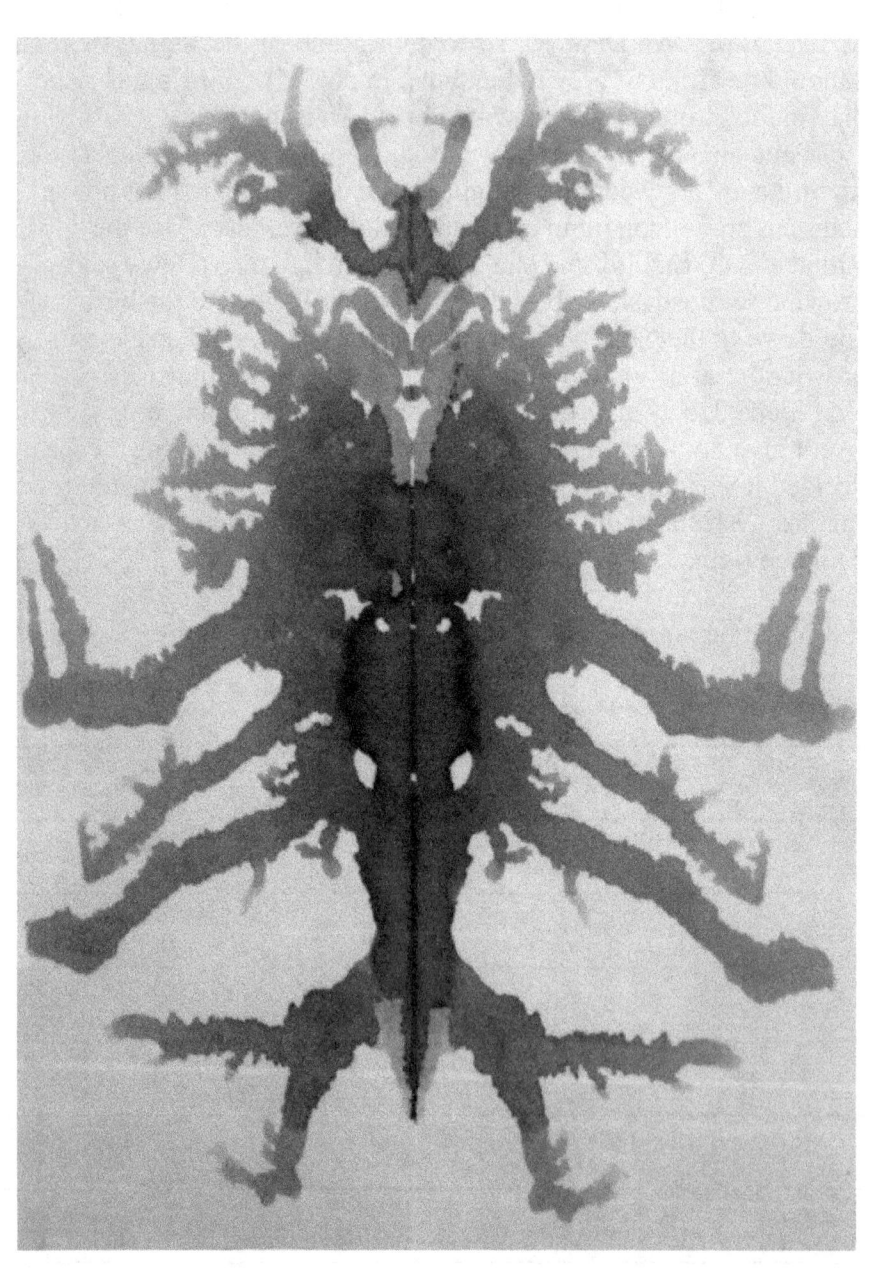

School had been interesting today. Teacher had taken us on an imaginary trip to Spain. I even dressed up in my colorful yellow scarf and circular skirt. My tap shoes were a hit at school, although teacher gave me "the look" when my feet wouldn't stay still during the presentation.

Walking up the driveway I noticed the fake rubber snakes grandpa put in the hedges to scare the birds. Sometimes grandpa would toss one of them high into the mulberry tree. I unlatched the gate and entered the yard only to see that one of the fake snakes had fallen out of the bushes.

I thought maybe I could toss it high like grandpa. As I reached down to grab it, is slithered away.

"AAAAH…! MOTHER !…. AAAAH….!

Mother heard my screams, and knew something was very wrong. She came rushing to the side door, swung open the screen door, and called out to me as she was stepping outside.. "What's wrong?"

"SNAKE, mom, it's a real snake!" I cried.

Mom quickly jumped inside the house, slammed shut the screen door, and as I heard her slip the lock into place she said, "Go around to the back door."

What do you think?

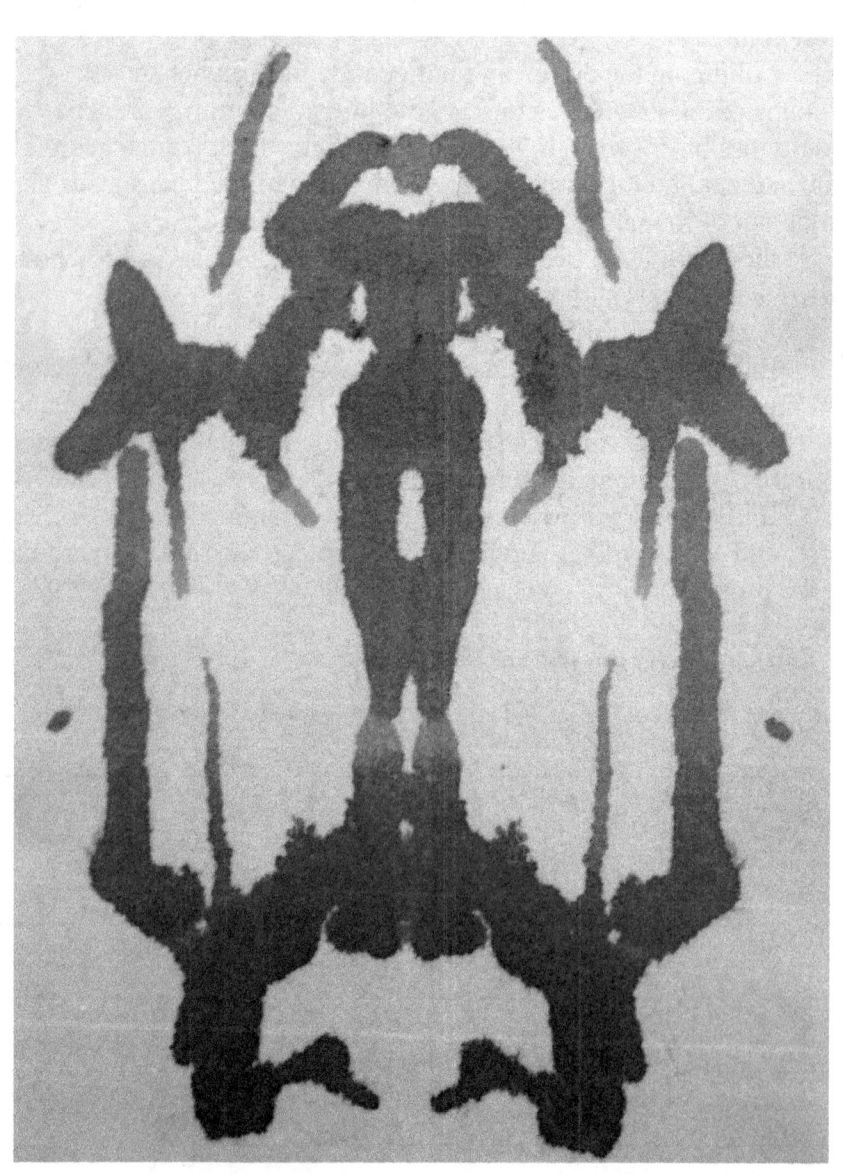

Grandma Ellen was a licensed therapist, skilled in the art of Swedish massage. So at least once during my visits I would get a massage. I did not exactly look forward to them. They were relaxing and felt good, except when grandma found a muscle knot. I remember laying on my tummy thinking if I didn't react, she wouldn't find any sore muscles. But, her skilled hands found them and worked over those areas, in spite of my protests, until the knot was gone.

During the 1940's they owned a Swedish Steambath and Massage business. My mom, Ester, and my uncle Gus went to the same school that grandma attended. So, the steambath became a family business. Grandpa ran the steam room and did general maintenance. A bath was fifty cents and a massage was also fifty cents. Ester and Gus and grandma were the massage therapists. Ester, a petite lady, often spoke about the heavyweight wrestlers that were her customers. Massaging their super bulky shoulders and muscles was a real workout for her. But the wrestlers were generous. They left her a one dollar tip!

What do you think?

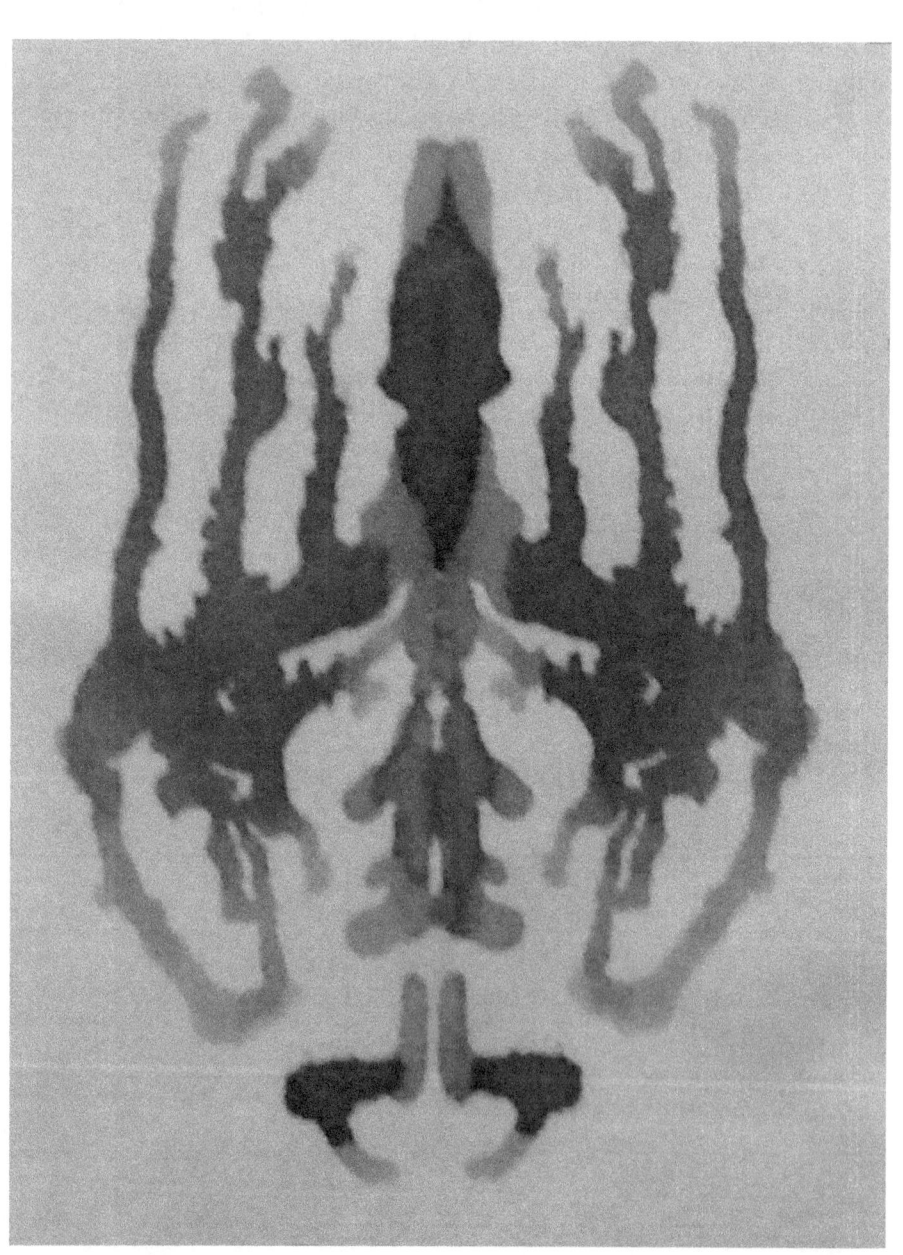

Ink! Ink! What do you think?

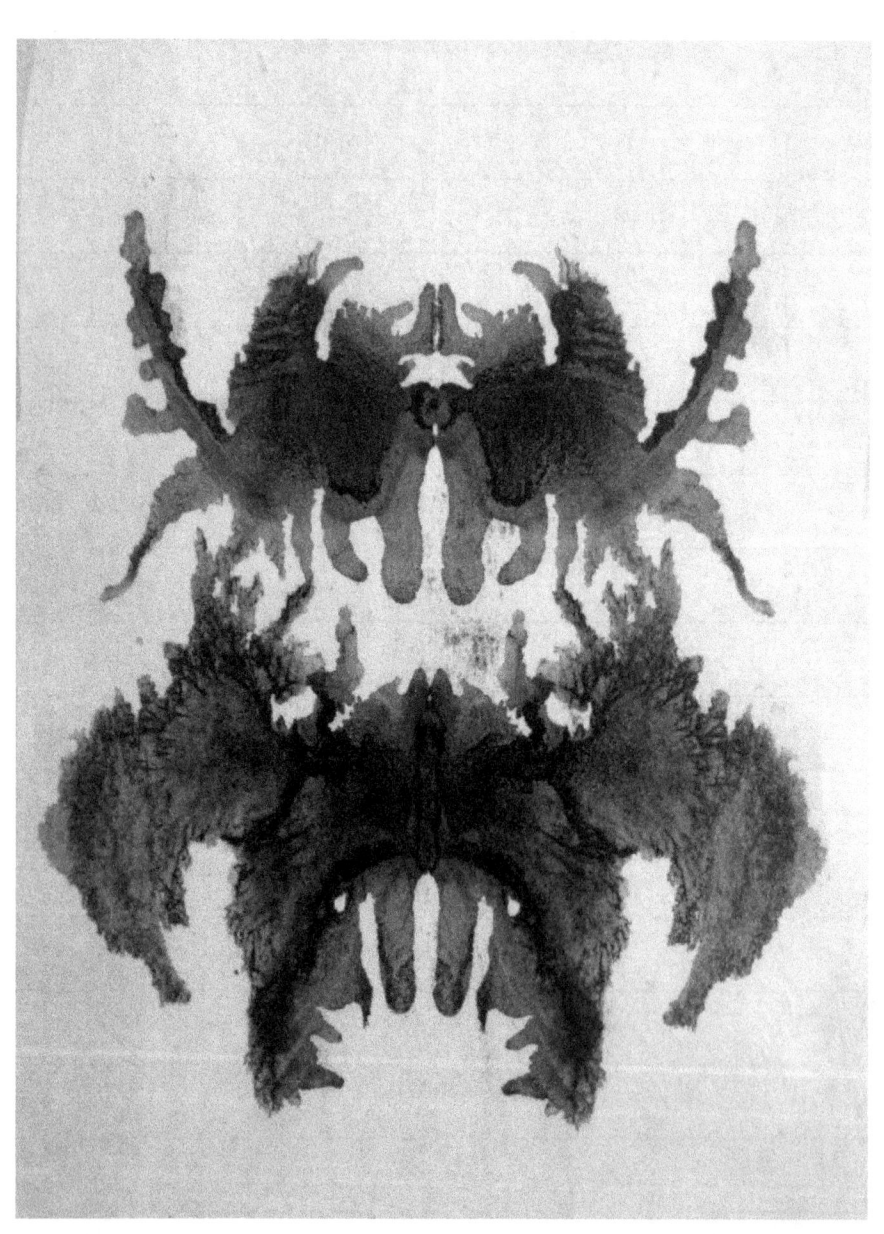

"What was that?" She sat up on the edge of the bed. Elizabeth reached for the matches and lit a candle. It was too dark in the small bedroom, so Elizabeth made her way into the living room. She was looking for more candles. Thank goodness we bought all of these candleholders and a good stock of candles. Jeremy, her big brother, thought she was being silly and a "fraidy cat." But mom had let her pick them out anyway.

"There! That sound, where is it coming from?" Elizabeth quickly lit two more candles. It was tapping and thumping and the sound was coming from every corner of the room. Suddenly the front door blew open. Elizabeth froze for a second and then she quietly closed the door. All was silent. No more tapping. Standing still, Elizabeth's eyes searched every corner of the room. With no warning her candles blew out. Darkness again.

Trying not to scream, she made her way back to her bedroom. "Maybe if I just get under the covers and close my eyes tight." The bed was cold now, but Elizabeth didn't care. With a shiver she quickly covered her head with her pillow. In the morning "I'm going to talk to Papa!"

What do you think?

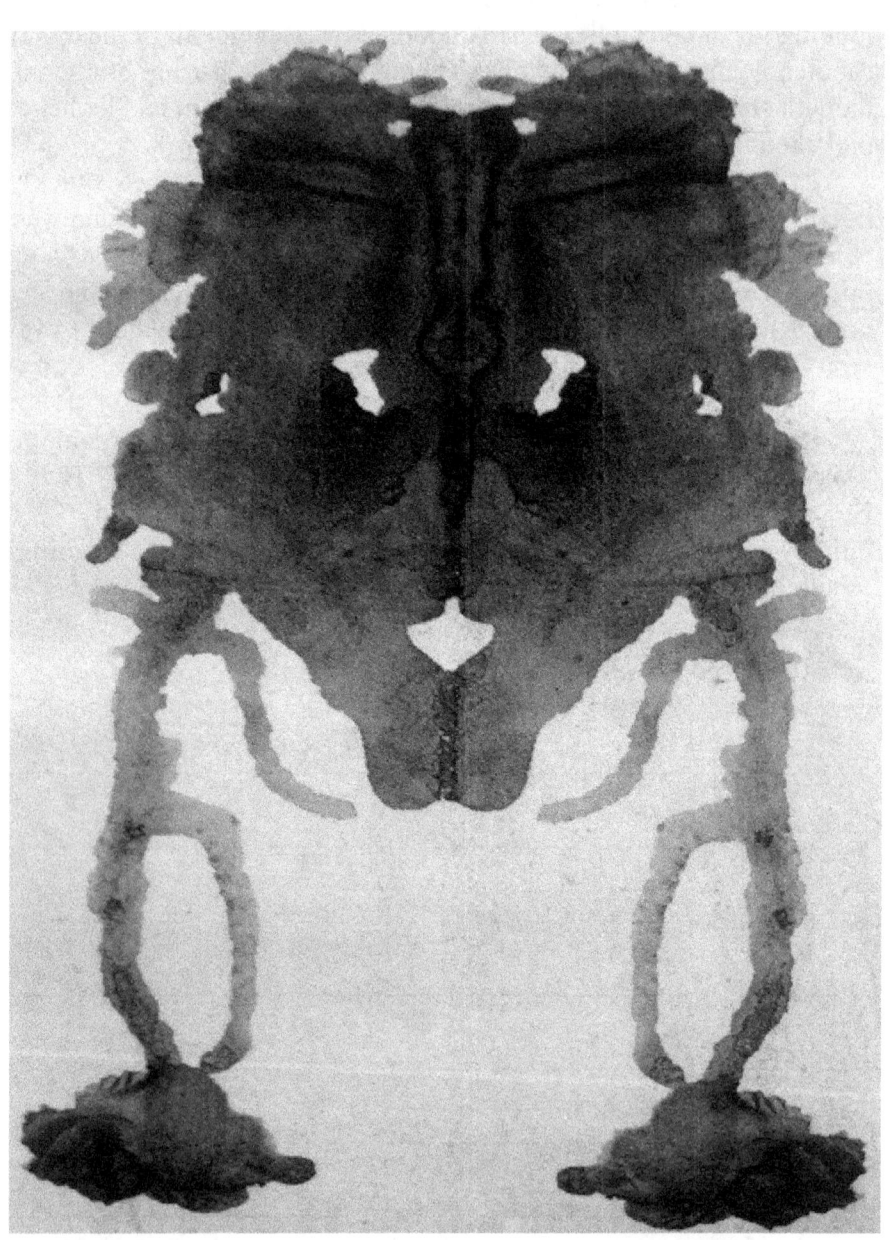

The five dollar bill was crisp and new in my hand. I even thought Lincoln was smiling just at me. Grandma Ellen's real estate friend had given it to me for my birthday. It was summer and my birthday wasn't until November, but I smiled and said thank you. Grandma's friends always had a dollar or two for me. Of course, they made sure grandma saw them give me the money. Or maybe I should say, grandma made sure they all chipped in for her only granddaughter. This happened whenever she had them over for coffee.

Walking across the tracks to the department store, my mind was dancing around with all kinds of ideas. What can I spend my money on? A doll? A necklace? Maybe that cute stuffed teddy bear I saw in the window last week. Wonder if I have enough money for the teddy bear?

As we entered the store, my shoes made a tapping sound. The smell of the hardwood floors and polished counters over took me. I felt like a queen. I thought what fun it would be to take my shoes off and slide down the shiny aisle in my socks. But then again, I guess a queen wouldn't do that.

What do you think?

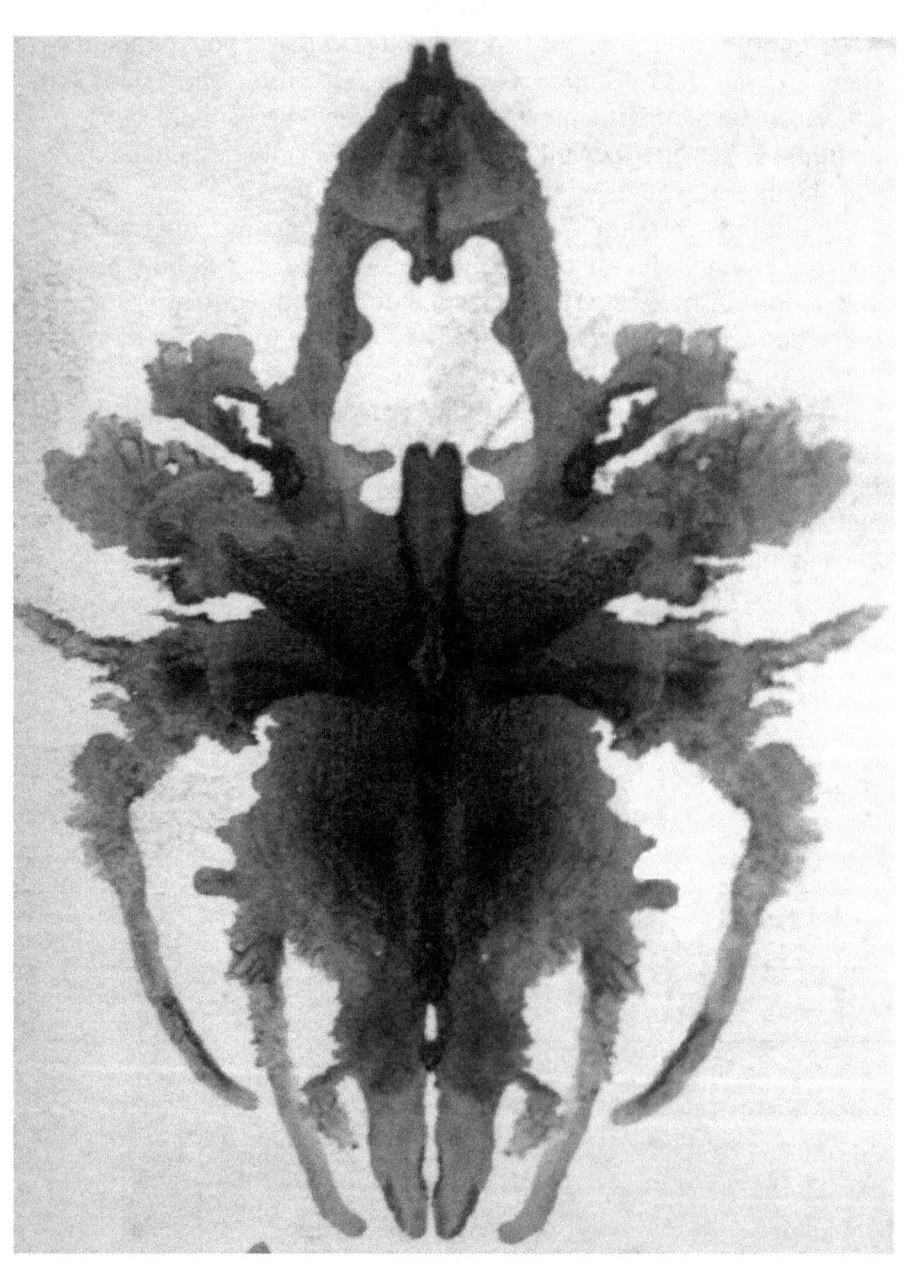

Did you hear the one about the lady that broke her toe trying to swim in her bedroom? Well, Daisy June loved to swim, but could not dive. The pool in her backyard didn't help. She was a belly-flopper. No matter how many times she tried, Daisy June could only belly-flop.

One evening while she was home alone, "Why can't I dive, everyone else can?" She started dwelling on the problem. "I just need to stand straight, put my hands together above my head, slightly bend at my waist, then bend a bit more and gently dive into the pool." The more Daisy June thought, the more she was sure she could do it. Standing in her living room, she practiced every move except the dive. "I know I can do this!" Daisy June's confidence was building.

Daisy June was ready. But it is was late at night and not smart to swim alone. "Bingo!" The next thing she knew, Daisy June was climbing onto the end of her bed. There she stood straight and tall on the footboard. Her waterbed, a perfect place to practice a dive. It will be soft with a little bounce. Staring straight ahead, she put her hands together above her head, bent slightly at her waist, then dove into her waterbed.

A perfect belly-flop! And the bounce was good, too. Up Daisy June flew into the air and then down onto the awaiting waterbed. Her big toe slammed on the footboard. Ouch, still all alone, Daisy June drove to the hospital.

What do you think?

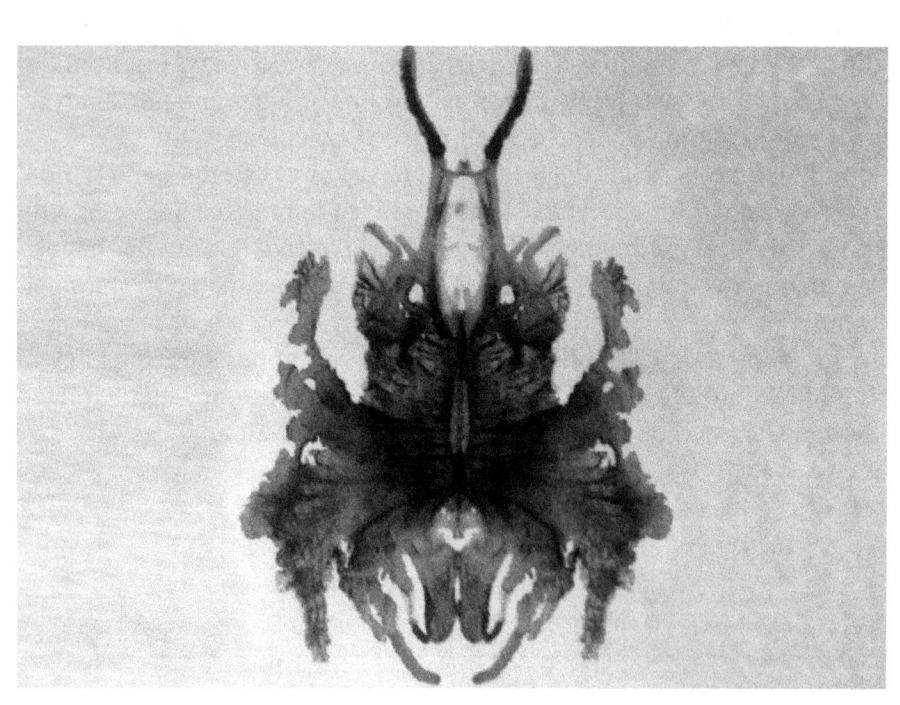

Grandma walked everywhere. So, when she announced it would be fun to see the state capitol, I panicked. "Are we going to walk all the way?" "Goodness, no." She explained that we would have to catch the PE train to the city and then catch a bus to head north. This road trip might just be fun.

So we walked to the P.E. tracks where we caught our train to downtown, and then made our way to the Greyhound Bus station. Still a lot of walking. Boarding the big bus was quite a sight to see, I was young and grandma was only four feet two inches tall. The driver had to give her a bit of a push. On board, she rented a pillow for me. When it was time to transfer to another bus, she insisted on taking it. Apparently the pillow was not transferable like us. I was a little embarrassed as grandma argued with the man. "I rented this pillow for the trip!" "No, ma'am, you have to get a new one when you change buses." Then I think she dared him to yank the pillow from behind my head. Anyway, I got to keep the pillow until we reached our destination.

What to you think?

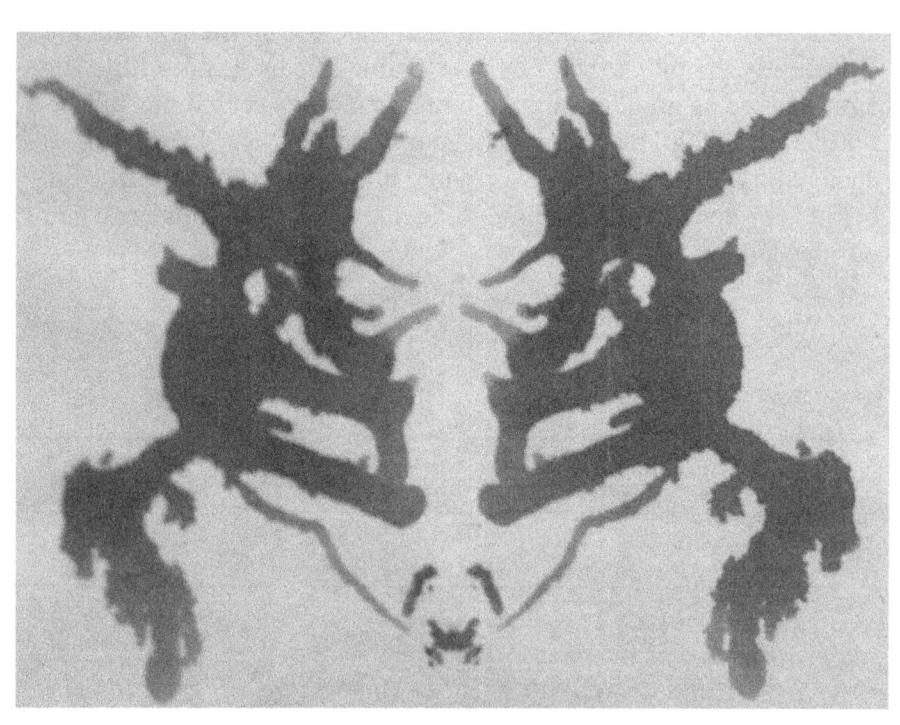

As we got off the bus, we could see the Capital building. It was late in the afternoon, so there was no time left to go sightseeing. We grabbed a sandwich at the station. There was one hotel fairly close by, so we headed that way. The sun was beginning to set and I was exhausted. Grandma approved the hotel room, got a key and up the old elevator we went. Room 302 was going to be home for a few nights.

I woke up hungry. "Grandma, what are we going to eat?" "Where? You mean where are we going to eat?" she answered. We quickly dressed, and headed down the street to a diner. "Do I get coffee this morning?" Grandma frowned at me and said, "Milk." After eggs and bacon were consumed, no coffee for me, we walked to the Capitol building.

I had to hold on to grandma's hand as I looked around. The dome was so high up there that it was a dizzy, but awesome sight. The marble floors felt cold and made squeaky sounds as people rushed by us. After the tour we walked to a local drugstore and sat up to the soda fountain counter for big juicy hamburgers and a malt.

We walked all over town enjoying the sights. My feet were starting to hurt. On our way to room 302 we stopped and bought some bread and baloney. "There," grandma said, "we have breakfast for tomorrow." Wait, baloney for breakfast?

What do you think?

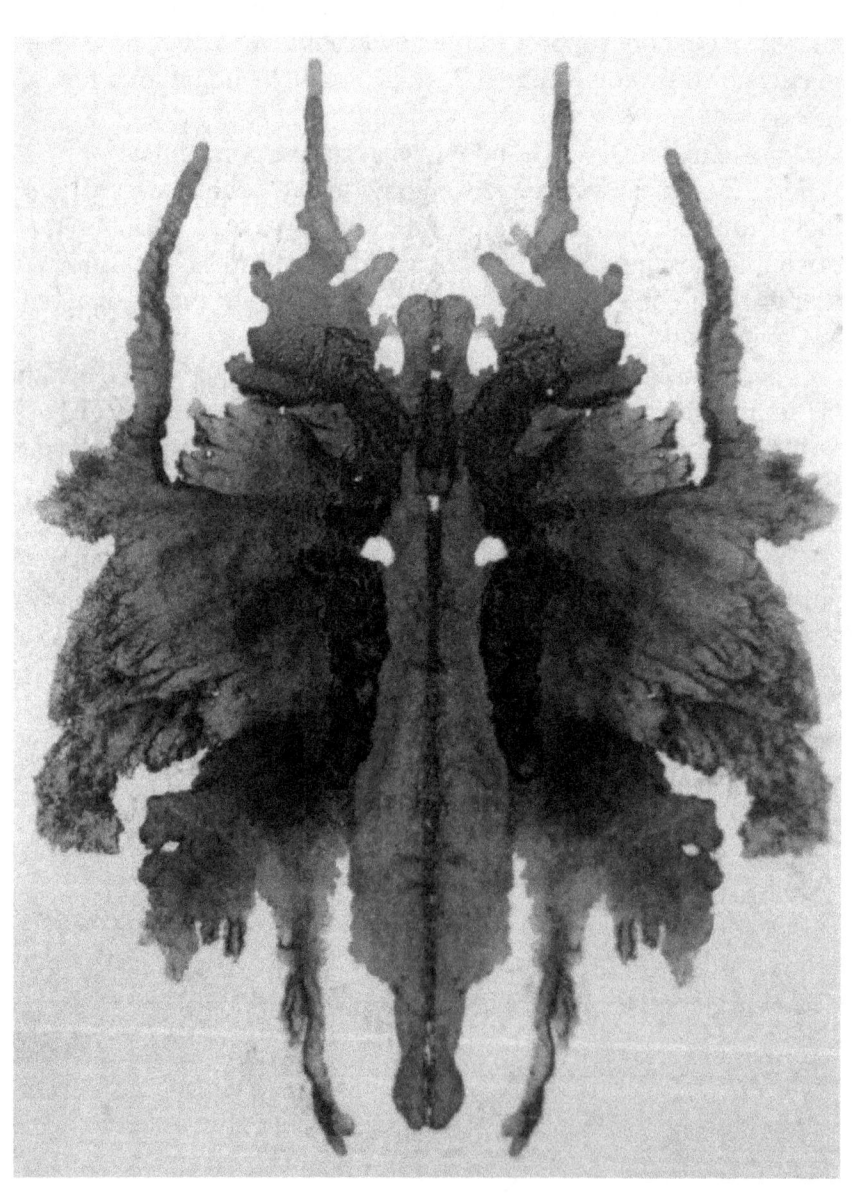

Early in the morning we were back on the big bus again. The forest scenery was so dense that the sun just peeked through occasionally. A deer dashed along side my bus window, then suddenly turned away and disappeared into heavy moss. Grandma was excited about our next stop. She was telling me about the zoo, and how it was suppose to be the largest in the state. Grandma got us a hotel room for two nights. Apparently she knew a lot about this town and figured we would have a good time. Our first stop the next morning, of course, was the zoo.

Grandma was acting funny as she made faces and silly noises at the caged animals. I was embarrassed, but soon joined in the fun. Grandma was laughing and having such a good time. This zoo was bigger than any I had seen before. The lions looked fat and lazy. They laid in the sun not moving a muscle, except for an occasional swishing of their tails. A black bird dove out of the trees and tried to swipe some hair from his mane. The lion barely lifted his head and gave a wimpy roar. The monkeys were more fun. They got as close as they could and returned grandma's silly faces. We spent the whole day at the zoo.

After hamburgers and milkshakes we went back to the hotel. We played cards until it got dark. Can you believe it? There was no TV!

What do you think?

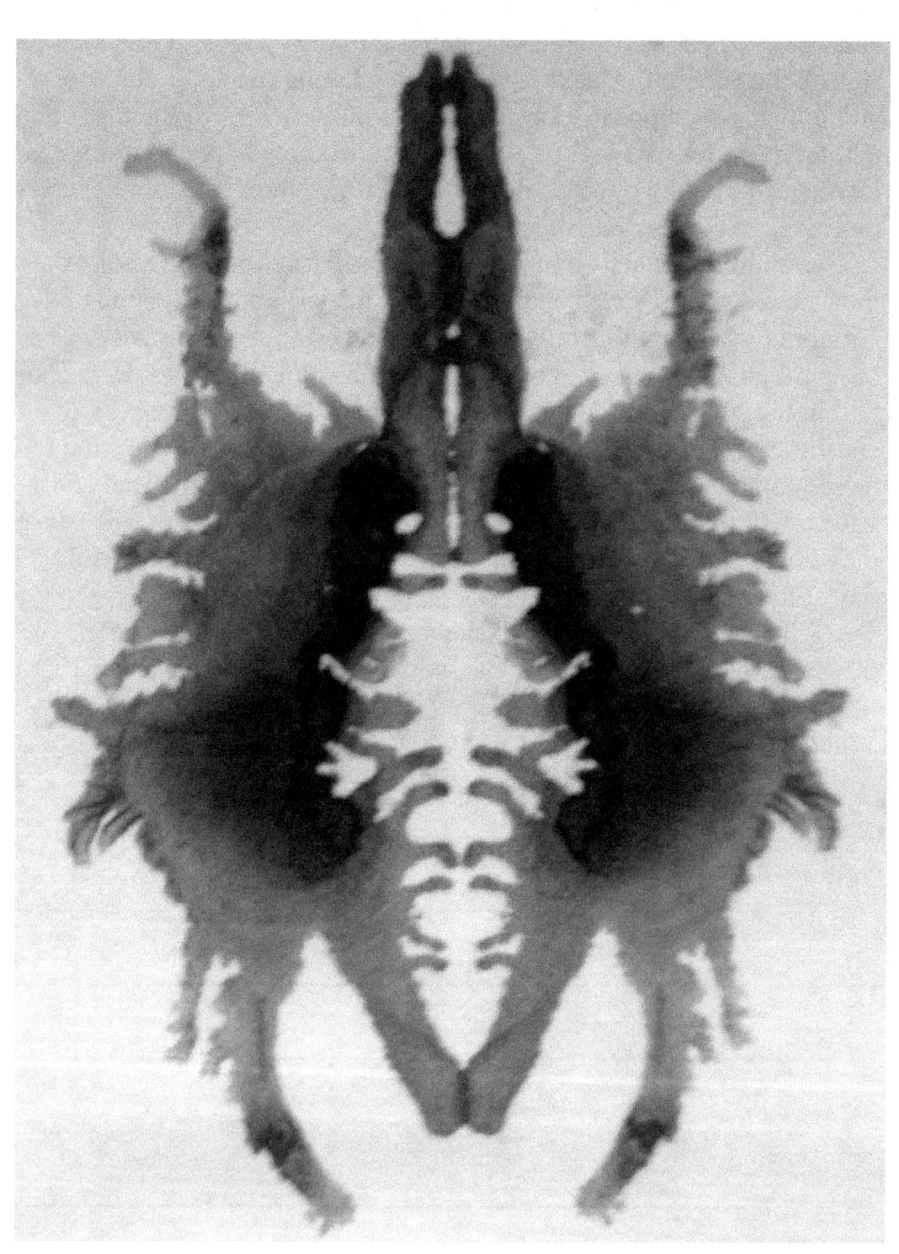

There it is. Sister finally found her favorite red shirt way in the back of the closet. It wasn't her favorite shirt, but it went with the blue jean skirt she wanted to wear. Sister needed to hurry, it was her turn in the bathroom. There was only one bathroom, and she had to share it with her two brothers..

Mom called that breakfast was ready, so she decided to get dressed after she ate. Oatmeal again, oatmeal at least three times a week. It was good and hot. Mom had to go to work and didn't have extra time during the weekday mornings. Her brother checked the date on the milk carton. He refused to drink any expired milk, even if it just expired this morning.

While the boys finished their breakfast, sister hurried to get dressed. With her jean skirt on, she slipped her red blouse over her head. Admiring it in the hall mirror, she started feeling something funny was going on. It didn't feel right. It felt kind of cool. Turning around she noticed there was no back to her red shirt. "MOM" she yelled.

Sister ran to the kitchen. "Mom, what happened to my shirt?" "Oh," mom explained, "your brother needed a red cowboy scarf for school a few months ago." Apparently it still looked good on the hanger after she cut out the square, so mom put it way in the back and forgot about it. Should sister be mad at mom or her brother?

What do you think?

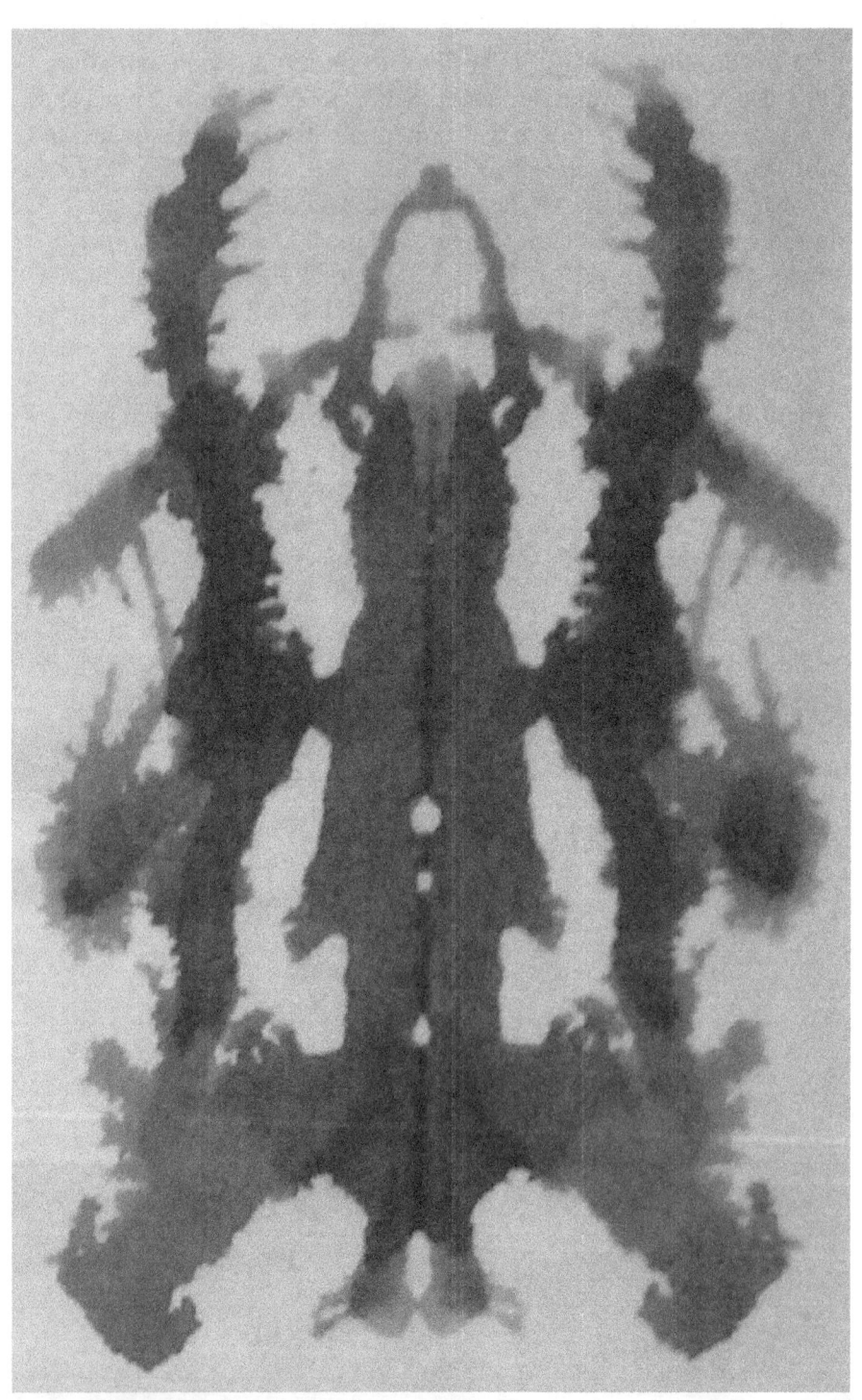

Ink! Ink! What do you think?

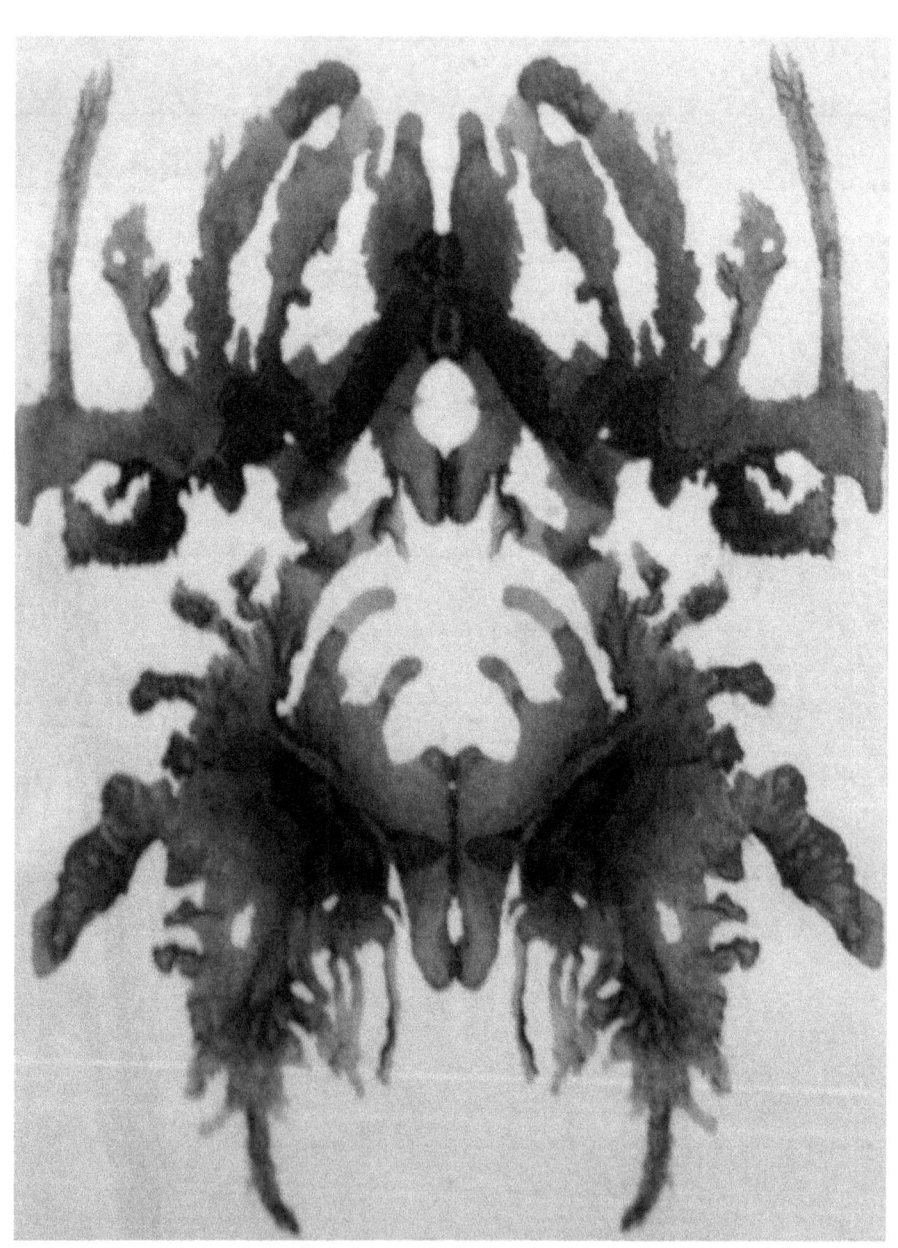

Behind the garage at grandma's was a large apricot tree. But even more special than that was the extra building that housed a steambath. Grandpa built it with two tiers of benches. Three maybe four people could sit.

A trip to the desert found us looking for large boulders. Grandma knew exactly what size she needed. We hauled a ton, or what seemed like a ton to me, of desert rocks home. These were put in a giant cement cylinder. It was designed so that when a gas fire under it was lit, the rocks would begin to warm. It took about thirty minutes for the rocks to get super hot.

When grandma was a little girl, a steambath was a regular winter tradition. After a quick shower, one entered the steambath, wrapped themselves in a towel, and sat on a wooden bench. Every so often someone would pull a rope that splashed cold water on the hot stones. Steam, foggy steam appeared. After about fifteen or twenty minutes, they ran outside and jumped into an icy lake, or they just rolled around in the snow.

A steambath at grandma's in the summer time was different. Grandpa heated the stones, I took a quick shower with my bathing suit on, and sat with grandma for a muggy steam. Then I ran out of the building, and surprise, grandpa threw a bucket of ice water on me!

What do you think?

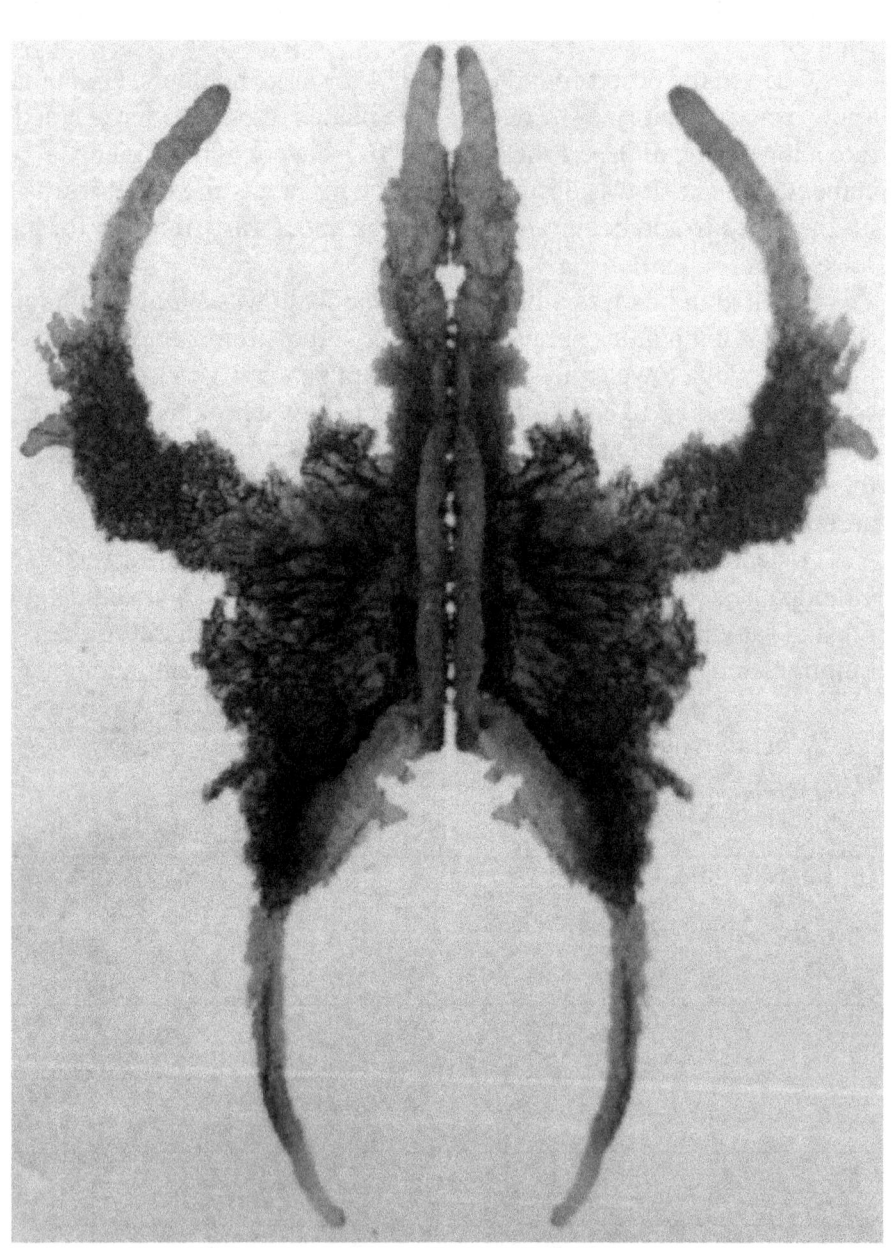

"Find the clothespins, and put them over by the laundry baskets," grandma ordered. Oh how I hated wash day. Grandpa was moving the old washing machine out into the yard. "Grandma, can I climb up into the apricot tree?" "No, we are doing the wash right now." "Hmph, okay."

Since the old washing machine was non-electric, I got to turn the crank. The wash tub would then swish the clothes around. Grandma sliced her home made soap into the tub. I am not about to give you her recipe for that soap. Trust me you don't want to know. When it swished around long enough, grandpa removed the cork from the bottom, and the soapy water headed for the iris bed.

Now clean water was hosed in and the laundry would be rinsed twice. After the final draining of the water, everything was squeezed between two built-in rollers, then the wrinkles had to be thoroughly shook out. That was just the first load.

Grandpa strung rope from tree to building, building to house, house to tree, and then back to the house. I grabbed a pocketful of clothespins and began the familiar routine of hanging everything up. The ropes swung quite low so it easy to reach. When one section was full, grandpa grabbed a long board with a notch in the end. The notch fit the rope and grandpa raised the laundry high into the air. The sheet waved like flags on a windy day.

What to you think?

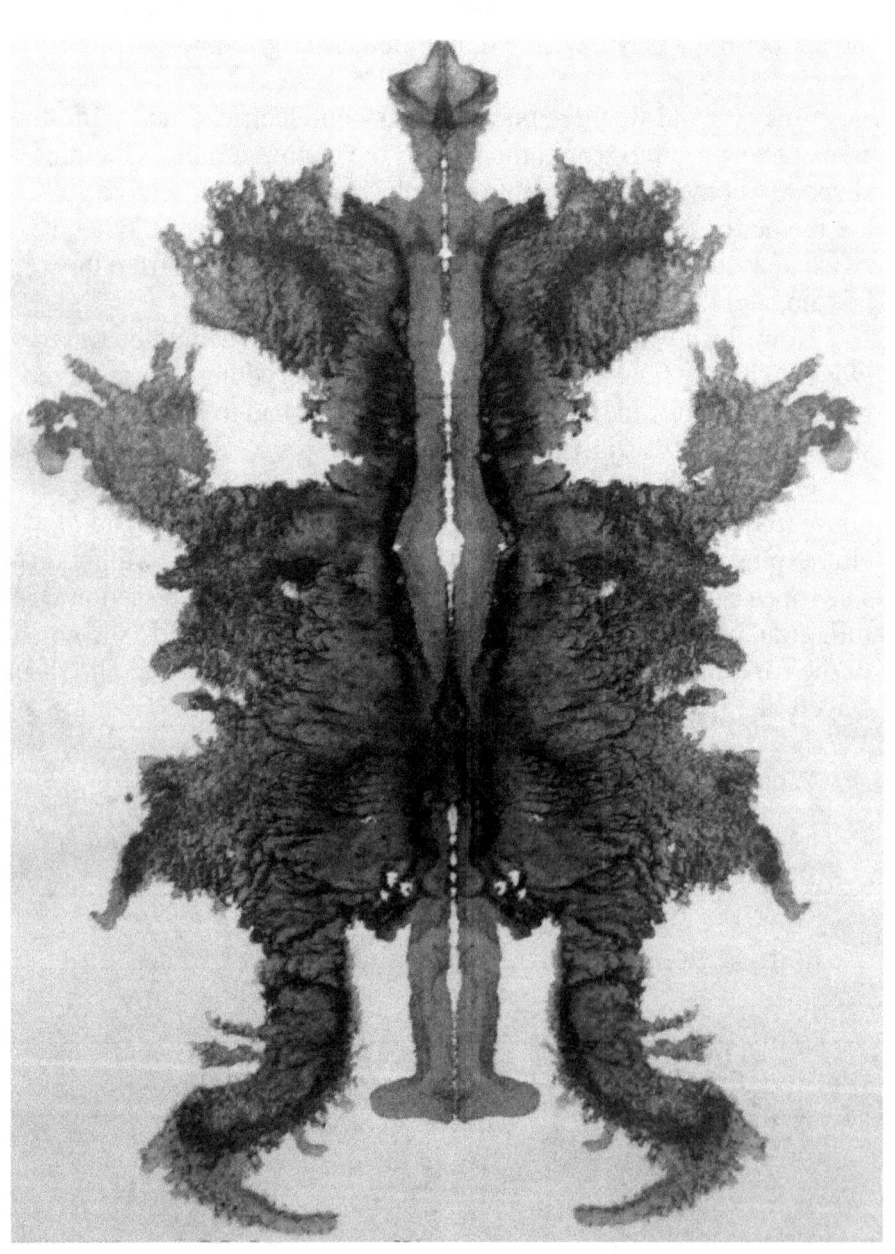

Did you ever stop to think about music? Yes, I am talking about music and the different sounds that have to meld together just to make a tune? All those different instruments; flutes, saxophones, trumpets, violins, and drums. How do they all blend together in such a way to produce the swaying sounds that make us want to dance?

Music writers can feel a tune and play it. Just like that. Can you? Can I? No, I am afraid I am not musically inclined. Grandma gave me a piano and lessons. She enjoyed me plinking away a simple tune. Don't you know she sat in her chair and dreamed of me being a concert pianist. But, after all those lessons I still could not play more than "chopsticks." Real musicians can find the right place on the piano or guitar to play their sound. When they really get going their music gives us the beat, and we get to dance. Tap, tap, tap go our feet as we feel ourselves joining the band. And then the melody plants itself in our head, and we can't shake it. You know, that tune that you hum all day long?

What do you think?

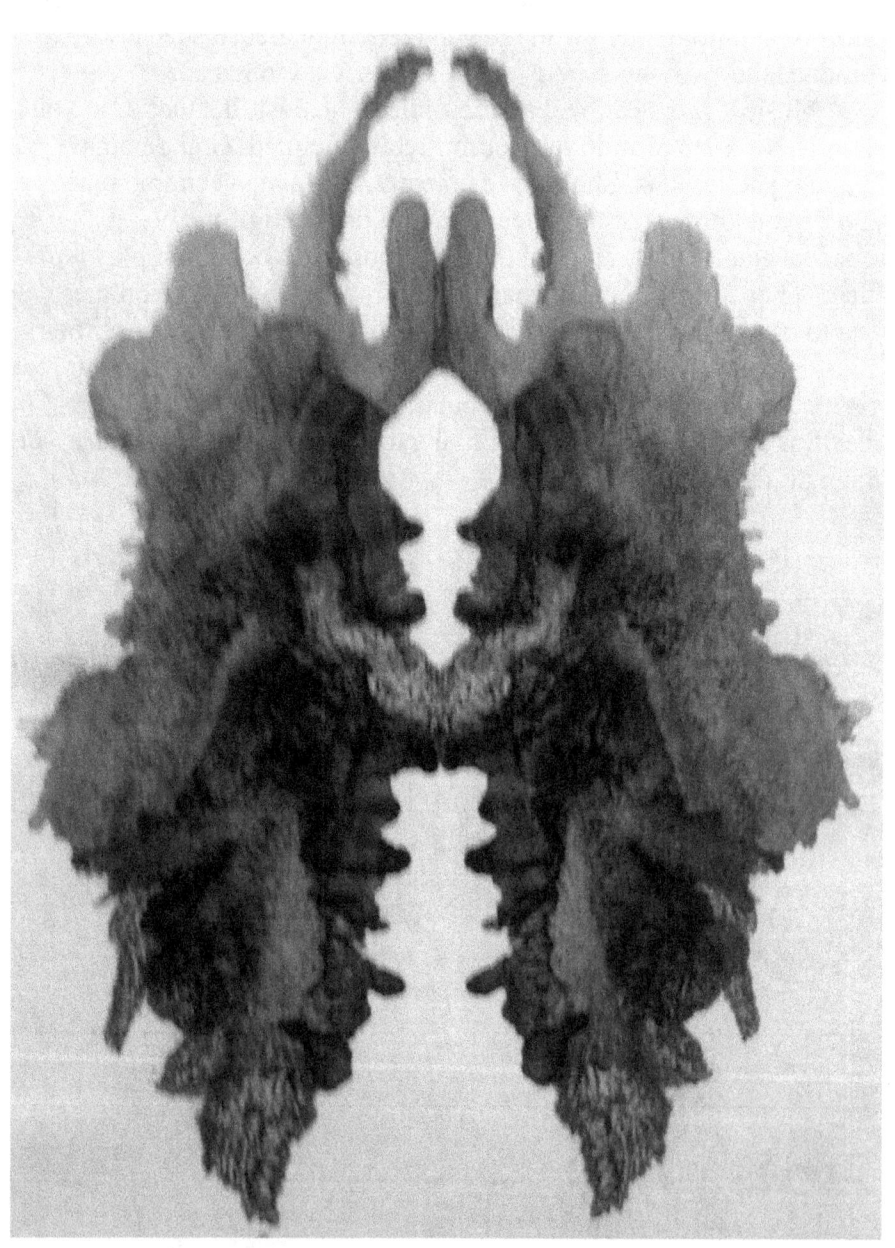

When daddy first started driving a big rig, he was hauling hay to the dairy farmers. Back then when a cow had a calf, the dairy farmers could not be bothered with it. Daddy would be unloading their hay and the farmer would wander over and ask, "You want this calf?" "Sure." So he loaded them in his cab and took them to his mother. Grandma Ida saw to it that they got plenty of milk and loving. Soon there was a number of calves in grandma's care. As the calves grew, her hobby was getting out of control.

Grandpa bought a bull to put out in the field. More calves were born and grandma was in charge of them. We became dairy farmers. Daddy continued to drive hay trucks, and now was making deliveries to his folks. The bales of hay would get stacked almost ten feet up. There is a story of my aunt Mary being chased by the bull. She had no place to go but up. No one really knows how she got on top of the bales of hay, but there she was. Rumour has it that the bull laid down at the bottom of the stack and took a nap. Poor aunt Mary spent the afternoon ten feet up.

What do you think?

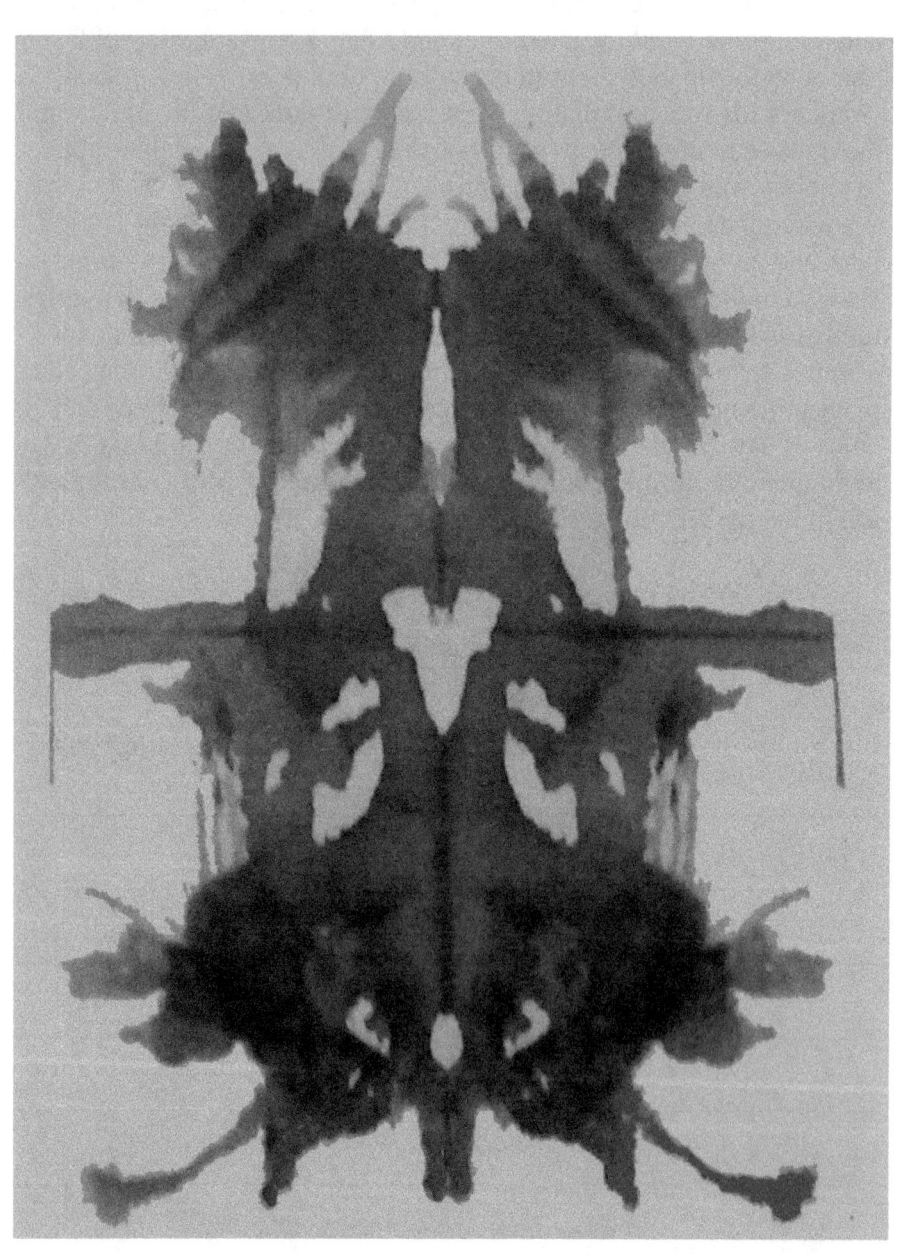

Ink! Ink! What do you think?

Her name was Scarlet. She was the most beautiful red colored filly in my backyard. Scarlet was not alway this great looking. Born and raised on the open range, she was a wild horse. We paid fifty dollars for her. A veterinarian checked her out and recommended oats and vitamins. Even though I was not raised around horses, I could brush her and walk with her around the corral. Scarlet was timid and so gentle..

Everyday, I fed her the extra oats and talked gently to her. One day, Scarlet was a little friskier than usual. Then suddenly she broke out into a run around backyard. I stood in the middle afraid to move. She would stop, look me over, and then take off again, kicking up her heels. I managed to run to the dog pen, where I felt safer.

Scarlet began to think this was a game. She came up to the pen and begged me to come out and play. I didn't move. Off she ran kicking and throwing her head in the wind, only to return and beg. On one of her moves, I manage to leave the pen and get to a tree. Now, Scarlet and I were dancing around the tree. When she wasn't looking I escaped the corral to our house. She still just wanted to play. Guess those extra oats worked.

What do you think?

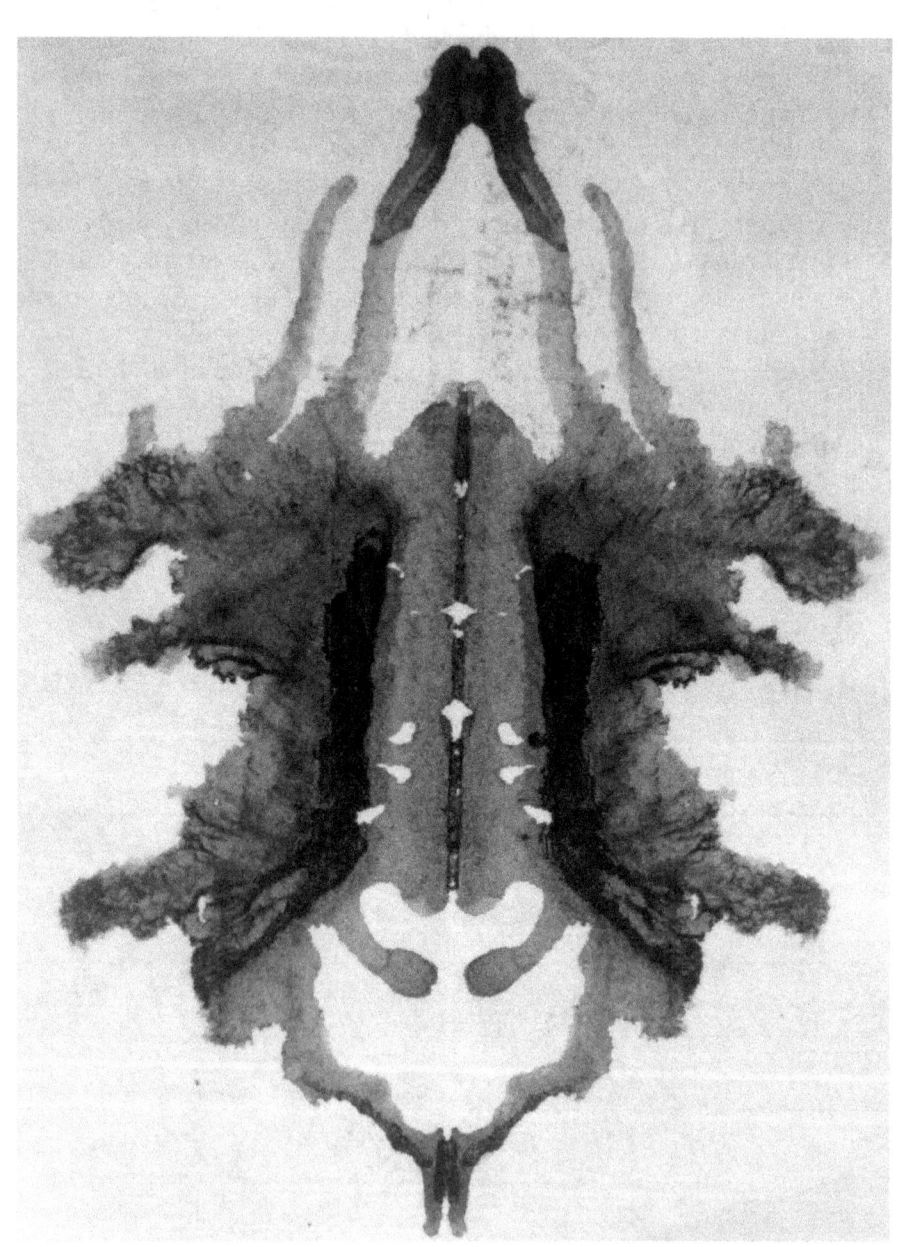

One day I went to a friends house to play ball. The neighbor boy, Georgie, called us over to his backyard hideout. He wanted to show off his chemistry set. He wanted us to watch his experiment. First, he put a liquid in the tube, then followed it with colored powder. It started to bubble and gurgle and turn bright purple. He seemed happy with that. As he continued his experiment, Georgie started telling us a story of a dog that was turned into a cat. Dog into a cat?

You see, this dog was looking for his lost ball when he ran into Hondo, the magician. Seeing a bowl of food, dog forgot about the ball and headed for the food. As he reached it, the floor opened and dog fell down into a hole and was trapped. A yellow cat approached, "You can get out of here if you will just pretend to be a cat." "How can I do that, I am too big to be a cat." "Just say meow." the cat instructed. "Meow, meow, meow, me….."

Right then in the middle of the story, Georgie dropped his jar of bubbling purple goo. It splattered everywhere. My tee shirt had purple spots on it. Then the purple spots started to spread, and big holes appeared in my shirt. It didn't get to my skin, but my shirt was a goner. In fact, I was a goner. I left quickly, hurried home, and threw away my tee shirt, before mama saw it.

What do you think?

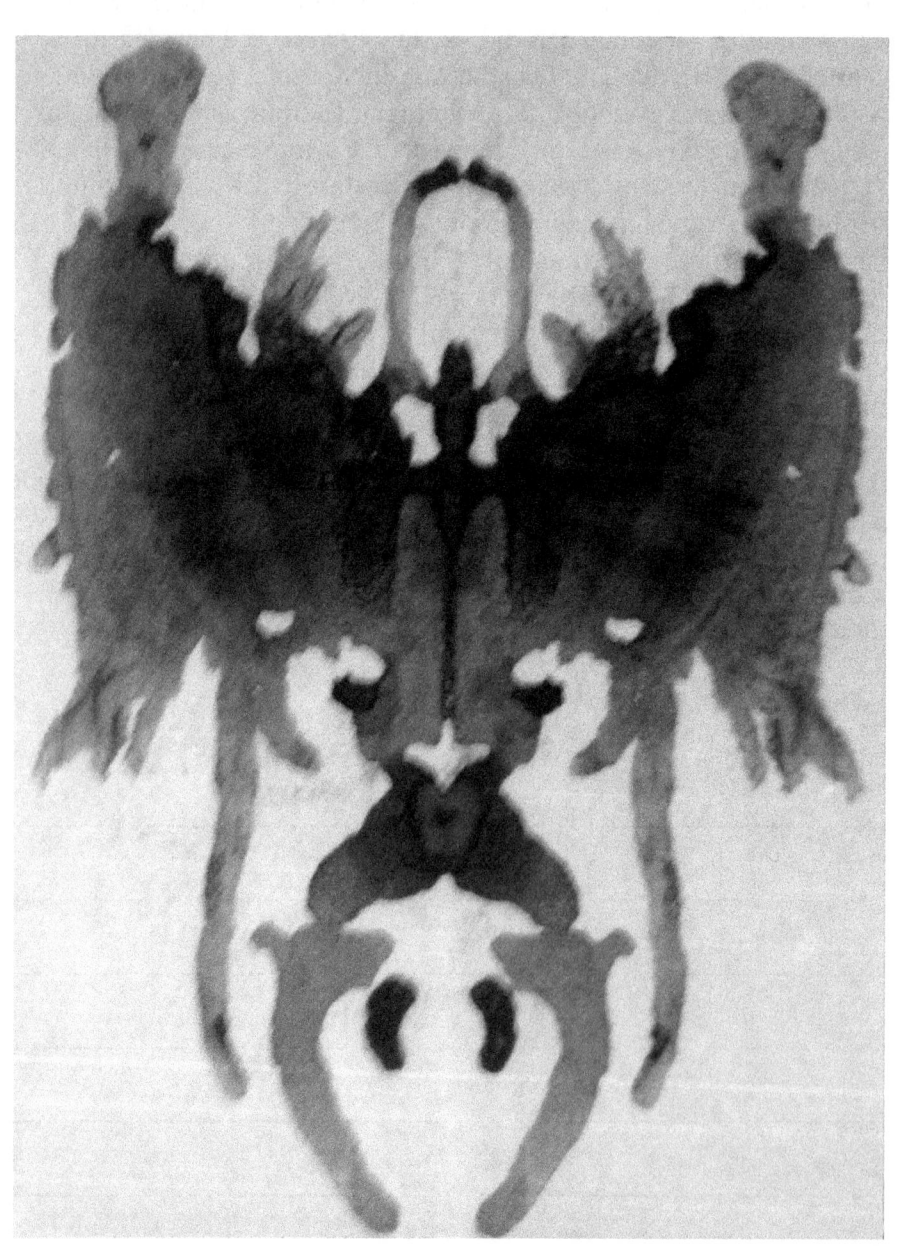

The two-weeks at grandma's house was almost over. I was anxious to go home. The morning stretched into noon as I waited on the porch steps. Watching a caterpillar make his way across the walkway, I grinned. The cement was hot and it appeared to be moving fast. As it reached the cool grass, I heard the family car. It purred as daddy slowly maneuvered into the driveway. Daddy was a good driver.

Mommy got a big hug. I was excited to tell her about the my adventures with grandma. But first, we headed in the house for coffee. I remembered to take my first sip from the saucer and exclaim "Aaah!" Grandma smiled her approval. Mommy just rolled her eyes.

After a round of goodbyes, we were ready for the two hour drive home. I settled in the back seat with my thoughts. Looking out the window I realized we would soon pass the grocery store with a pony ride in the parking lot. Sometimes daddy would stop and let me ride. Would this be one of those days?

Slowly the car turned into the parking lot. Look at all the ponies going around in a circle tethered to a pole. Excited I wondered which one was mine. Hurry daddy, I like the black and white one. Hurry daddy, before some other kid claims it. On board my palomino stallion, I rode off into the sunset.

What do you think?

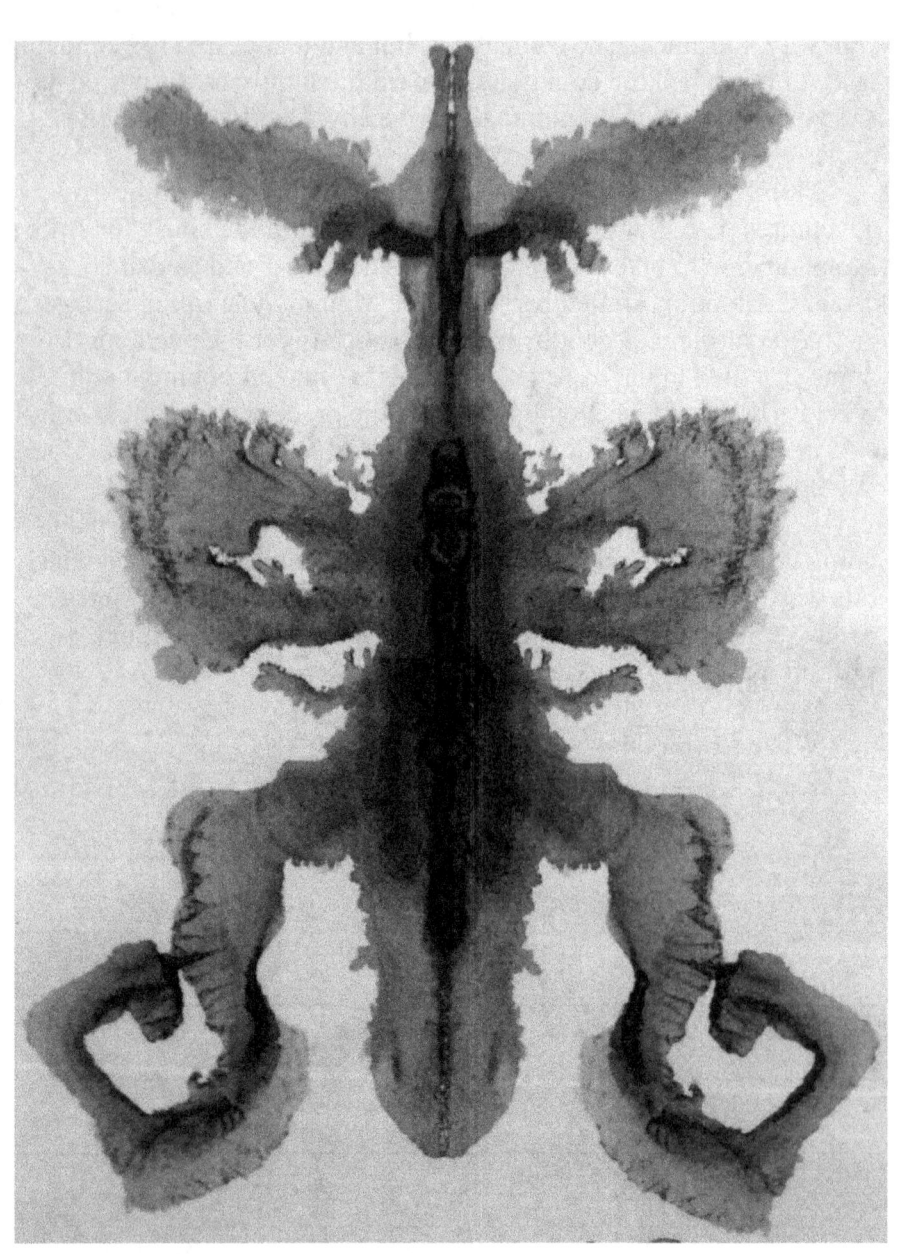

Just how strong do you think I am? Can I lift the piano over in the corner of the room? Maybe I can hold the car up by the front fender for twenty minutes.

What do you think?

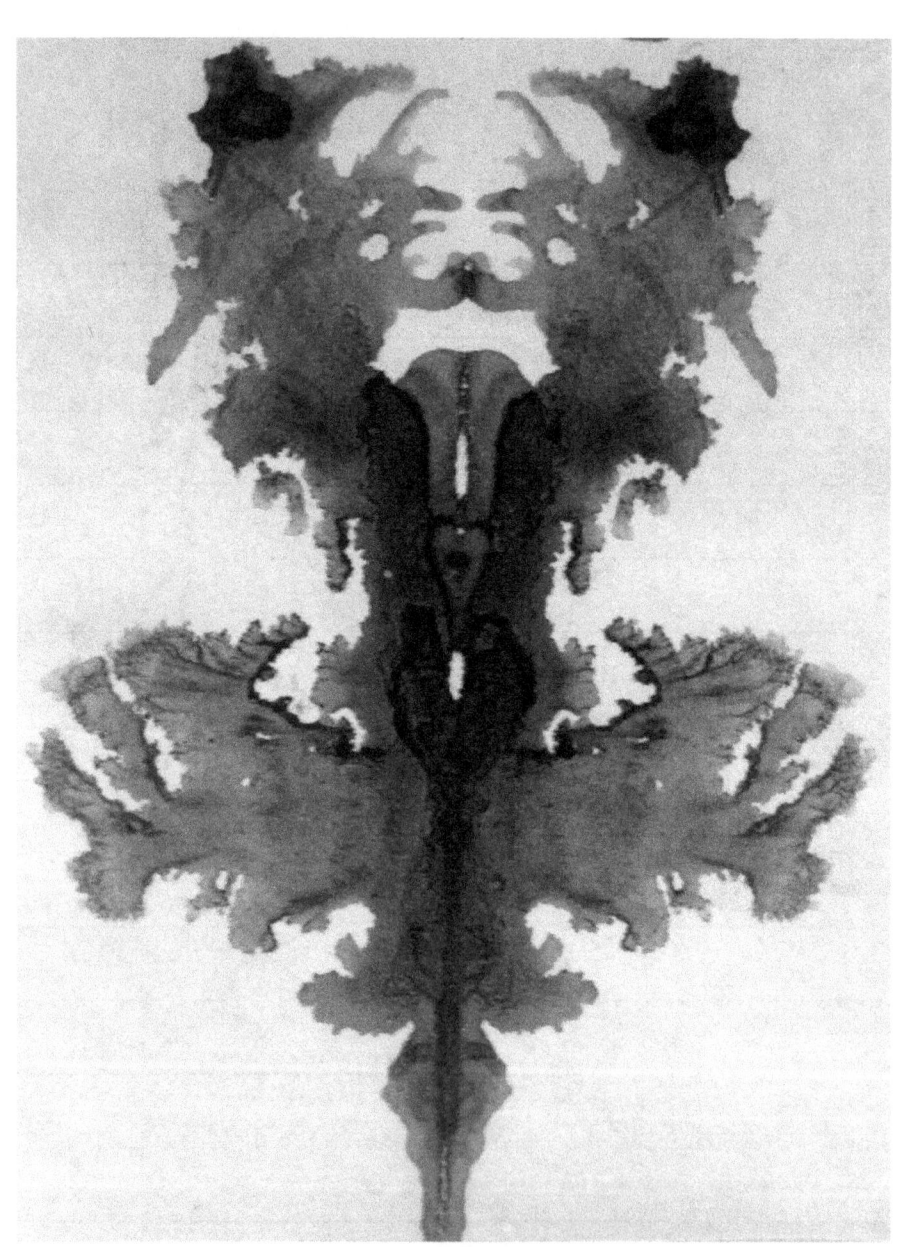

When I was five it was really difficult to play at my other grandparents house. Grandma Ida had chickens, and a goose named Lucy.. That goose did not like me. Whenever I tried to cross the yard Lucy would appear from behind the bushes and chase me. She like to nip at my legs and untie the bow at the back of my dress.

Grandpa Axel told me to stand up straight and walk past Lucy pretending that I was not scared. That never worked. One day I came up with a plan. Maybe I could lure Lucy into the chicken house and latch the door behind her. Then I could play at the fishpond and not be bothered by Lucy. As I left the house, I pretended not to care about her, trying to whistle my way across the yard. Sure enough, Lucy appeared. I ran fast. She waddled faster. Lucy caught my dress hem and wasn't going to let go. I kept running straight to the chicken house. Opening the door, I swung myself around. Lucy was still hanging on as her webbed feet left the ground. "Squaak," Lucy let go as she flew through the door. I latched it. Then I pretended to throw away an invisible key.

Grandma appeared at her back door as I skipped by. "Did I hear Lucy? Is Lucy alright?" She was concerned. "Oh, grandma, she is fine. Lucy just wanted to play with the chickens."

What do you think?

The fabric section at J.C. Penny's was particularly of interest to grandma as she was a seamstress. Made all of her own clothes. Come to think of it, I don't think I ever saw grandma in a store-bought dress. There was fabric for nightgowns, dresses, tablecloths and pillows. Every two years or so grandma would completely reupholster the couch. We would search out the "4 yards for a dollar" fabric, finding just the right yardage to make my yearly nightshirt.

Back at grandma's house, I learned to sew using her Singer treadle sewing machine. Had to get your feet moving just right to keep that needle going up and down. My nightshirts were really very simple: two yards of lightweight fabric folded in half, sew up sides leaving plenty of armhole room, cut a section out for my head, then hem all the loose edges. I remember them looking like hospital gowns, except mine weren't open in the back.

What to you think?

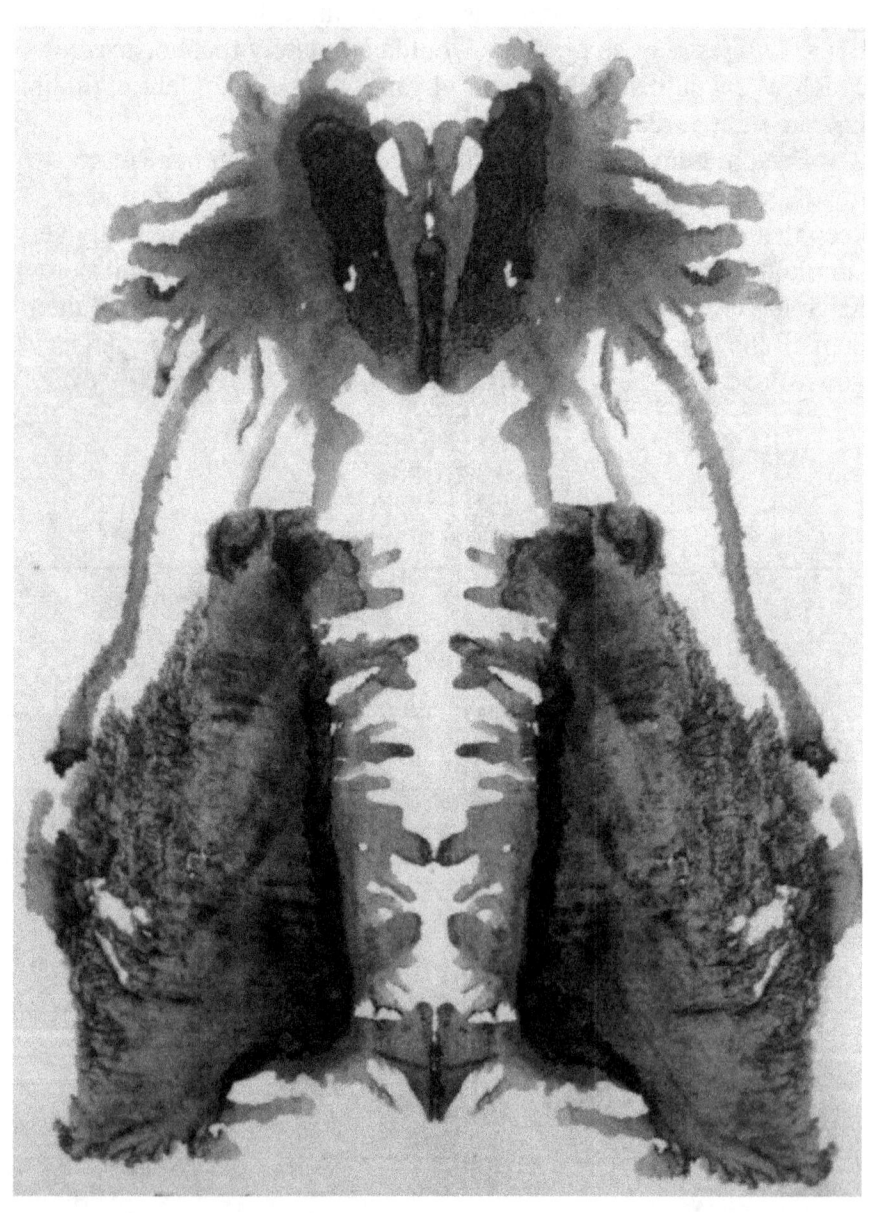

Choc Taw was a cute little puppy, that grew into a large German Shepherd. A brave dog, always on guard, his life was good. He had the run of the house and his yard. He was very much in charge, or at least thought he was. This story is about his fear of the vacuum cleaner. He hated it and was afraid of it at the same time.

Choc Taw was not allowed on the furniture, but his favorite spot was on the green couch. At night he would quietly curl up on it. His blonde hair accumulated in one corner, for all to see. Mom came up with the solution.

She laid parts of the vacuum cleaner on the cushions. "That will keep him off," she thought.

That night she heard Choc Taw cross the room and jump onto the couch. As he jumped up, the pieces of vacuum cleaner wedged into the back of the couch. Choc Taw had no idea they were there. Mom could hear him sniffy around until he discovered the parts. He yelped, flew off the couch, knocked over a table, and cowered in the corner unable to breathe.

Mom put a pillow on the floor and did her best to calm him. Choc Taw closed his eyes and tried to sleep. All night long, about once an hour, he woke up yelping and breathing hard. But, Choc Taw never got on the couch again.

What do you think?

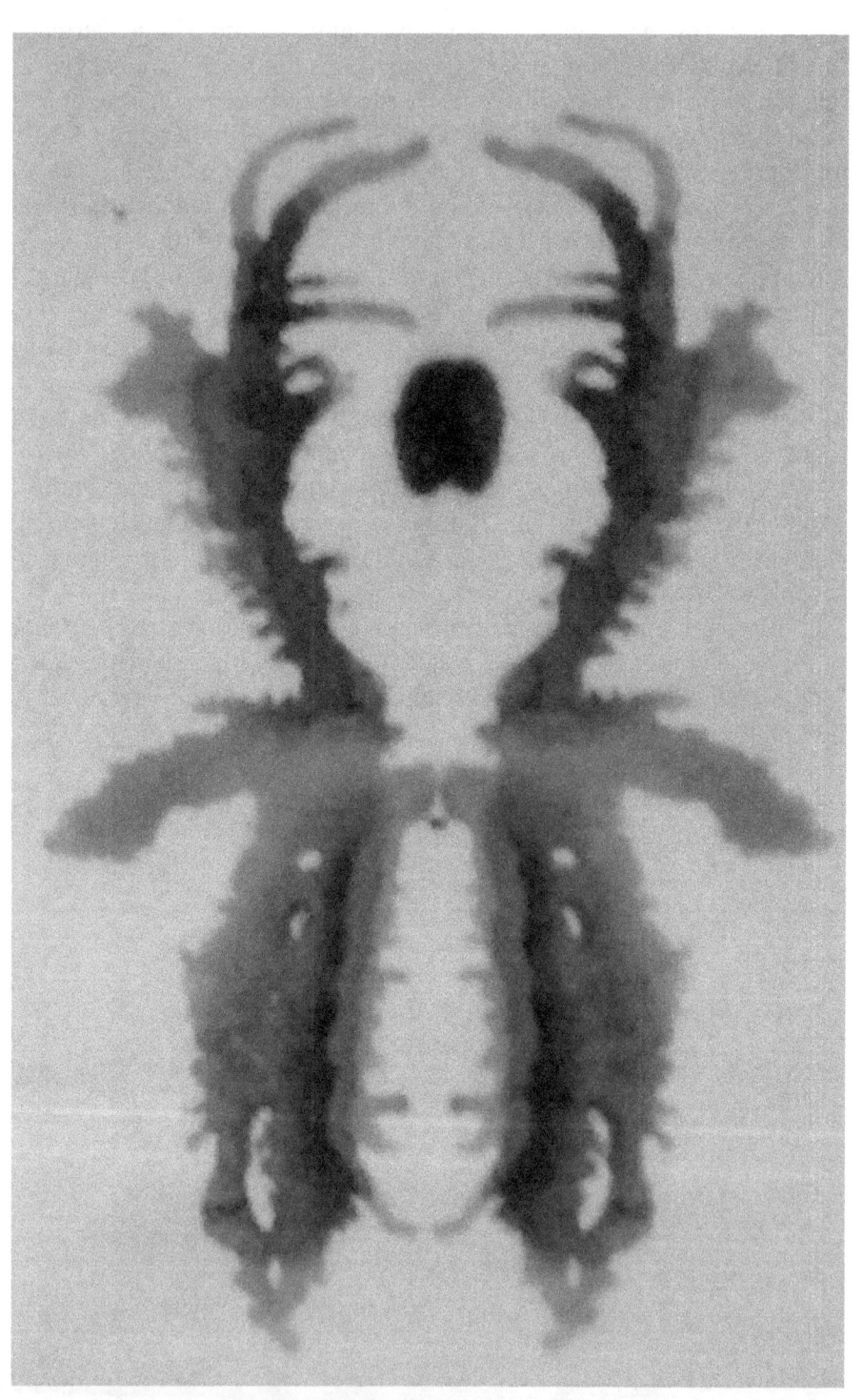

Ink! Ink! What do you think?

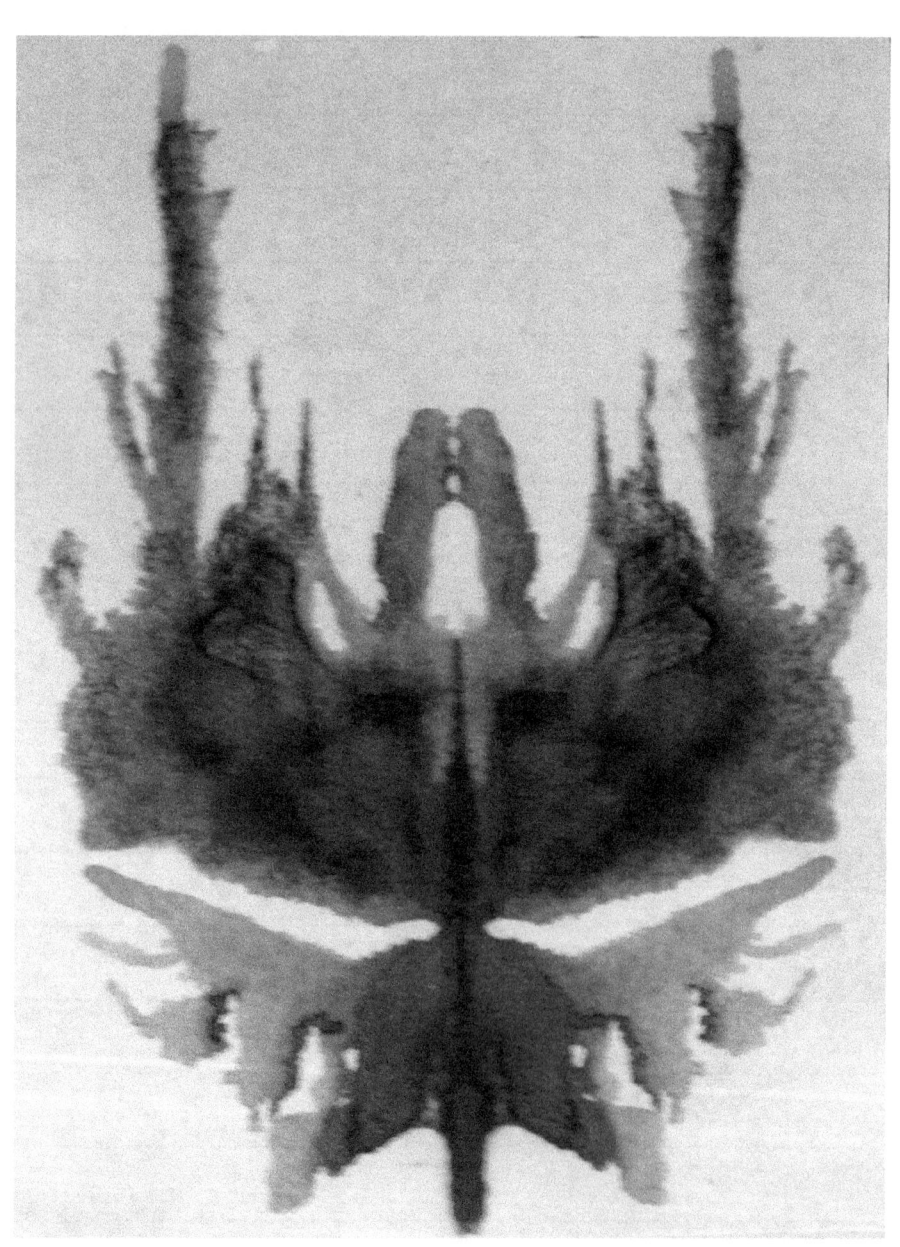

We were moving to California. It was a long and sometimes boring ride. All of a sudden, you could hear the excitement in mom's voice. "Look, kids, the river!" We looked. "When we cross the river we will be in California." We kept looking. "Here we go this is the stateline, hold your feet up high in the air as we cross. Hold'em, keep holding, just a little longer." My tummy muscles were beginning to ache. "There, we are across the river and across the stateline. We are now in California."

As we settled back into regular passenger positions, I didn't think the scenery had changed much. Then mom started talking about California. How much fun we would have at the beach, and hiking in the mountains, and on and on about our new home. But, she felt it was her duty to share one special rule with us. In California, no one under the age of twelve was allowed to chew gum. Gee whiz, why hadn't she told us this before?

After a short summer we were enrolled in school. One day my sister came home with an important question for mom. "Mom, today at school, Tommy Smith was chewing gum." "Okay, so Tommy was chewing gum." "But mommy, you told us that no one under the age of twelve could chew gum in California."

Mom just smiled, then chuckled, then looked a little guilty. "Oh sweetie, I was just pulling your leg."

What do you think?

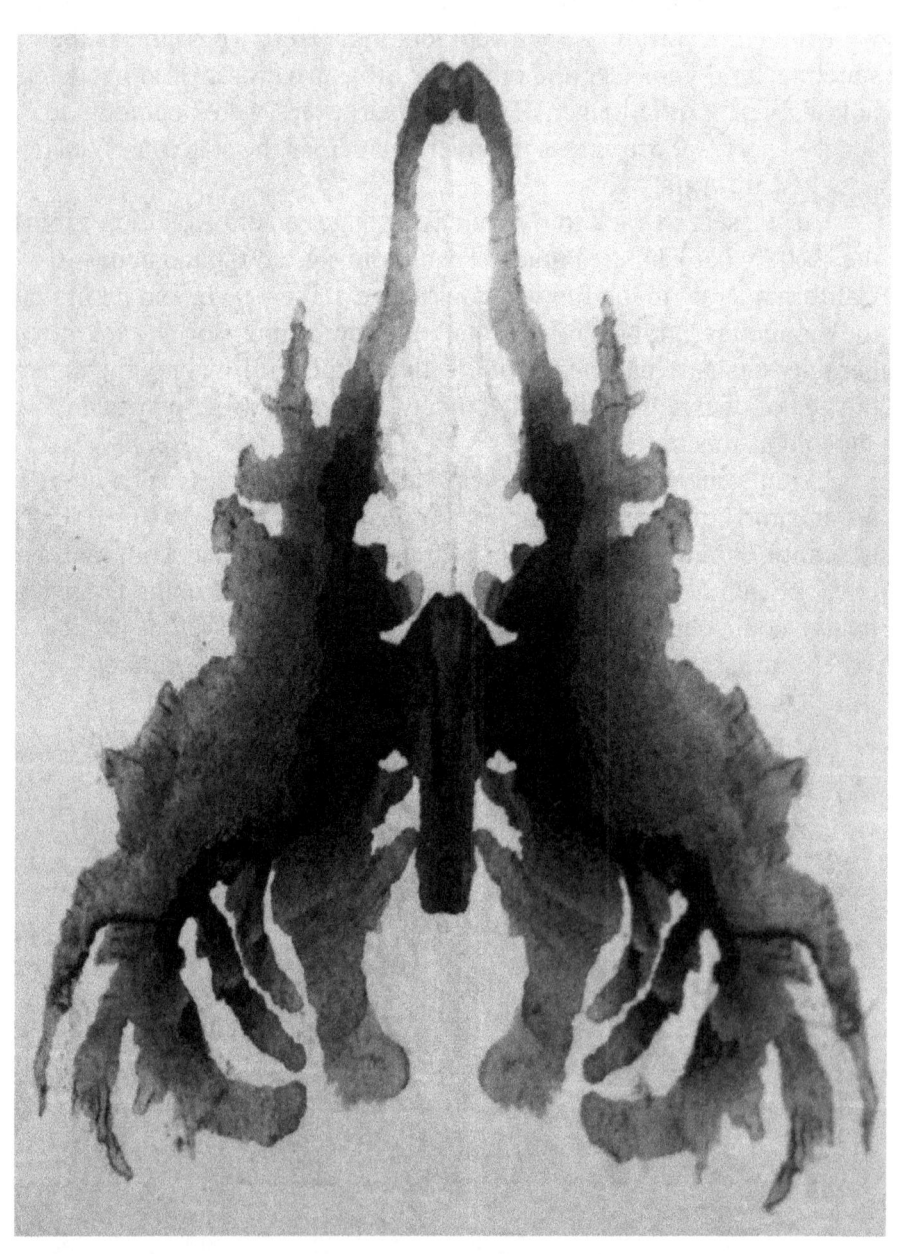

We were riding rental horses down the old river bed. My horse was named Red; don't know why, because he was really an ordinary brown horse. Every other month, my friends and I would rent these "stallions" and pretend we were great horsemen. The river never had much more than a trickle of water here and there, but, it made us feel like we were out in the country. Never mind that we could hear the cars whizzing by on the freeway above us. We still could pretend.

Remember, these were rental horses, and we had them for just an hour. If you rode for thirty minutes, you'd think that you should turn back. But, no, we learned the hard way, turning back too soon, would get you to the stable in fifteen minutes. Then, when you returned to the stable, the horses instinctively felt you should get off. They no longer wanted instructions from us novice riders.

And I'm sure the horses probably knew how far they had to go before they could turn back. After the first half hour, they began to get harder to control, kind of looking back at the trail. Maybe they were looking at each other, deciding which one would make a break for it. As soon as they were facing the stable, it was a wild time for us. Probably the best part of the ride.

What do you think?

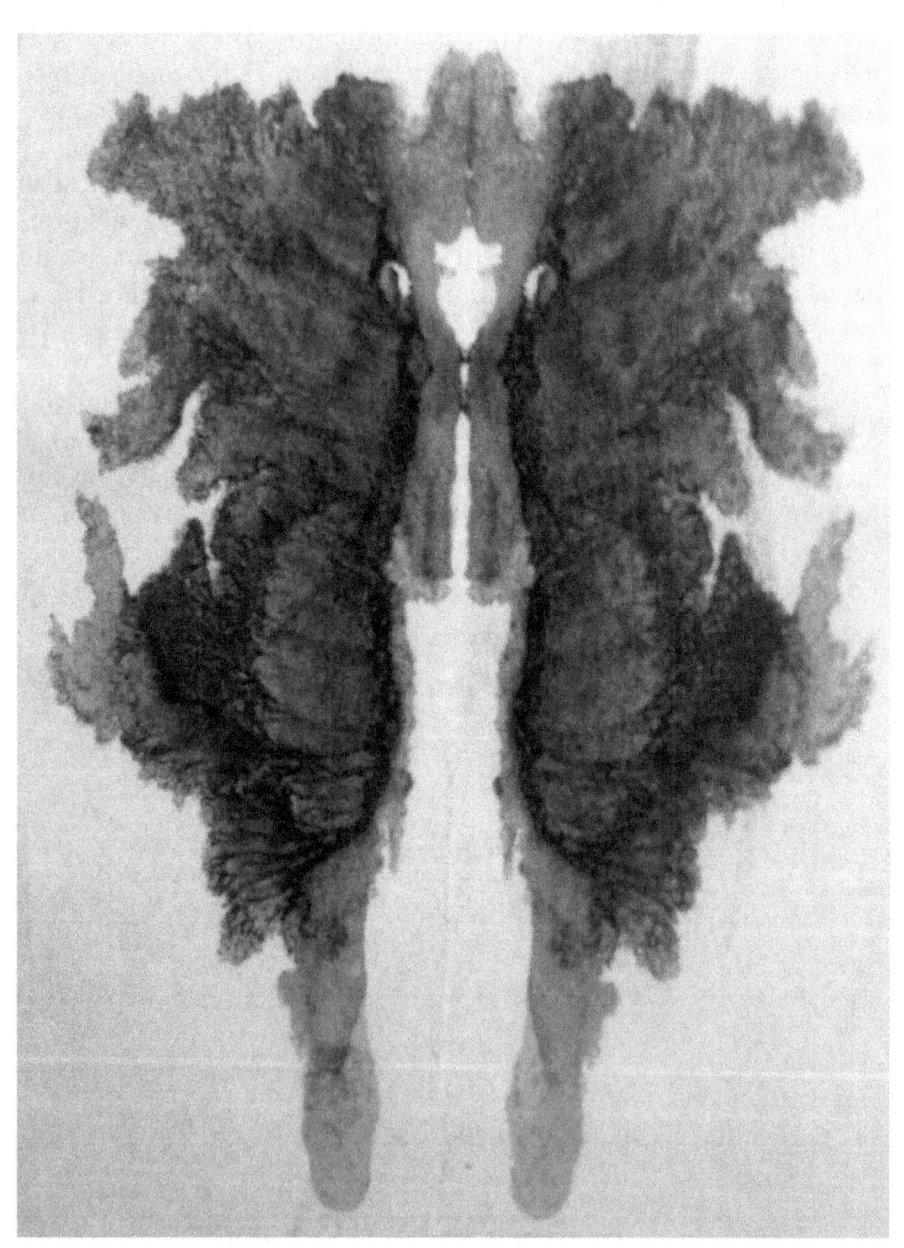

"Get your things packed up we are going camping." Sister was scurrying around packing her jeans. I wasn't sure. This probably was mom's idea. She was always trying to do "family things" with dad. "Where are we going?" "To the lake for one night. Maybe you boys and your dad will catch some fish." Dad never took us fishing before, why now?

When our orange van pulled into a campsite it was already late afternoon. Cool breezes off the lake felt good. We hiked, played in the water, and built mud castles. It looked like dad was having fun teaching us how to skip rocks across the water. Dinner was hot dogs with marshmallows for dessert.

Finally time to get our sleeping bags out. "Where's the tent?" "We don't have a tent. You and your sister get to sleep out under the stars." "What? Just me and my sister, where are you and mom sleeping?" "We need to sleep in the van with your baby brother."

This wasn't right. We moved our bags close to the van. Mom didn't look too happy about the arrangements either, but she kept assuring us that it would be fine. Sure, fine! Out here with the bears, bugs, night creatures and who knows what else. Sister was scared, I needed be the brave one. "What was that?" A creepy sound over by the burned out campfire. "I don't know, just cover your head and go to sleep. Dad said it would be okay."

What do you think?

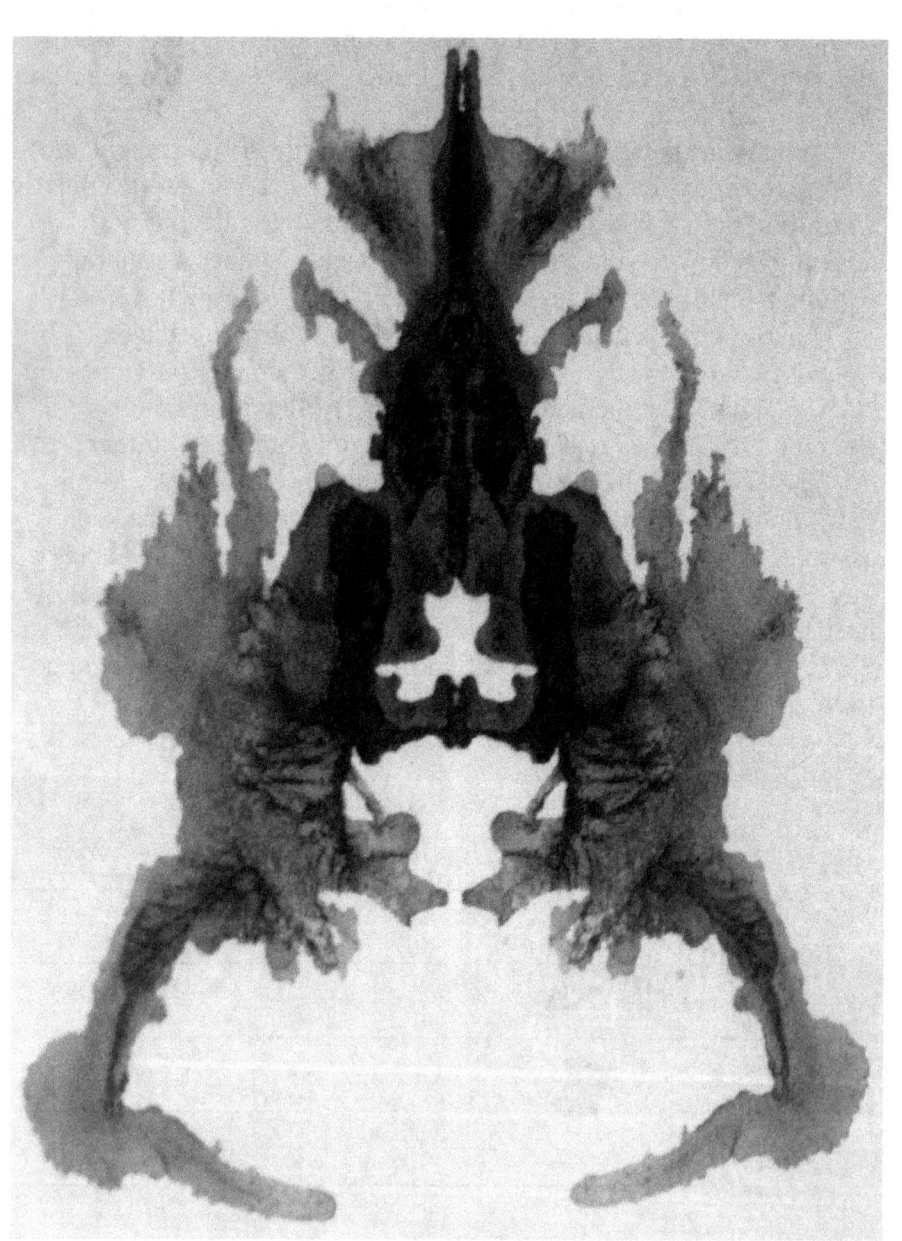

O Christmas tree, O Christmas tree… You may have heard that familiar song. In fact, you might be humming it right now. The real meaning of Christmas gets lost in the hustle of the season. One of the magical times is driving through the neighborhoods looking at the decorations.

Checking out the Christmas trees in the house windows is my favorite part. Trees can be small or ridiculously tall. They come in all shapes and colors. I've seen pink ones, and red ones. Green with fake snow are my favorite. There was one tree that was so tall as it sat in the big picture window that it went through the roof and continued toward the sky. A clever homeowner.

Can you see the Christmas tree? The one with red birds chomping away at the berries and nuts high up in the tree. Hiking through the forest, it is fun to try and spot the perfect tree. Over there, look, that one is a little lopsided. Looks like the sun never hit the other side. We wouldn't want that one for our house.

Farther down the trail we see a bushy tree. Getting closer to it causes several squirrels to jump in every direction. We jumped, too. That was close. Now the tree doesn't look as bushy as before. It just looks empty and sad. Maybe if we step away from it, the squirrels will return and it can be a happy tree again.

What do you think?

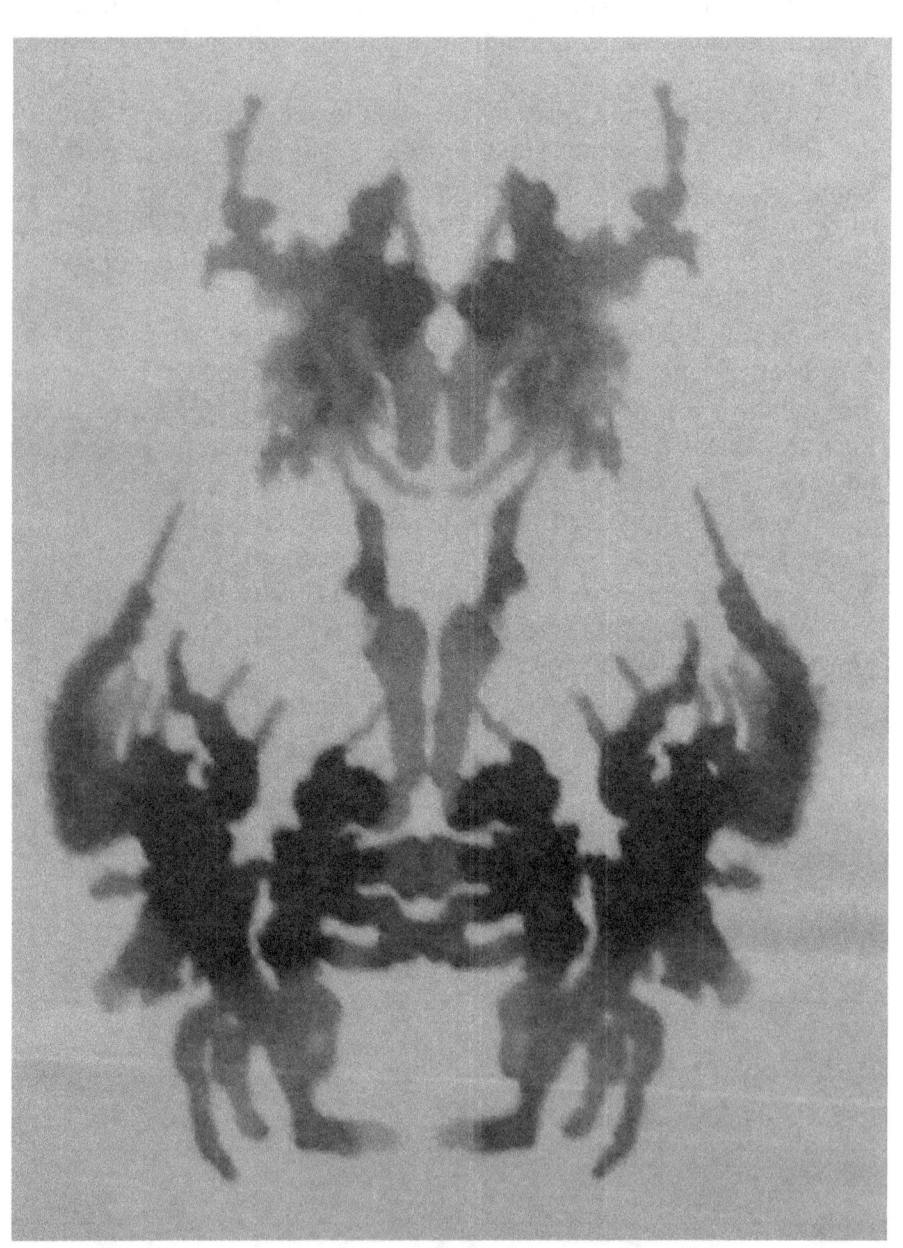

Ink! Ink! What do you think?

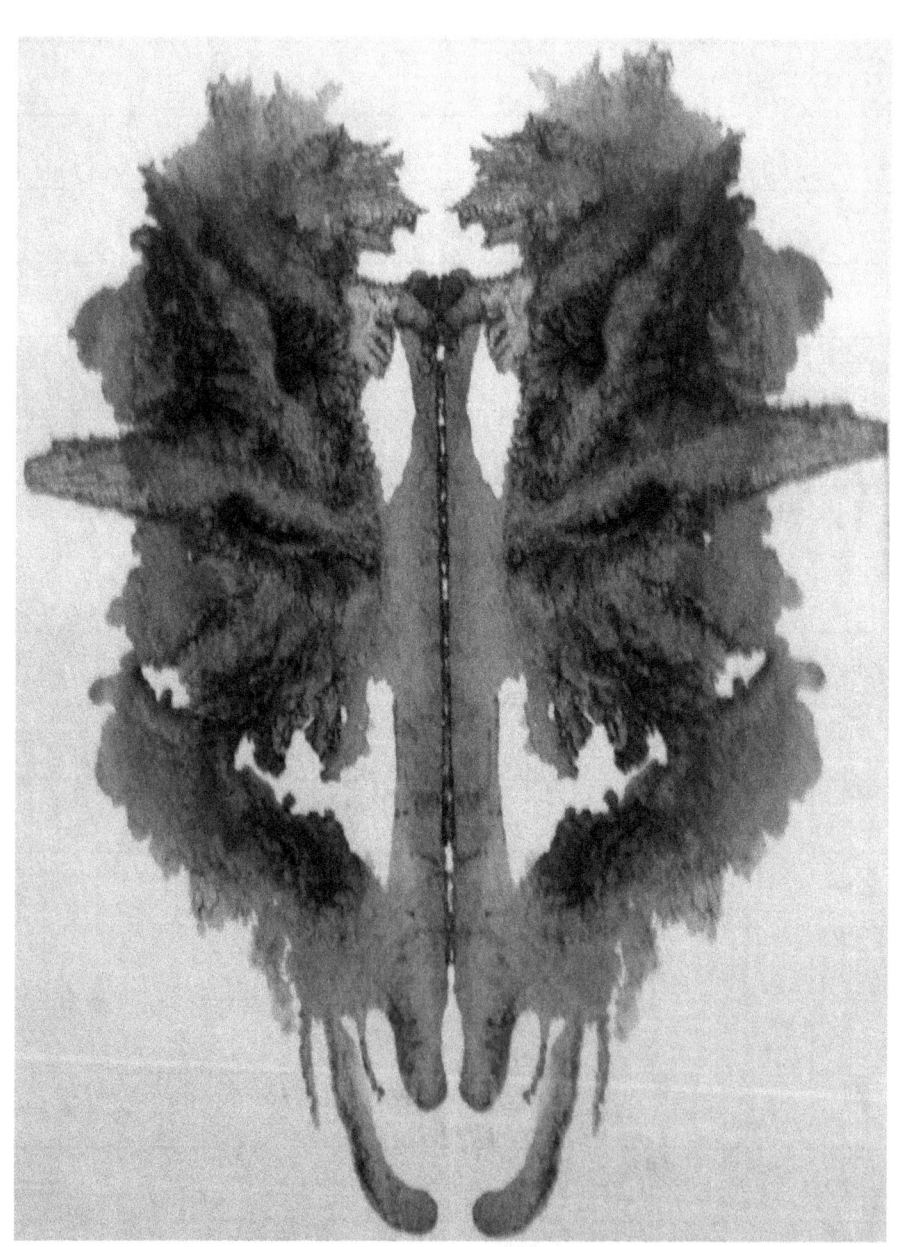

Didn't you see all the cactus? Cactus, everywhere. This desert is covered in cactus. Don't know why mom told me to run away from the safety of the rest area. She simply said to head over to the tree as fast as I could. I ran, and as I was running, I tripped on a piece of broken log.

I wouldn't have tripped, except for the horned toad that was about to be smashed by my foot. When I spotted him it was too late to change my direction. I was going to land square on his back. My body unwillingly stiffened, which made my leg straight. As my stiff leg came down, the toad simply hopped out of the way. But, I was still in "EEEK it's a toad mode," so my stiff leg hit the ground so hard that I tumbled into the nearest cactus bed.

I got up and tried not to cry. As I returned to the van the pain was traveling up and down my leg. I had to move very slowly. My brother and sister were making fun of me. Mom was sympathetic to my plight, as she could see that my blue jeans were full of cactus stickers.

There was no way I could sit down. I had to just stand there while mom plucked cactus stickers out of my jeans. She slowly turned me around, making sure she found them all. This all happened because Mom wanted me to get some exercise.

What do you think?

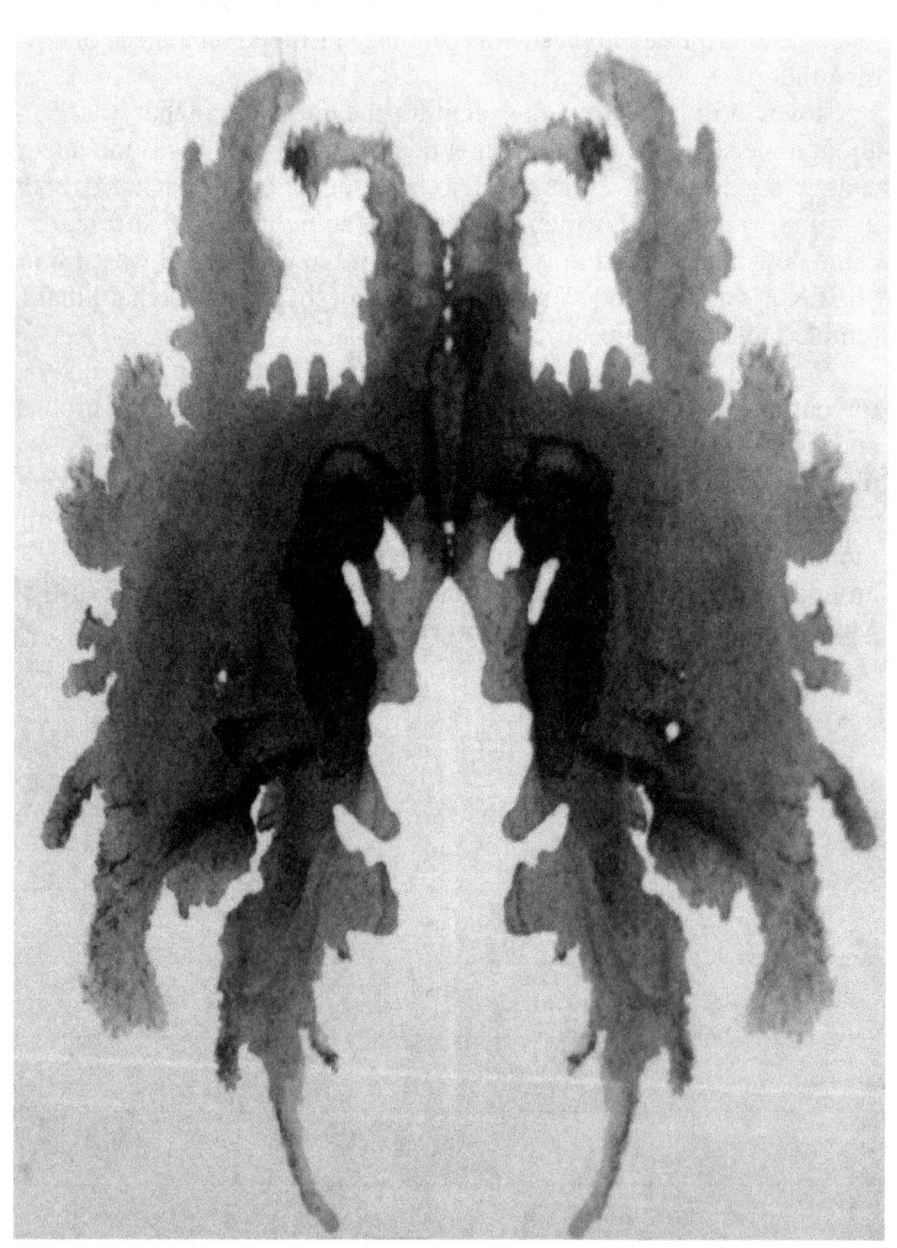

As she played her saxophone she was standing right across from the cutest guy in the band. When he realized that she was watching him, he picked up his horn and played the same tune. The room was filled with glorious sounds.

What do you think?

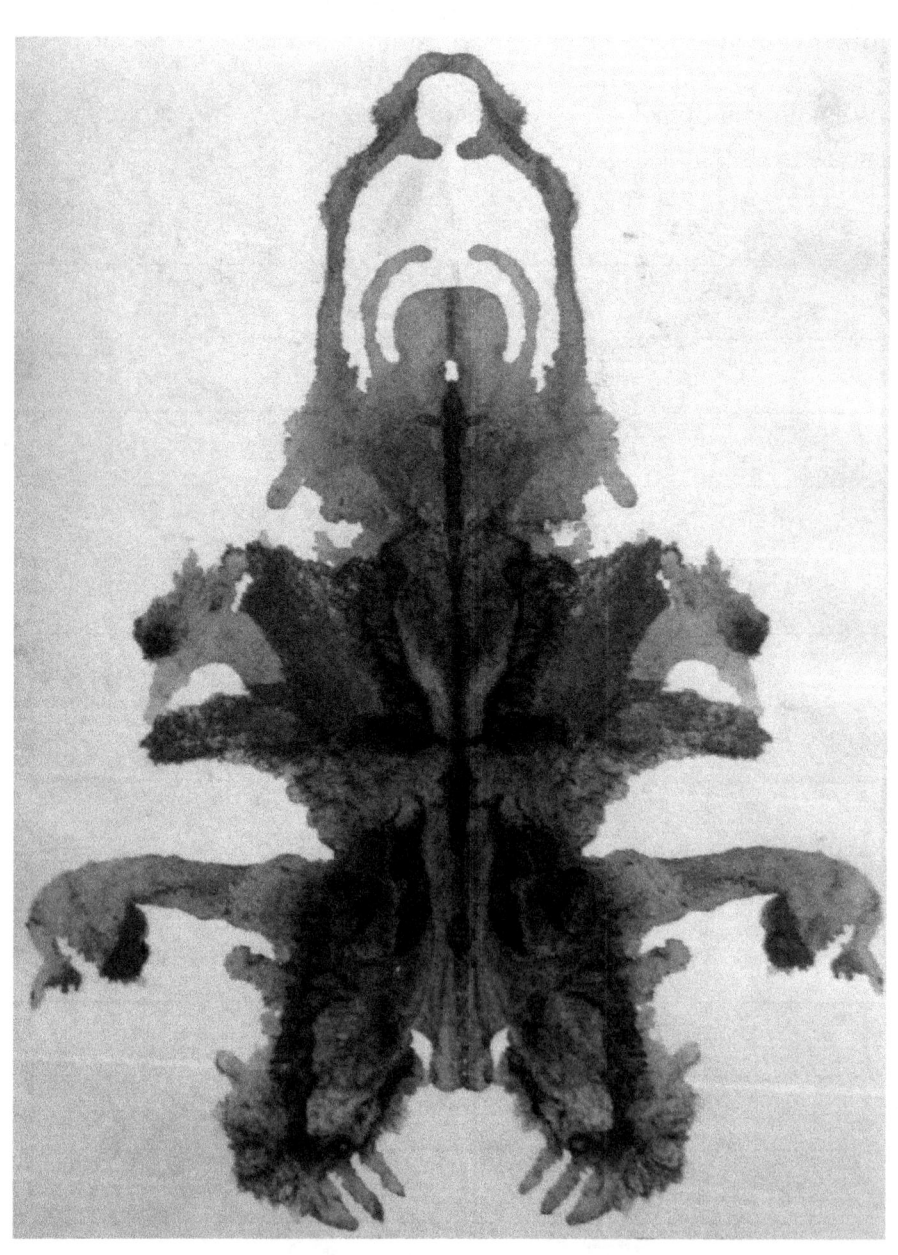

You see it, don't you? ...The big toe, right there in the middle of the ink blot. Makes me remember growing up, and all the stubbed toes I got. All of the neighborhood kids went barefoot everywhere that we could. By the end of summer, my feet were hard as rocks on the bottom. We ran, played baseball in the street, and jumped rope with bare feet. So naturally, every other week or so, "Ouch," I stubbed my big toe.

One day we were up on the roof of my house. Daddy put out a ladder and we got to climb up there with him. Slowly and carefully we made our way up the slopping roof to the top. There we sat down to enjoy the view. The mountains looked closer, the tops of trees swayed faster, and the birds seemed to be beckoning us to soar with them. It was an exciting adventure for a ten year old, looking down at the world.

But, sure enough, climbing our way down the ladder, I caught my big toe on a wooden rung. "Ouch," It snagged the nail and bit into my skin. "Mom, get out the iodine, I stubbed my big toe, again!"

What do you think?

Look at this ink blot. It keeps changing every time you look at it. Sometimes it just takes blinking and poof you see something different. Think about it. When a group of people are staring at the clouds, everyone sees something different in the clouds

"There, I see a pair of shoes walking on a cloud."
"I see a man with a gavel in his hand."
"Look, over there to the right, that is a puppy dog chasing a ball."
"That looks like a mama duck with her babies following her."
"I see a pretty bow, that looks like it was tied perfectly."

As the crowd watches the sky, a slight breeze begins to change the formations. The clouds are drifting away. Some of the people begin to leave, while a smaller group decided to lay down on the cool grass and watch the cloud scenery go by.

"Now it looks like the ocean waves."
"Over there could be a dolphin jumping way up out of the cloud."
"I see a giant redwood tree almost ready to fall."
"Where?
"Over there, see how the wind is blowing it over?"
"A giant tree, a pair of shoes, a dolphin, and a pretty bow."

What do you think?

The house where I grew up was on a street with nine or ten houses on each side. The sidewalks were smooth in most places and perfect for skating. I had to wear sturdy shoes, so that the skates could be attached securely. Getting them to fit properly was really a scientific marvel.

The skate key was used to adjust the skate's length to match my shoe. The key also tightened the clamps around the soles of my shoes. After they were buckled on, they had to be tightened just right, or I could end up with one skate on, and one skate dangling from my ankle.

As I skated down the street, I kept my skate key on a string. I could have worn it around my neck like jewelry, but I usually held it in my hand. I dropped it occasionally, and could stop and pick it up. But, as we all skated by the house on the corner, we knew to beware. Their whole front yard was ivy, ivy ten inches tall in some places. No telling what lived in there.

Of course, you know what happened. Skate keys were lost in the ivy almost every week. No way to find them in that growth. I must have lost almost a dozen keys, and so did all the neighborhood kids. Can you imagine what they found in their ivy years later when they decided to just grow a lawn?

What do you think?

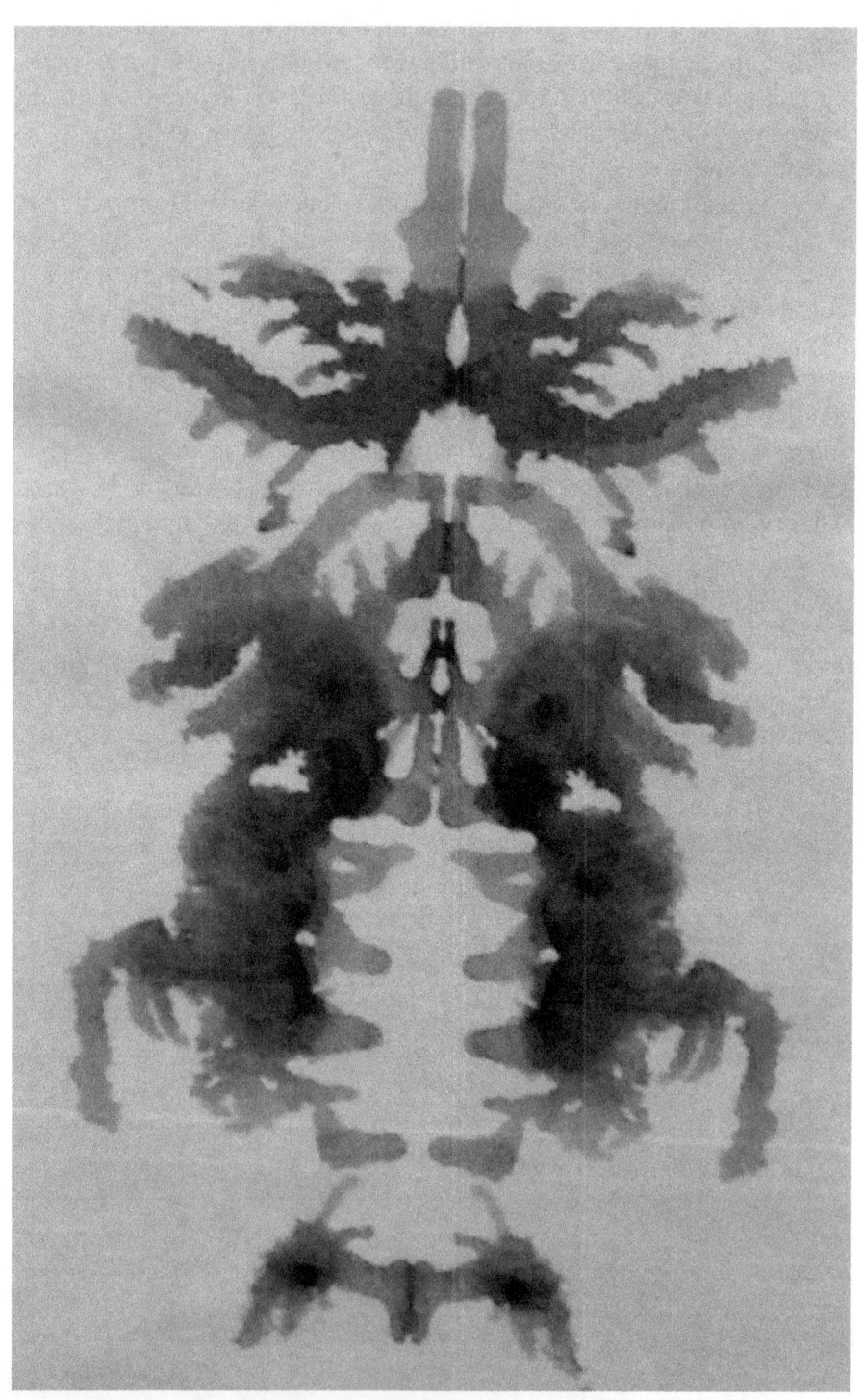

Ink! Ink! What do you think?

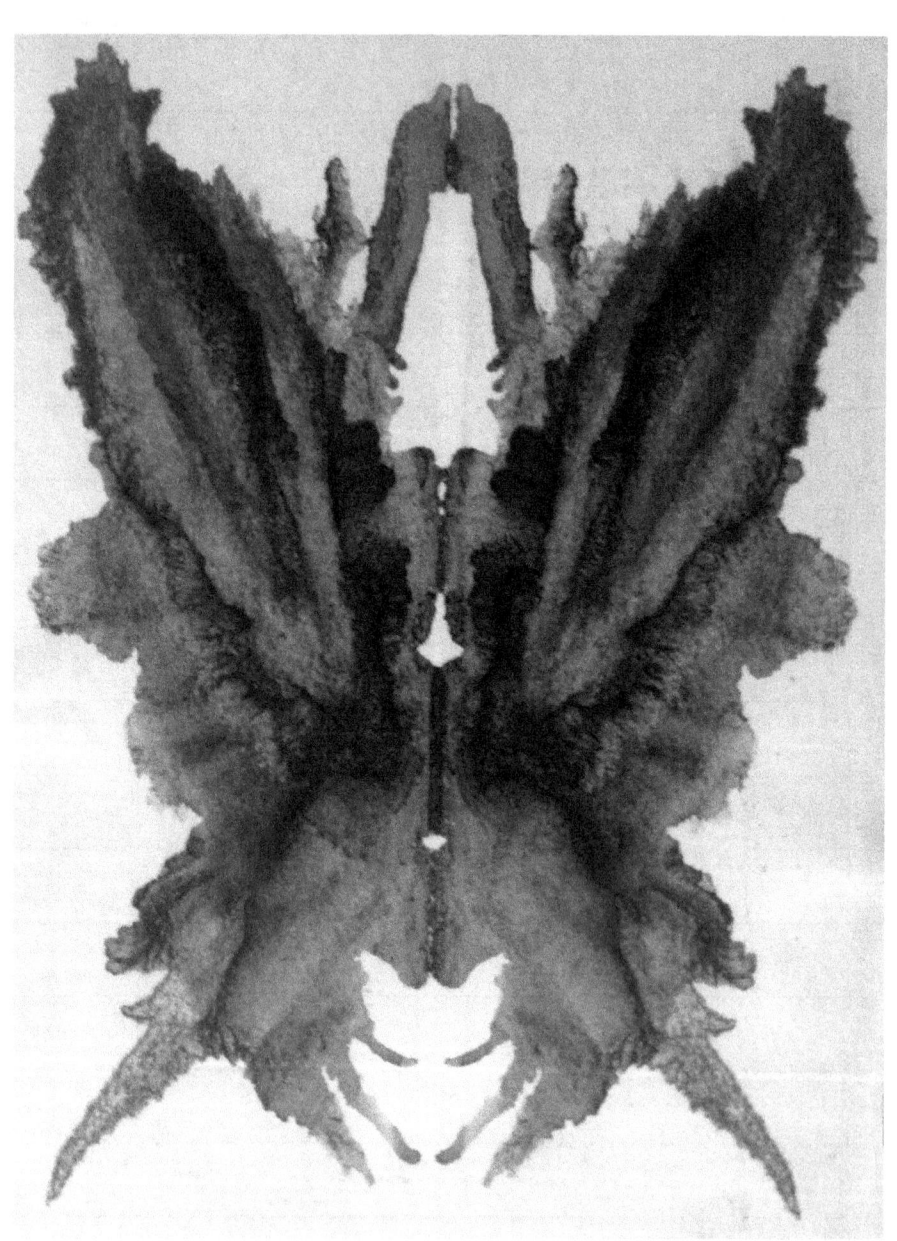

We were headed to Catalina Island to spend a few days. After a short train ride to the harbor, we arrived at the ship's dock just in time to buy our tickets. Grandma worked her way towards the front of the line. "Grandma, the end is back there." "Wah-toost" she said in her broken Swedish accent. I'm sure it meant be quiet. Anyway, she got our tickets, and I heard the ticket seller tell the next couple "sold out." My face was red, I looked at the ground, hung on to grandma's hand and boarded the ship.

Catalina was fun with grandma. We took the glass-bottom boat ride, checked out the old museum, saw flying fish, and found a hotel close to the small beach.

Our biggest adventure was a tour of the island. The bus driver, Josh, knew everything about the island and told some of the funniest stories. It was good to see grandma laugh. Suddenly, a buffalo appeared in front of us. Screeching to a halt, Josh identified him as "Billy G," the buffalo that acted like a Billy Goat. No amount of horn honking helped. We all got concerned when Billy G started pawing the ground. When his eyes locked onto Josh's eyes, we held our breathe. Slowly the Josh backed the bus up. Billy G stood still, then he appeared satisfied that he had won. Billy G snorted loudly and trotted off into the trees. Whew!

What do you think?

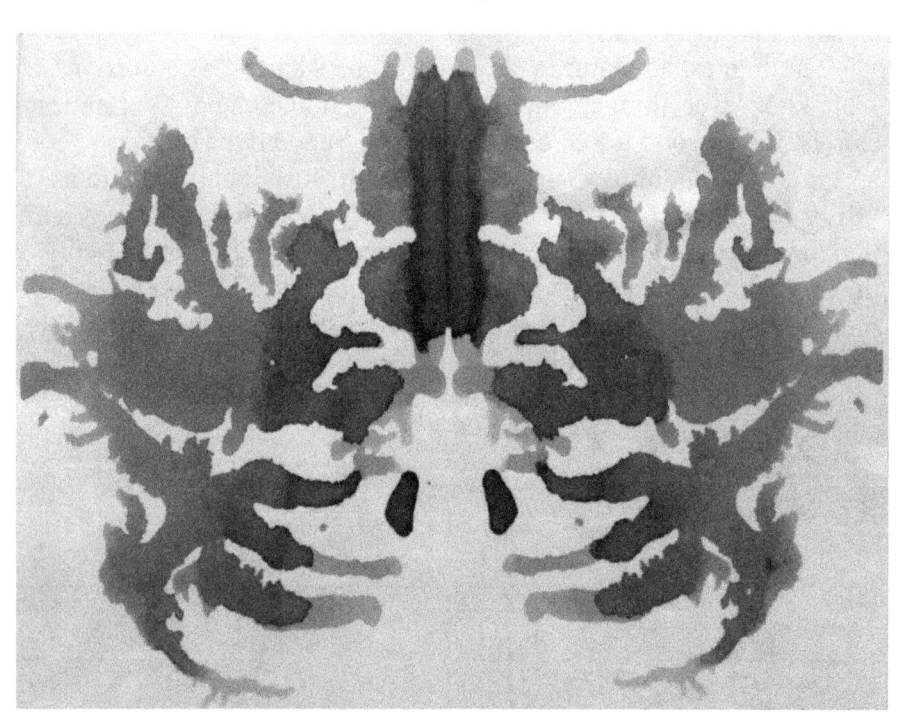

I think I see snowflakes. Do you see them? We grew up in a desert that produced a small snowfall every other year. Just enough snow to close the schools for a day. But, snow in the mountains was even more fun.

One long weekend we climbed in our orange van and headed to the snow covered mountains. We enjoyed skiing and playing in the snow As we left the mountain retreat, heading downhill, mom noticed that there were no brakes. Resting the brakes, mom noticed that the brakes returned slightly. Slowly she pulled off to the side to assess the situation. There she was on top of the mountain with three kids and no brakes. Slowly mom drove the van, almost coasting to the next turn out. After cars passed, she pulled out again and cruised on a bit further. So, slowly we came down the hill. When we arrived in the small town at the bottom of the hill, everything was closed. What was mom to do? Might as well keep driving.

Mom got on the highway, pulled in behind slow eighteen wheelers, and never applied the brakes. That weekend we drove from Santa Fe to Albuquerque, stopped for a wedding celebration, and then continued on home to El Paso. All with no brakes!

What do you think?

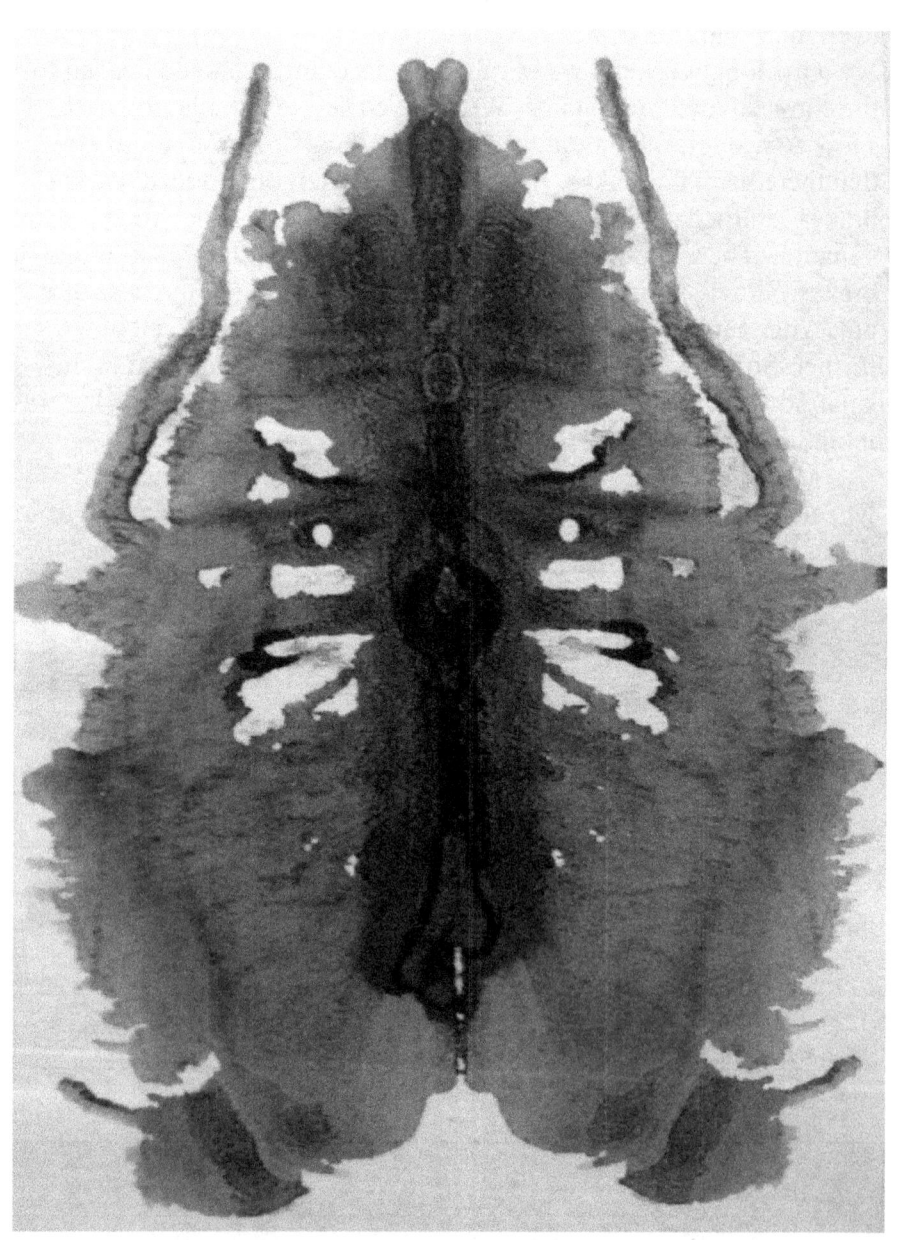

I shouldn't really complain about that old orange van. It took us everywhere we needed to go. It could be spotted anywhere in town. All our friends knew where we were, and never missed a chance to tell us they saw the "Orange Blob." Guess we kids should have kept our name for it a secret.

Faithfully, Orange Blob took us to Grandma's house in California every summer. There was no air conditioning, as we traveled the hot desert highways. The only windows we could open were on the driver and passenger side doors. We drank lots of water and survived several summer trips. One time it was a bit sketchy, Mom had to put motor oil in it every night. It became harder and harder to start each time we stopped at a rest area or a cafe. But, Orange Blob always got us to California and back home again.

These vacations were also an experiment in patience. One side of the van had no windows behind the driver. The other side just had a window in the sliding door. This meant that if mom saw something on the left side of the road, she would just say, "Oh, you can see it on the way back."

What do you think?

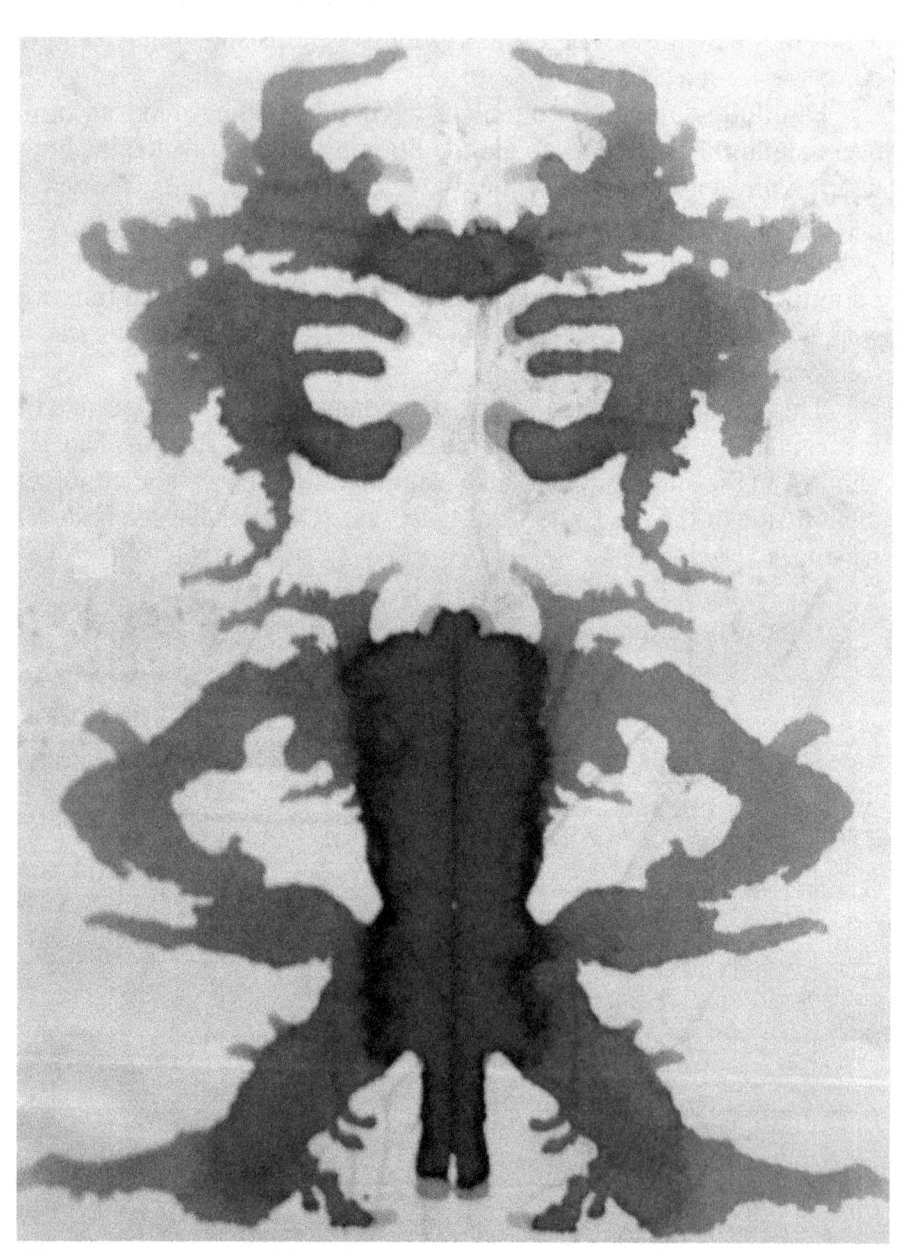

"Have you cleaned your room?" mom asked. "I will," was my answer. "Grandma and grandpa will be here in two days," mom replied.

"Have you cleaned you room?" mom asked. "I'm going to," I answered. "They will be here tomorrow," mom replied.

"Have you cleaned your room?" mom asked. Why does she keep asking me that? I know she has looked in my room. I haven't tackled it yet. "Did you hear me?" mom asked. "Yes, it's a mess, it'll take forever. I don't know what to do with it," I said. "Why do you think I have been reminding you? If you had started three days ago…" mom didn't finish the sentence.

I know she's right, but I wanted to play baseball with my friends. Then we all walked to the store for candy. Yesterday I was laying on the grass counting the pigeons on the telephone wires. Did you ever notice how they clump together, then one pigeon will shove another off the wire? The ousted pigeon then has to find another place to hang. Guess even a pigeon's life is complicated.

Anyway, Grandma will be here in an hour. Time to go into overdrive. This will fit in the closet, that in the drawers, these in the laundry basket, and I'll sweep this into the wastebasket. Looking around, it's shaping up. All that stuff will fit under the bed. Need to quickly dust and "tah dah" I'm done.

If Grandma doesn't open my closet or look under the bed, I'm good.

What do you think?

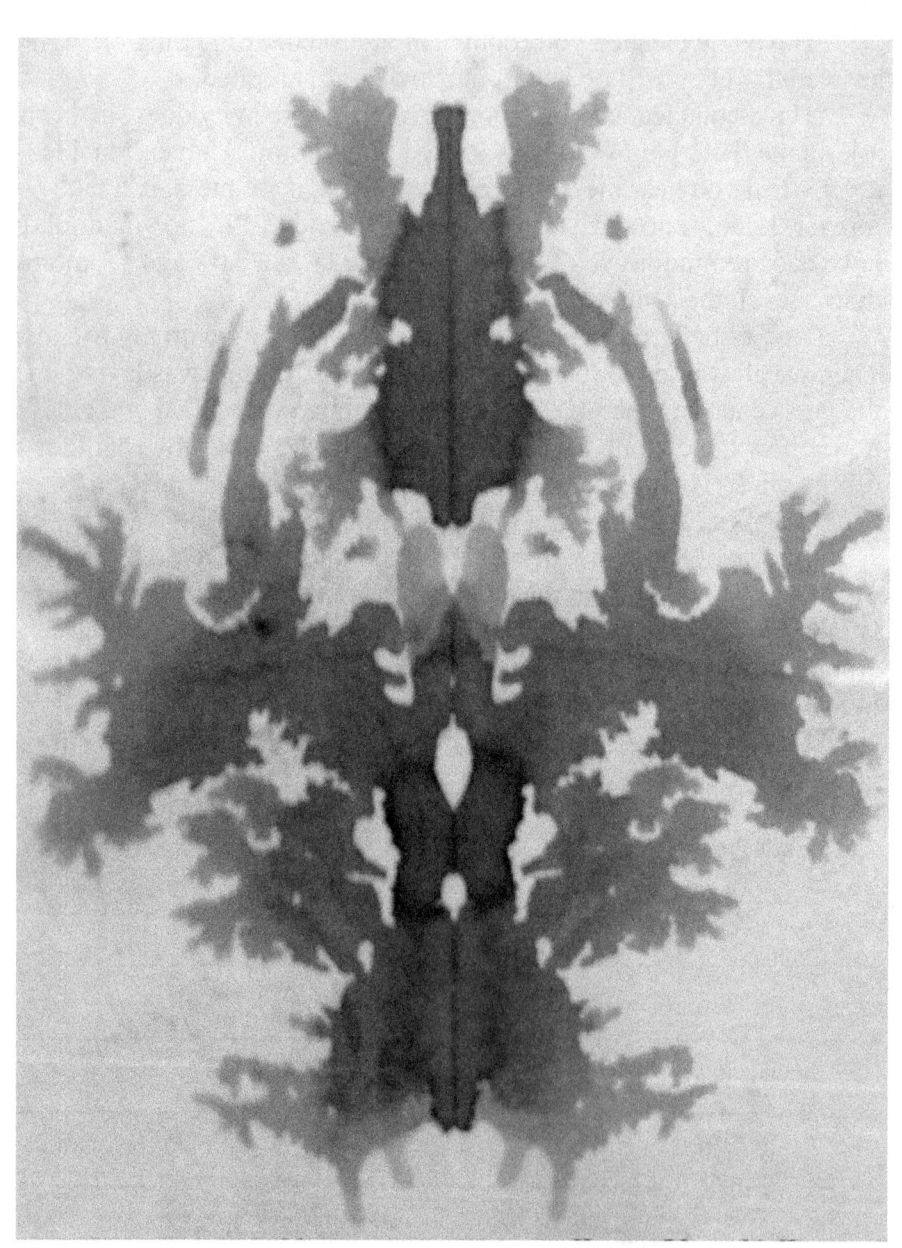

Daisy June was out to dinner with several friends, at their favorite restaurant. This evening the service was not the same. The waiter forgot to refill the water glasses, didn't put out enough silverware, and was having trouble taking their food order.

Finishing the meal, Daisy June was not happy. She never got her side order of okra. Checking the bill, the okra was there. Daisy June was not happy. She wanted to see the manager, she wanted to see the owner, she complained until the okra was taken off of the bill.

When they got in their car to leave, Daisy June settled down. Taking a deep breath she began to relax. As she pulled out a lipstick from her purse, she flipped down the passenger mirror and gazed at herself in disbelief. Oh my goodness! Right there on her tooth was the biggest piece of spinach she had ever seen. It stuck there and looked like it was cemented on her front tooth.

No wonder the waiter, the cashier and the manager were holding back their smiles. Can you imagine this insane sounding woman, ranting and raving about her dinner, while a piece of spinach made her a comic figure?

What do you think?

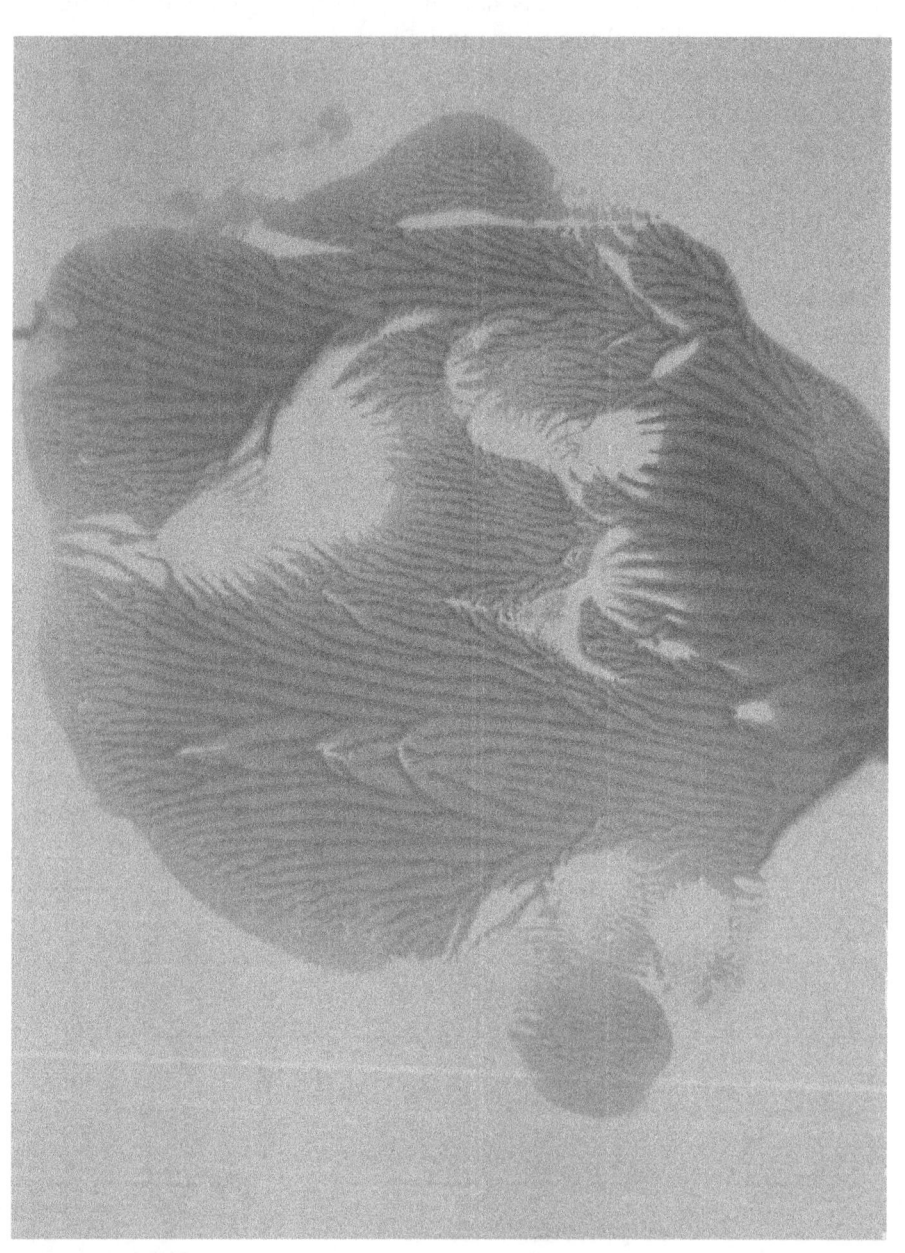

Creating these and finding the stories they tell can be a family affair! Here is one made by my great-grandson, Eli. If he were telling this "inky" story, he might create a tale of a young boy lying out on his backyard trampoline one warm spring afternoon, when he should have been doing his homework. As he gazes into the sky, he sees this strange fiery cloud moving in quickly overhead. Slowly he rises, preparing to run in to tell dad to come see, when, faster than he can run, the cloud whooshes down flooding his body with more power than he has ever felt before. The cloud returns to the sky, as fast as it came down, but soon the boy notices he can do things he has only ever imagined he can! BUT, if I am telling the tale, I guarantee mine is going to be of adventures by the ocean, where these beautiful sea fans make their home!

What do you think?

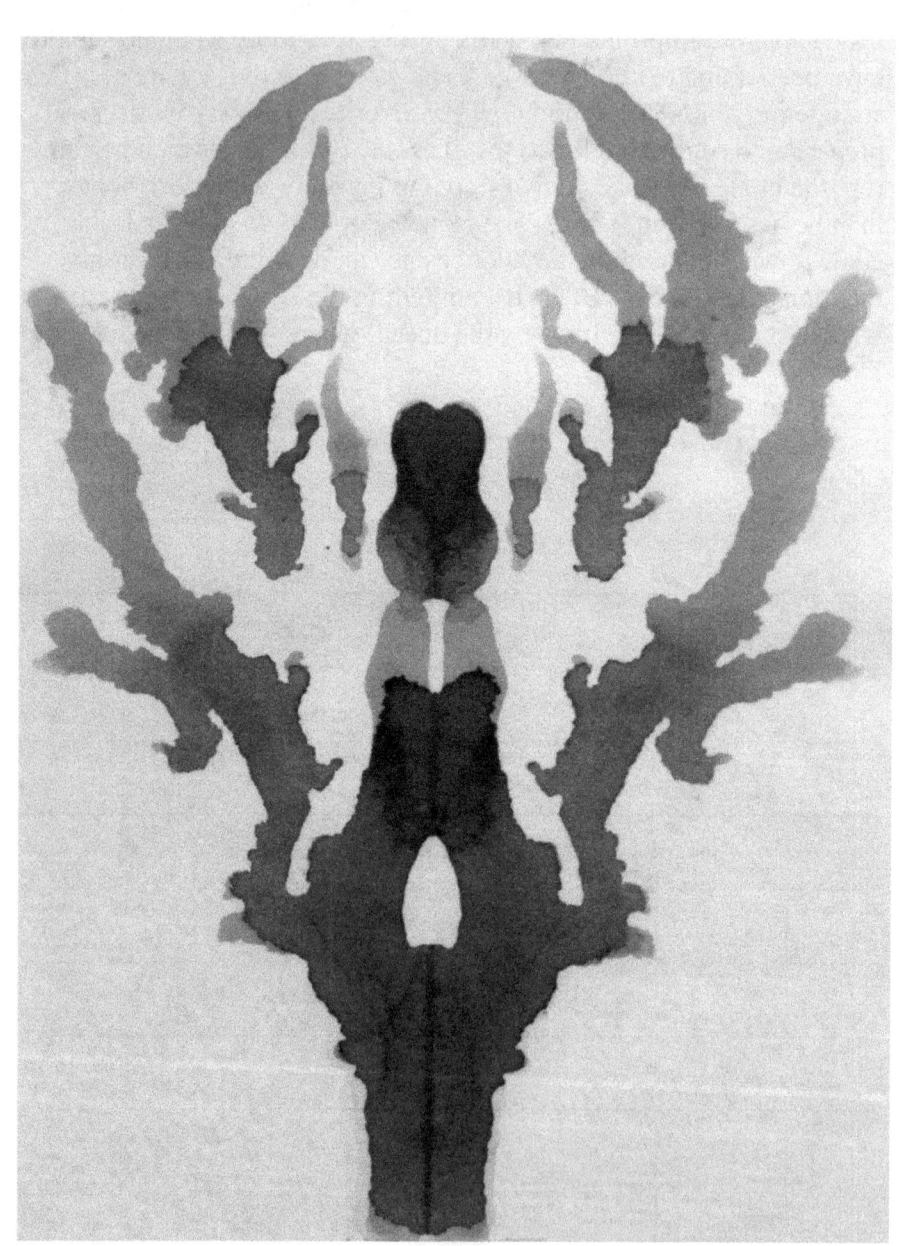

The swimming lessons were getting longer and longer every Thursday afternoon that summer. The brothers and sisters loved to bob up and down in the whirlpool near the center of the lake. Their swimming instructor was always yelling at them to return to their swim positions.

What do you think?

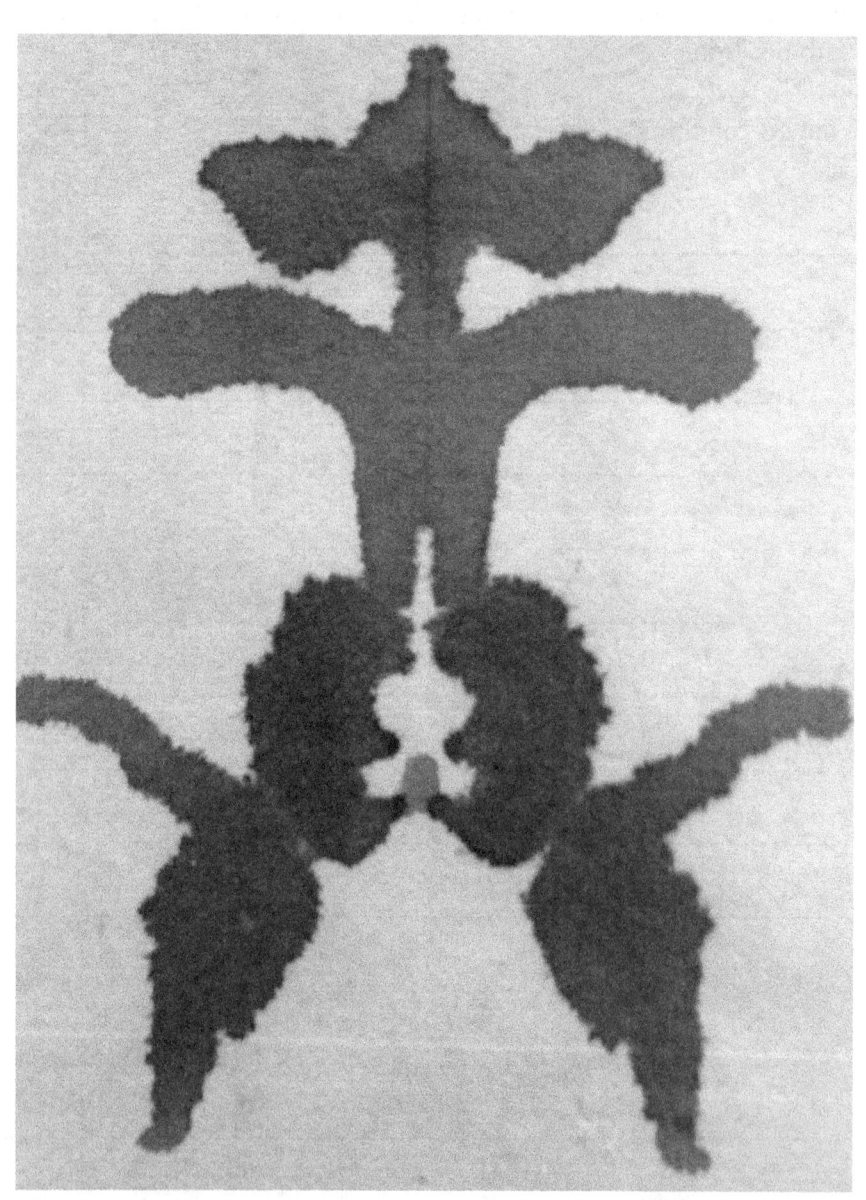

They all lived in a three bedroom one bath house on a busy boulevard. Comfortable, except he had to share a bedroom with little brother. No privacy for him. One day dad offered him the office room next to the garage. Perfect! His own room. It was larger, and definitely private. He could study, read, or just hang out by himself. In the storage room he found an extra desk and a chair. "There's the old waterbed," he thought, "wonder if it leaks?" He tested it out and decided it would work perfectly. Things were looking good.

Only problem, the bathroom was in the house. He had to go in to wash his hands, take a shower, etc. This would have been annoying except, no more sharing a room with his little brother. Besides, he did have to eat and watch television and occasionally talk to his sister in the house.

Life was good out in the office. Then one afternoon it happened. He went in to take a shower. Passing his old bedroom, he noticed toys, clothes, and books strewn everywhere. "Boy, I'm glad to be out of there," he thought.

The shower was quick. He didn't want to be late for the church youth group meeting. He stepped out of the shower, wrapped the towel around his waist, headed for the sidedoor, took the two steps in one giant leap and "oh my", the towel dropped. There he was, standing alone, as a tourist bus passed by.

What do you think?

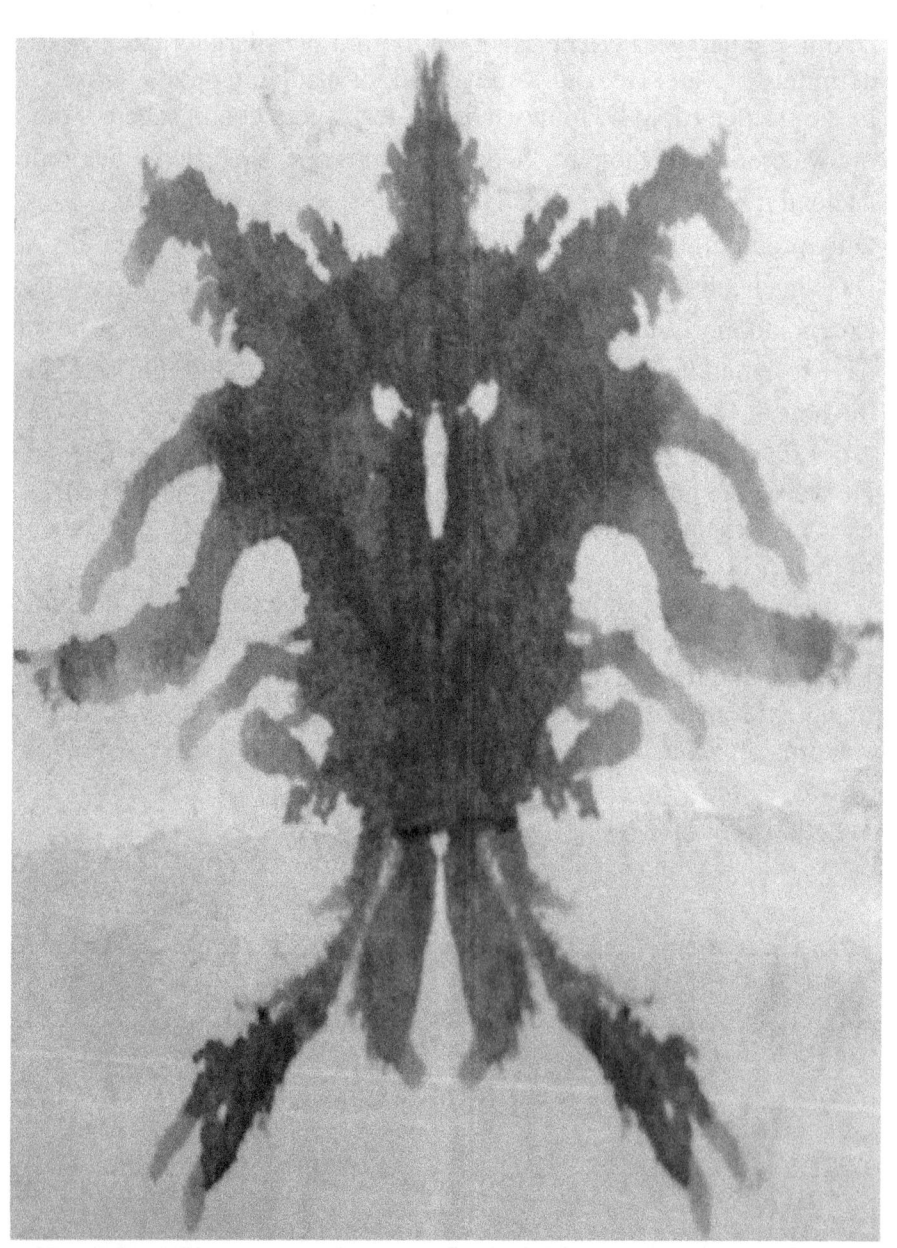

The band leader was tapping his feet as he held the baton high in the air. The students waited breathlessly for him to nod and start the music.

What do you think?

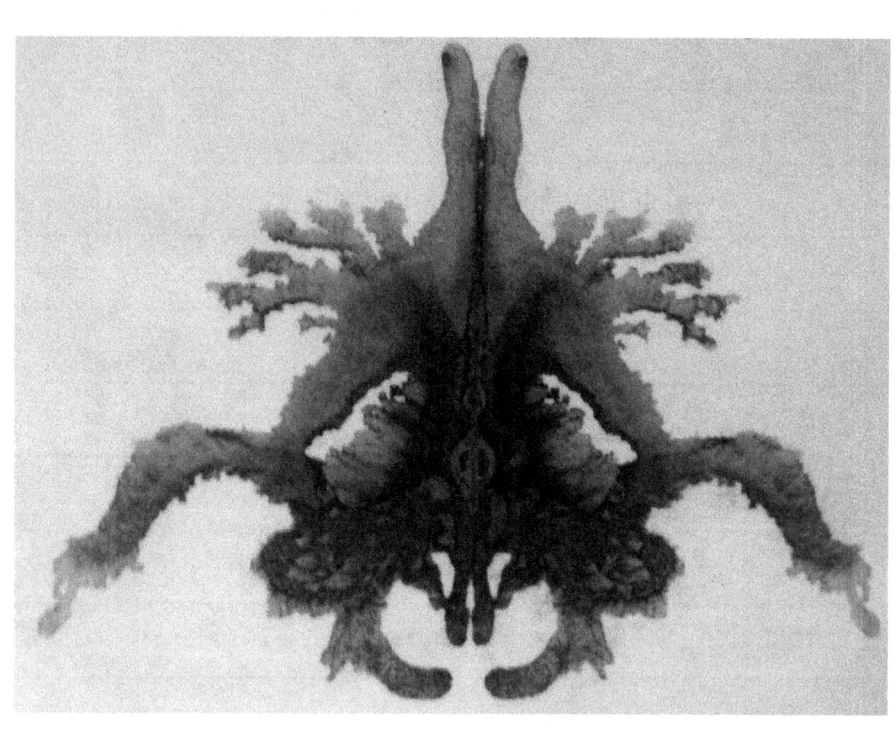

I really don't know when Grandpa Axel Rodes arrived in the United States. He was from a large Finnish family. In the early 1900's, he along with two or three of his brothers decided to leave the old country behind. Finland might have been his homeland, but he always referred to himself as a Swede-Finn. The two countries are as close as California and Arizona with a bit of a sea, almost like a large lake between them.

  When the brothers arrived here, it was the custom of many foreigners to change their names to sound more American. The "Skog" brothers picked the name Rodes. Only they each spelled it differently....Rodes, Rhodes, Rodas. Then they proceeded to go to different parts of America at a time when communication wasn't a phone call away.

  What this means is that I have no idea who my early relatives were or where they ended up.

What do you think?

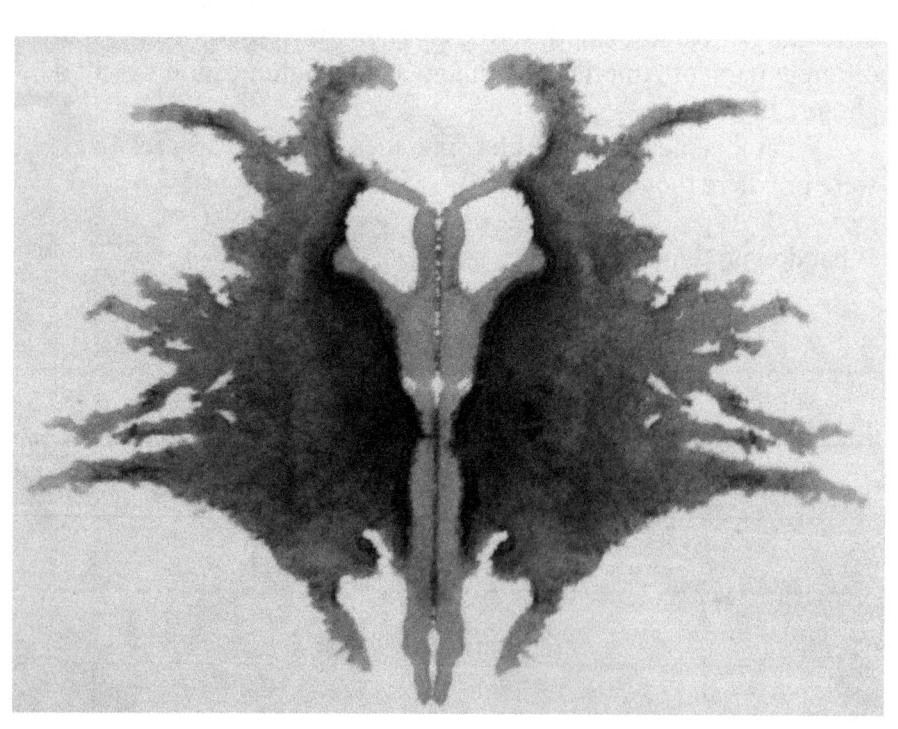

As a Swedish emigrant around 1914 my grandfather, Carl Gustaff Adolphus Svedman, arrived on a ship that was loaded with many different European nationalities. He slept in crowded quarters, leaning against the wall. Leaving Sweden, his father wished him good luck, handed him a gold pocket watch and said goodbye.

The ship made a stop in France to collect more passengers before setting sail across the ocean for America. It was sometime during this stop, that the gold watch was lifted from his pocket as he slept. While he was saddened by this theft, he was looking forward to his America adventure.

The lines were long when they arrived on American soil. Checking in, he was asked "How do you spell your name?" "S- double V- E- D- M- A- N." Grandpa answered. "Okay," the clerk said, "Swedman." By the time grandpa noticed that she misspelled his name it was too late. Double V in Swedish is the letter "V" not "W." So, for the rest of his life in America, my grandfather's name was misspelled.

What do you think?

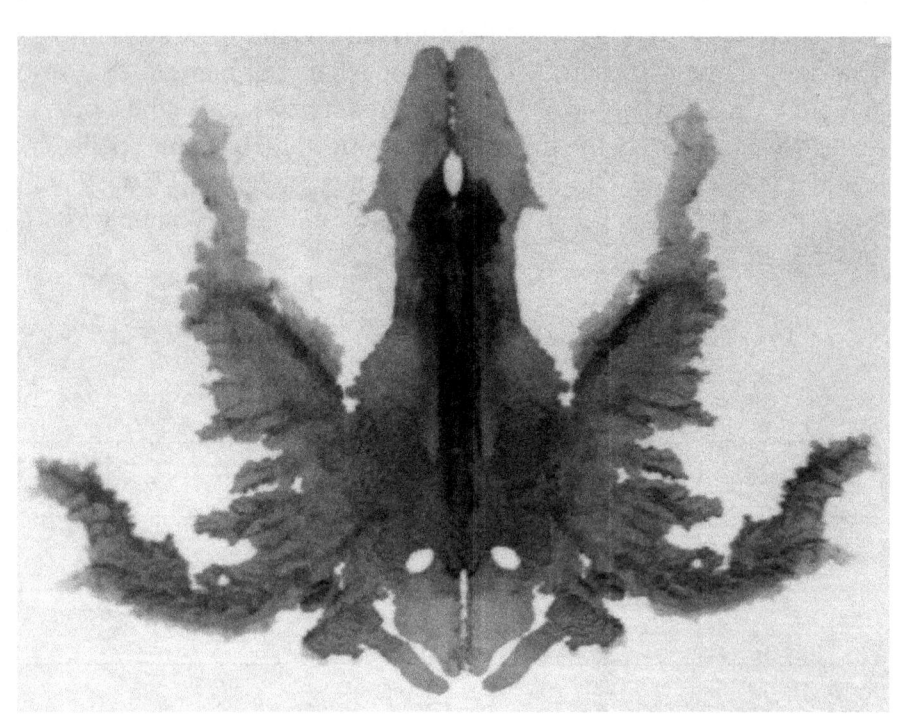

"Gee it's really hot outside," Lulu complained. "I think it is time to stay inside and cool down," mom replied, "and why don't you get out Monopoly, and play with you brothers?" "They don't play fair, they become partners and wipe me out." "Then play dominos," mom suggested.

Lulu yelled for her brothers to come in and play dominoes. They had been playing in the water and were getting mud all over the tile floor. "Stop that, you are walking all over my play area!" Lulu demanded. The mud was falling off of their shoes faster than she could clean it up. "Take off your shoes," she said, "and let's play dominos."

Mom entered the room and immediately sent them to wash up. She was fixing supper and wanted everything spotless before dad got home. "I'm hot," said Lulu. "Come here and get a slice of cucumber," said mom. Lulu danced into the kitchen where mom was slicing some tomatoes and cucumbers for a salad. "Hmmm, good," said Lulu as she munched on a bit of lettuce. "Want to cool down quickly?" mom asked as she forcibly twisted the end of a cucumber on Lulu's forehead. It stuck there.

The boys had washed up and were setting up the dominos, not to play, but to knock down. As Lulu entered the room they broke out laughing. "Lulu's got a green bump on her forehead," they exclaimed. "What is that?" "Where did it come from?"

Lulu just smiled and kept her cool secret.

What do you think?

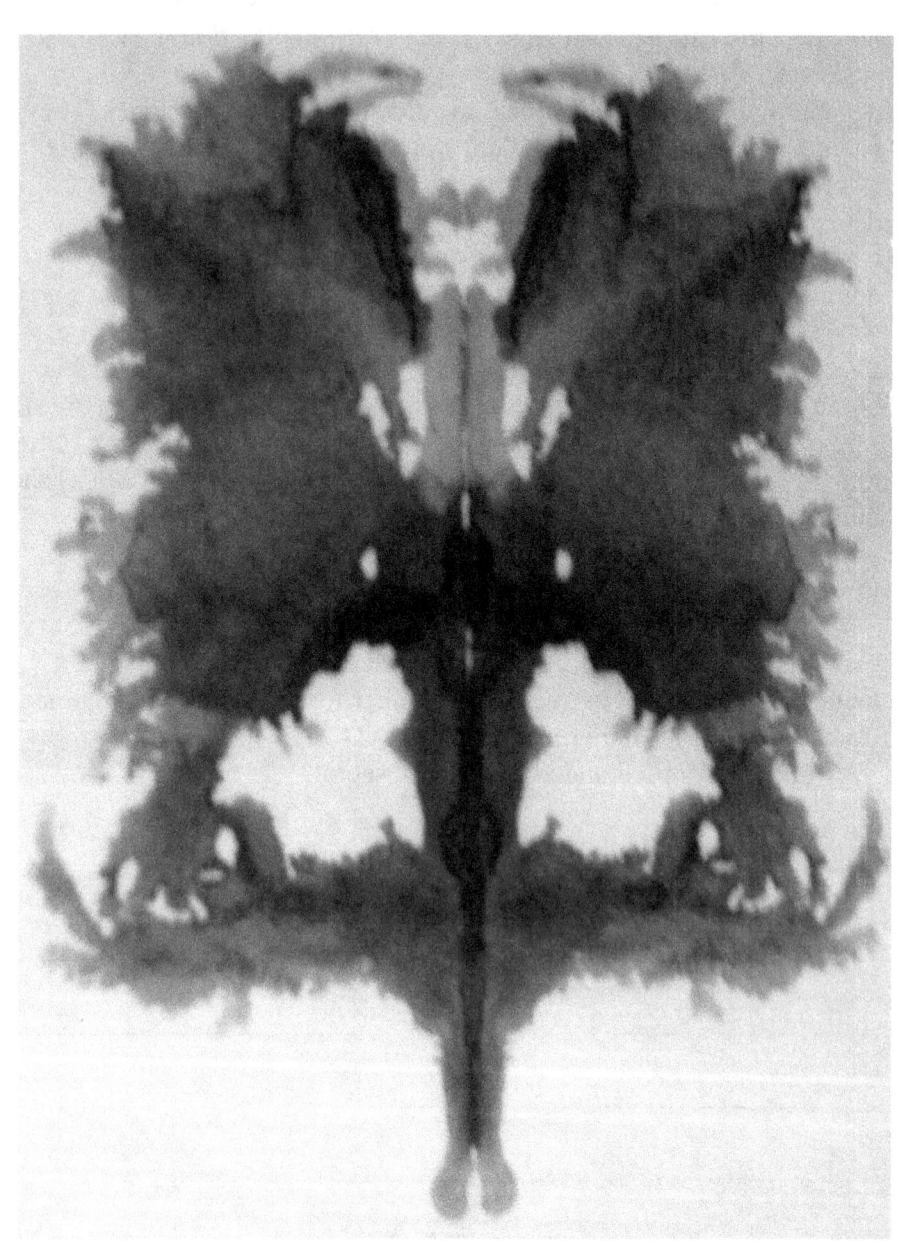

The dew was dancing on the flowers as the morning sun hid behind the mountains.

What do you think?

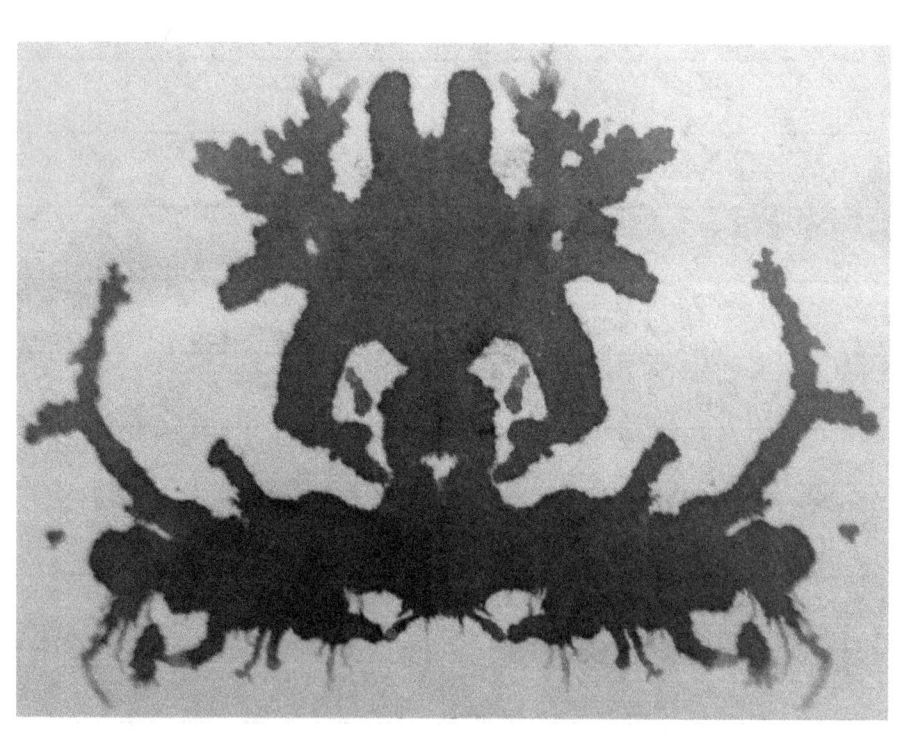

I have a splitting headache. I was riding my bike down the quiet road in my neighborhood. I cruised along putting my head down and guided my bike by watching the curb. As long as I was about a foot from the curb, I traveled slowly down the long street. Crash, I hit a parked car. This car had been way down the street. Apparently I was traveling faster than I thought. Ouch, I had to walk my bent bicycle home.

What do you think?

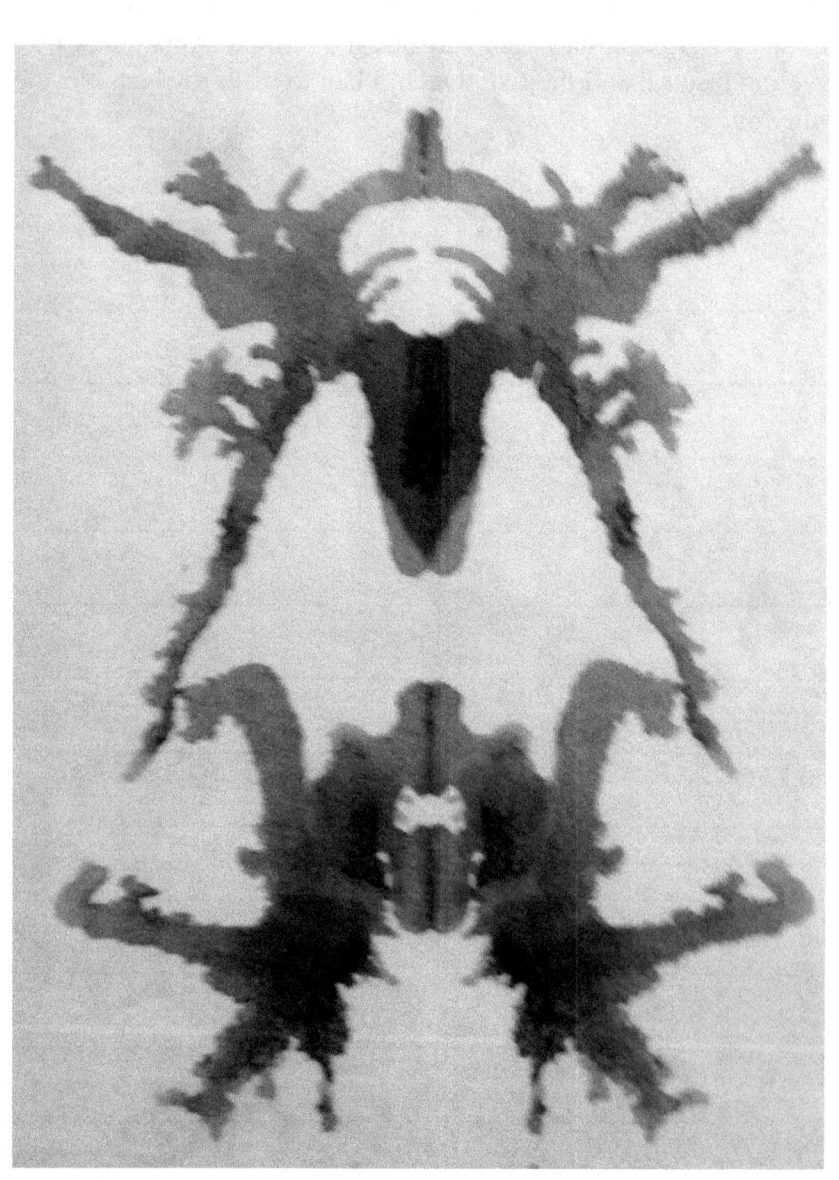

Ink! Ink! What do you think?

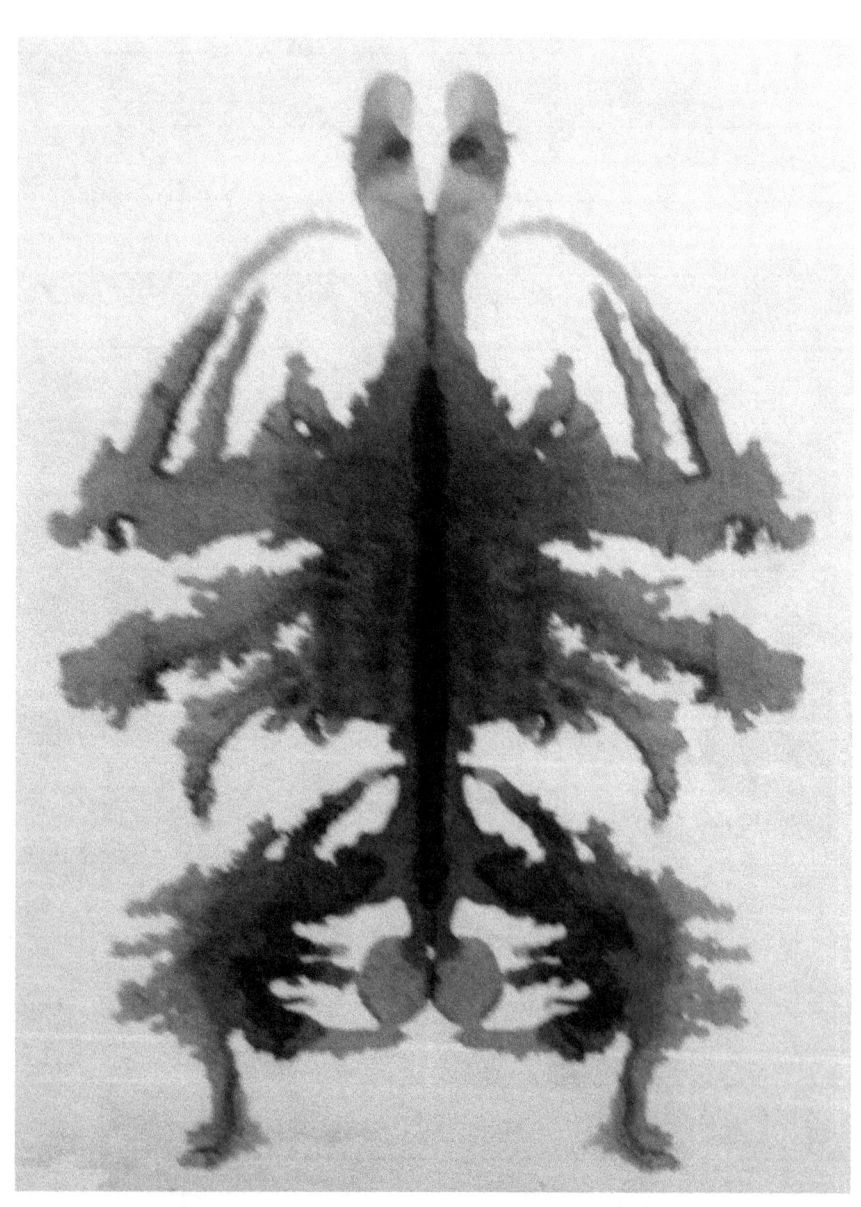

While the young couple sat under the Banyan tree the elves were dancing through the forest with glee.

What do you think?

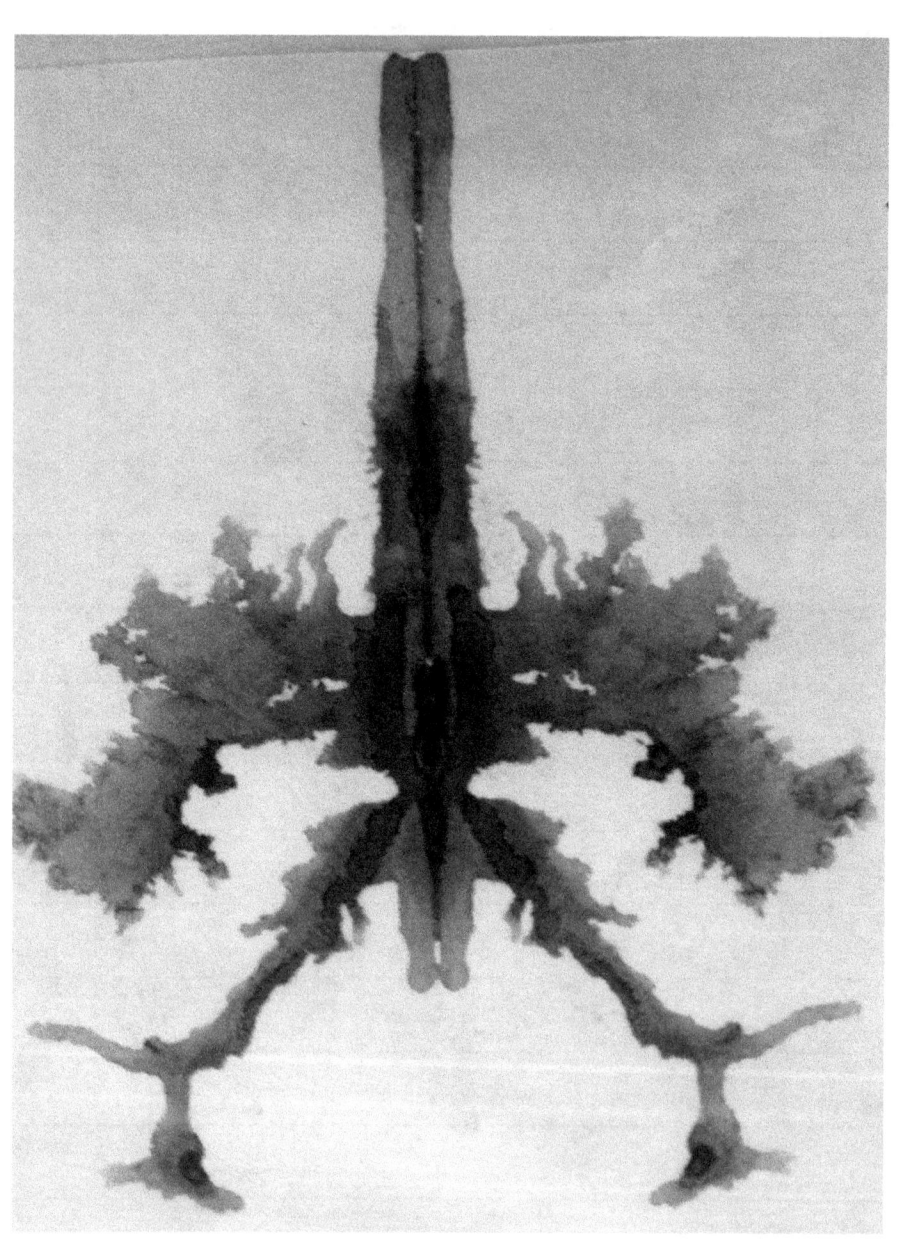

A tiny bud or a blooming rose
A butterfly upon my nose
Big balloons floating through the air
Funnel cakes at the county fair
Grandma's apron, Grandpa's pipe
Summer's strawberries, oh so ripe!

See what you will, See what you might
Who's to say what's wrong or right?

Lisa Engel Moore

What do you think?

Can anyone find the bottle opener? It was here last Thursday. Did it just walk off? It didn't have any feet. Or did it?

What do you think?

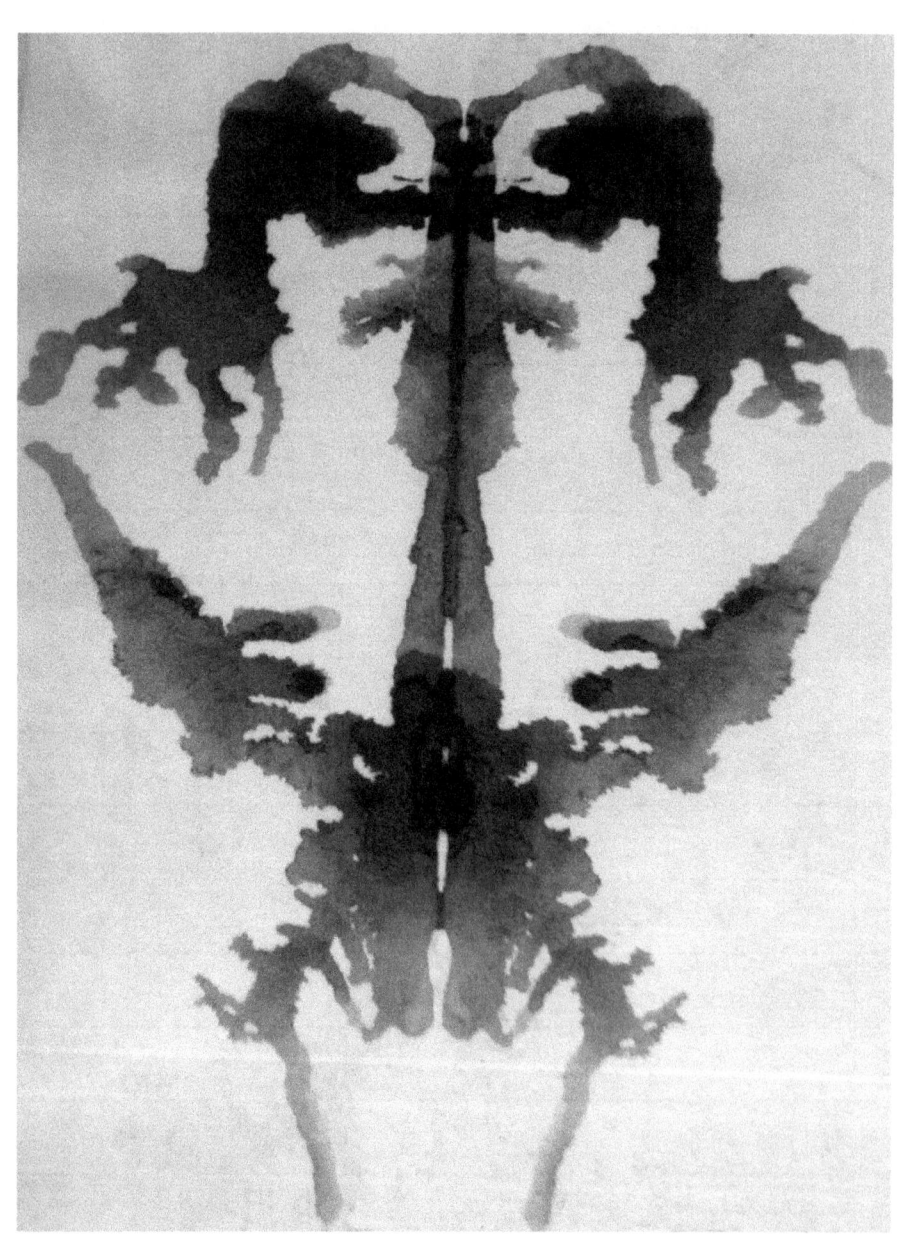

Growing up, I got to listen to my grandmother's stories about the "old country." She was raised in Finland, but was always quick to remind me that she was actually Swedish. "I am a Swede-Finn." she would declare proudly.

Her stories always had a moral point for me to decipher. "The little girl got sick from eating too much cake." "The little girl should never have gone into the bears cave." "The blonde little girl fell through the ice into the lake, because she didn't listen to her mother."

What do you think?

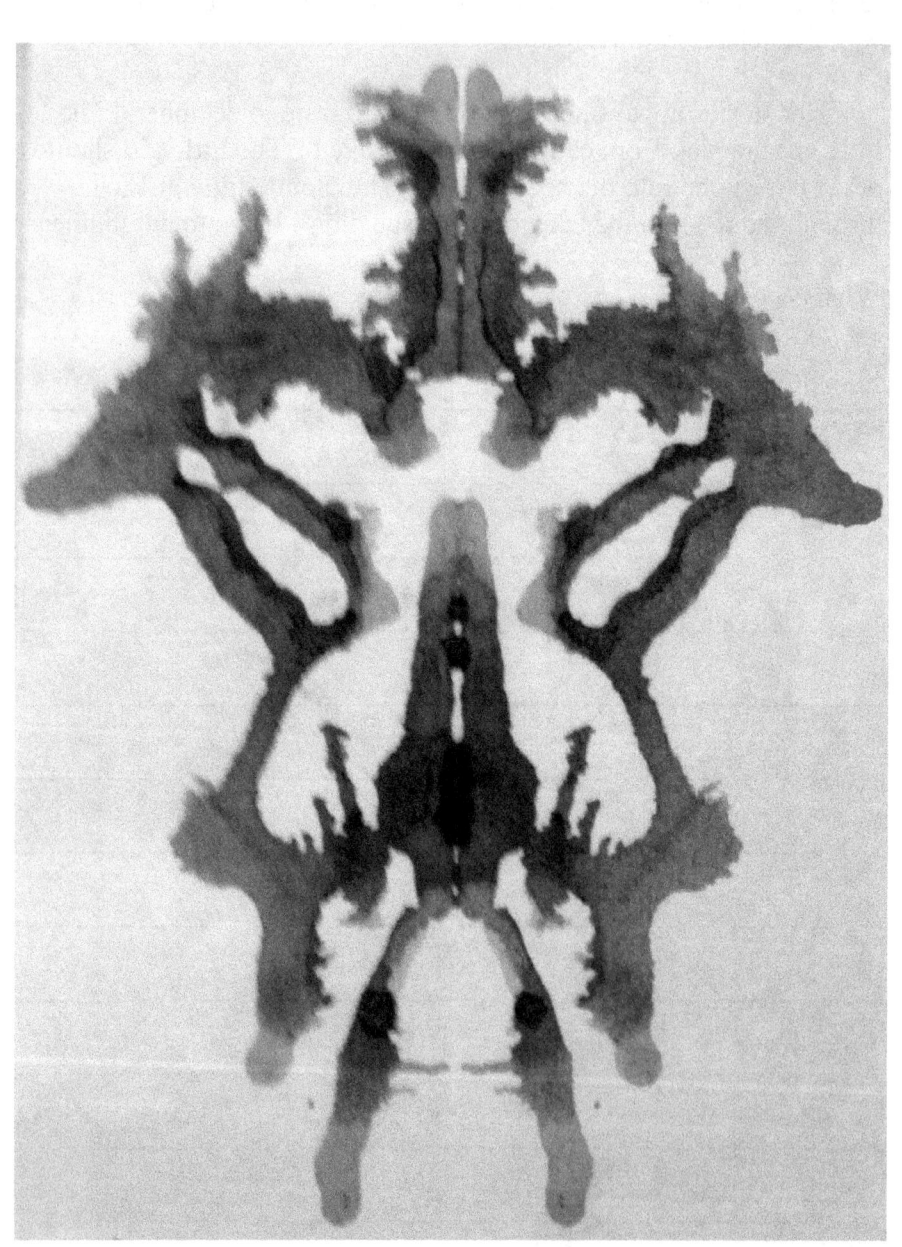

"Grandma, what do you see? "I see a whale playfully diving around his mother." "Wait, grandma, there are two, no three whales playing. And isn't that a mermaid swimming quietly by?"

What do you think?

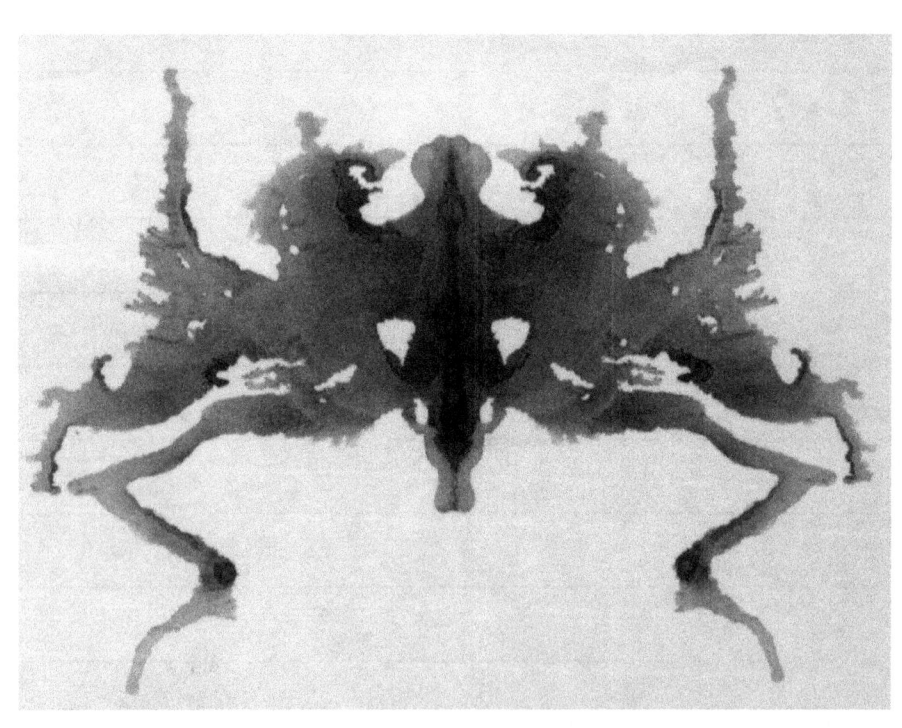

My grandfather's chicken coop was sometimes an exciting place to be. I sat for hours watching the chickens scratch the ground looking for worms. Sometimes they pulled up the longest, stringiest, and most gross black worms. Yuk. When this happened, the chickens played "tug of war" with them.

What do you think?

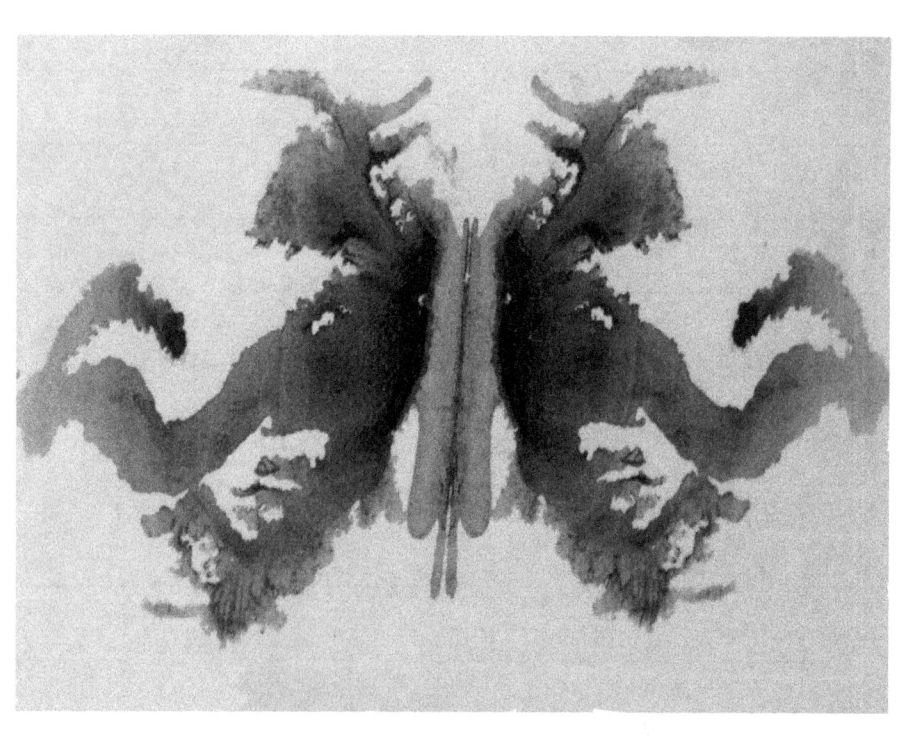

I know the best way to get this dresser up the stairs to the second floor bedroom is to use my back. I will have to take the twelve drawers out and set them aside. Then I am going to flip the dresser over on its smooth top. Lifting it onto the first few carpeted steps is the heaviest part. Once you start to shove the dresser up the stairs it slides easily. This is when I put my back on the side of the dresser and simple push it the rest of the way up. Daddy taught me this trick when we had to move the living room furniture around. Mama was always redecorating.

What do you think?

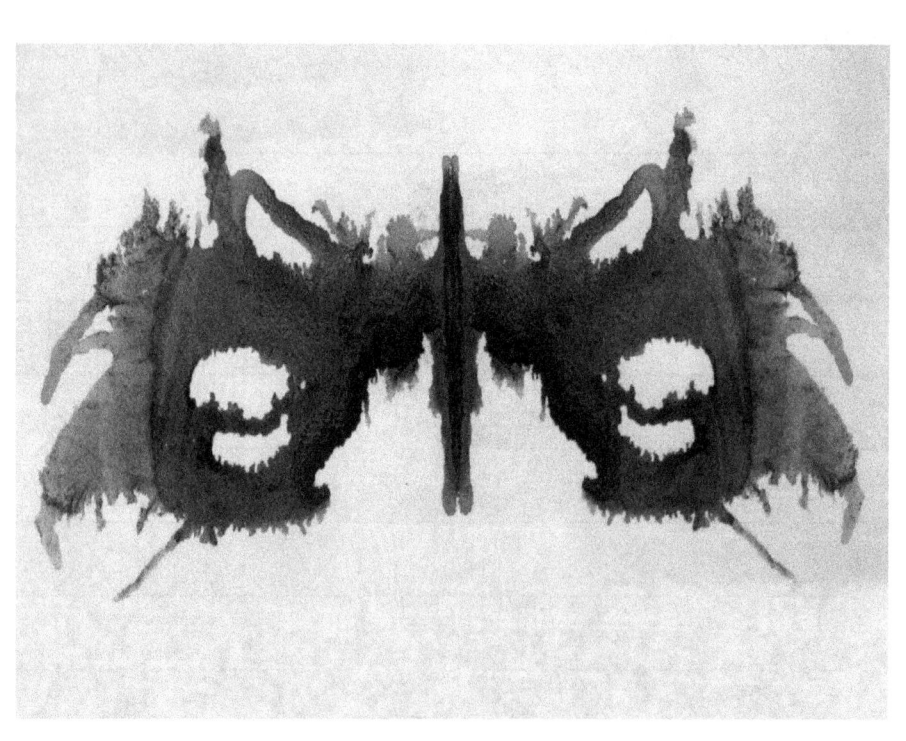

Dashing up the front porch steps I tripped. Oh ouch, it hurt. I sat down on the steps and examined my knee. No blood, but a small pebble had lodged itself deep in my skin. Can't show it to grandma. Her medicine cabinet held awful, smelly, goop. Grandma had some very strange ideas.

Above the kitchen sink there was a jar with cotton balls soaking in Boric Acid. The eye cup sat next to it. I had to stand over the sink, put the cup to my eye, tip my head up and then (oooh) open my eye. Grandma stood right there until I rinsed both eyes. If she hadn't used the word acid, it might have been so scary.

So, this pebble in the knee incident? I chose to suffer through the pain. It remained in my knee four or five days before it just fell out.

What do you think?

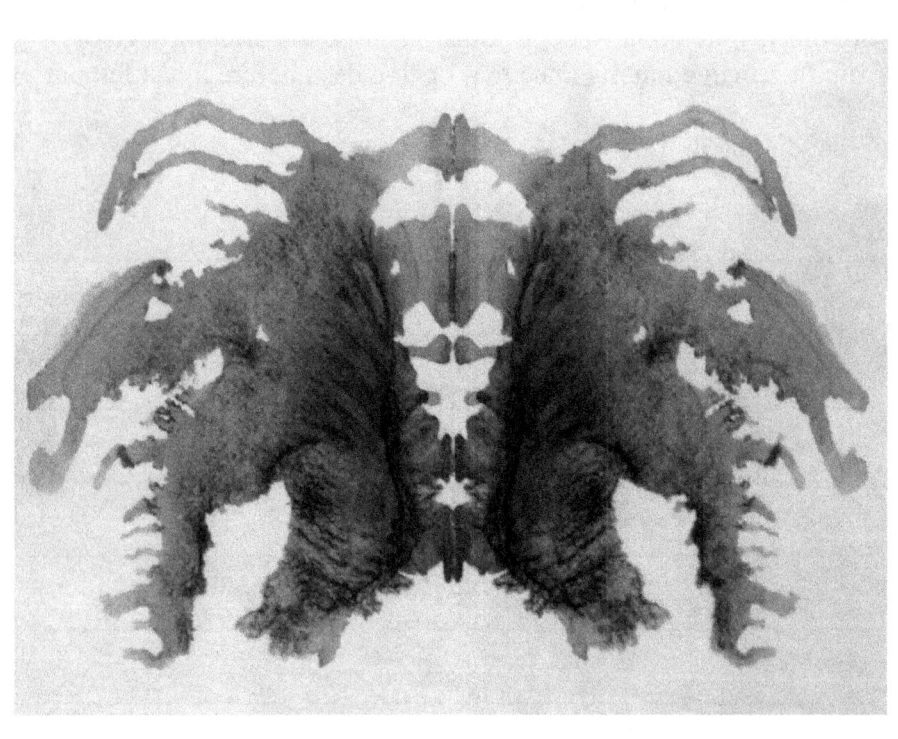

Ink! Ink! What do you think?

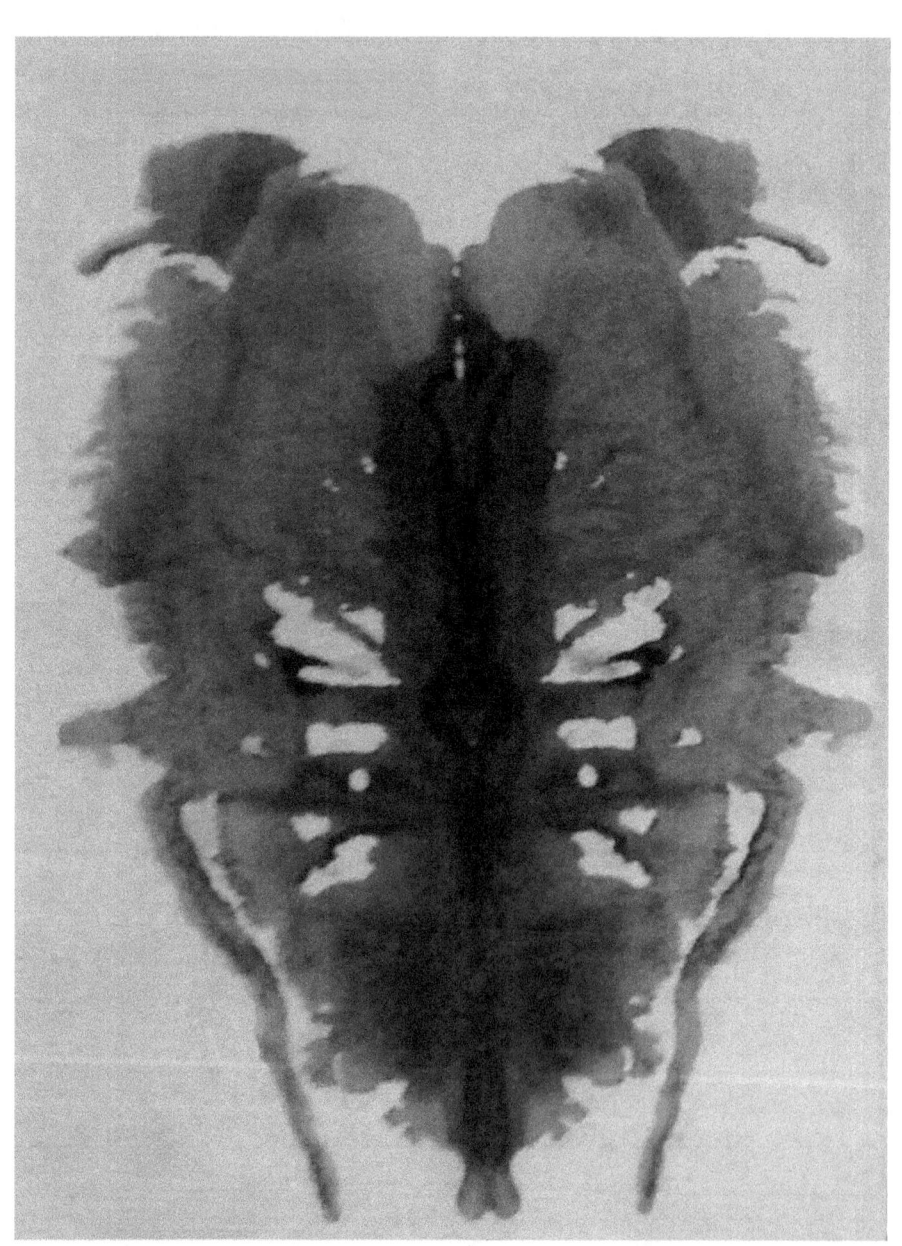

This causes me to remember grandpa's big nose. His nose was large, but very slender on the sides. It made him look very distinguished. My mother had a cute stubby nose. Me? I have an ordinary nose.

What do you think?

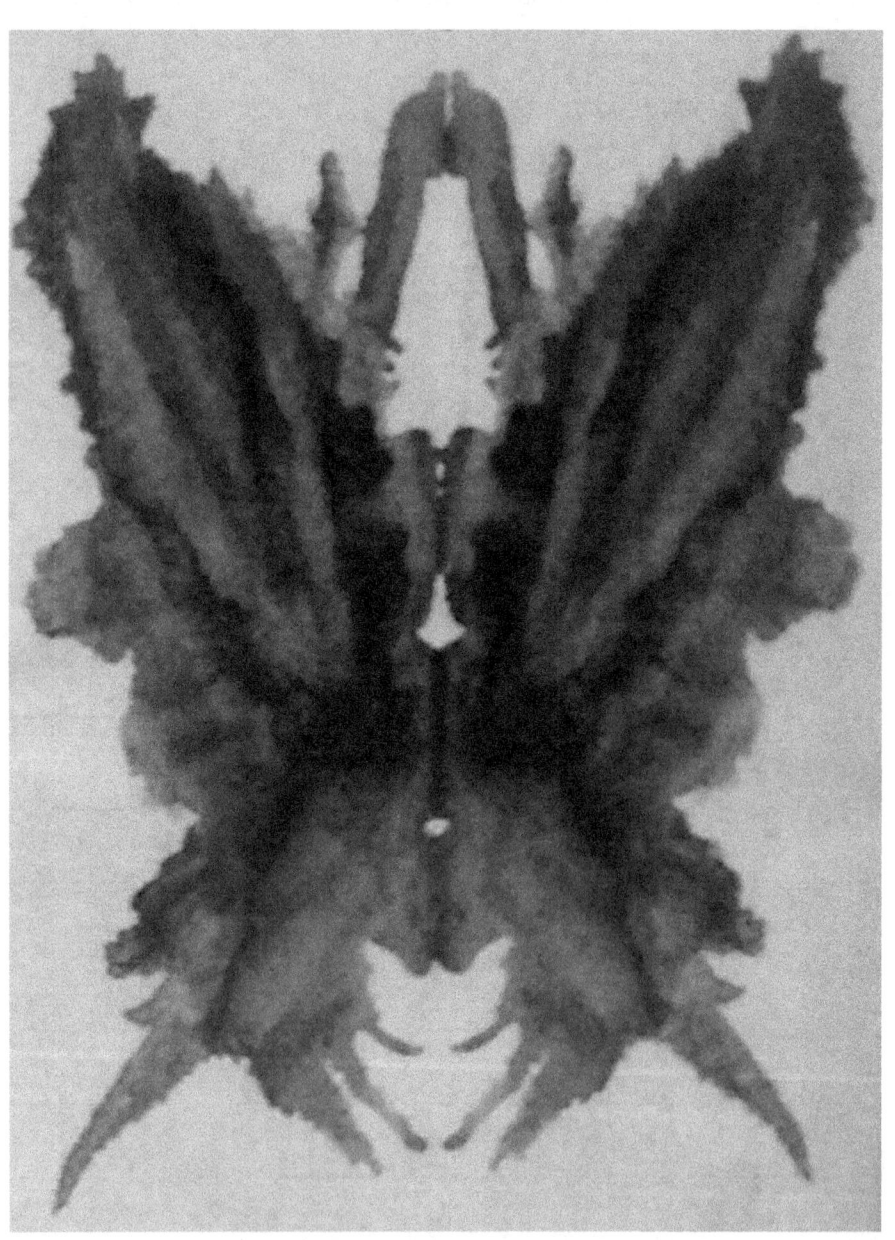

My first trip to the dentist was an adventure that had me wringing my hands. When the dentist put those clampy-looking things in my mouth, I heard the banging of bells in my head. Why was my mother putting me through this?

What do you think?

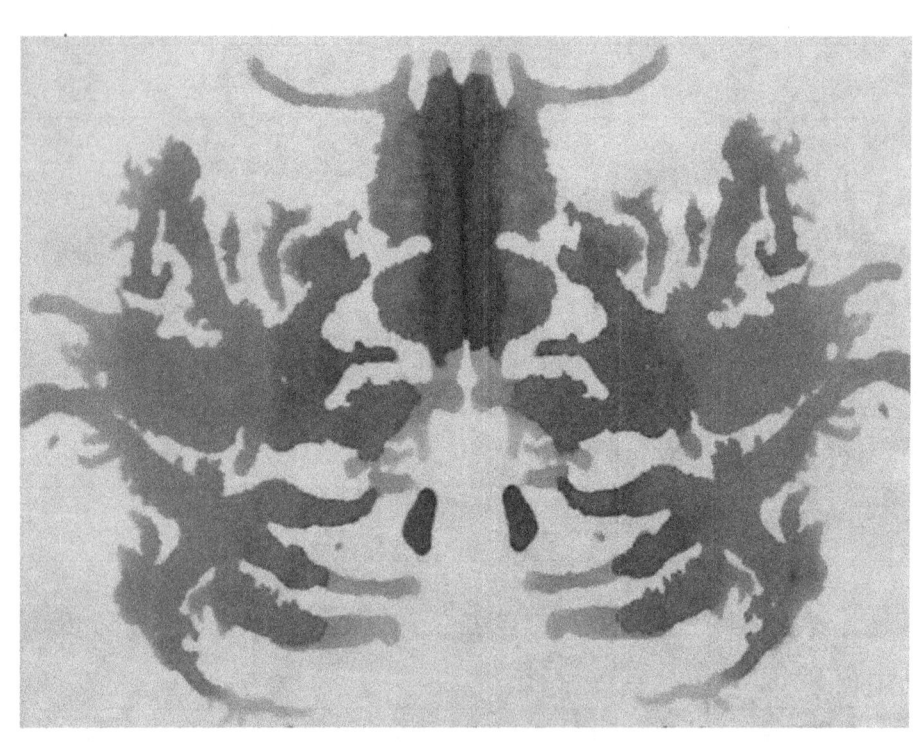

The whole classroom was loaded onto the bus. We were on our way to McKinley Elementary to meet with another sixth grade class. Looking around the bus, I saw lots of red neckerchiefs around the boys' necks. We girls were wearing our big circular skirts. A couple of students had their cowboy hats on their heads. Teacher had instructed us to dress western like. This was square dance day.

What do you think?

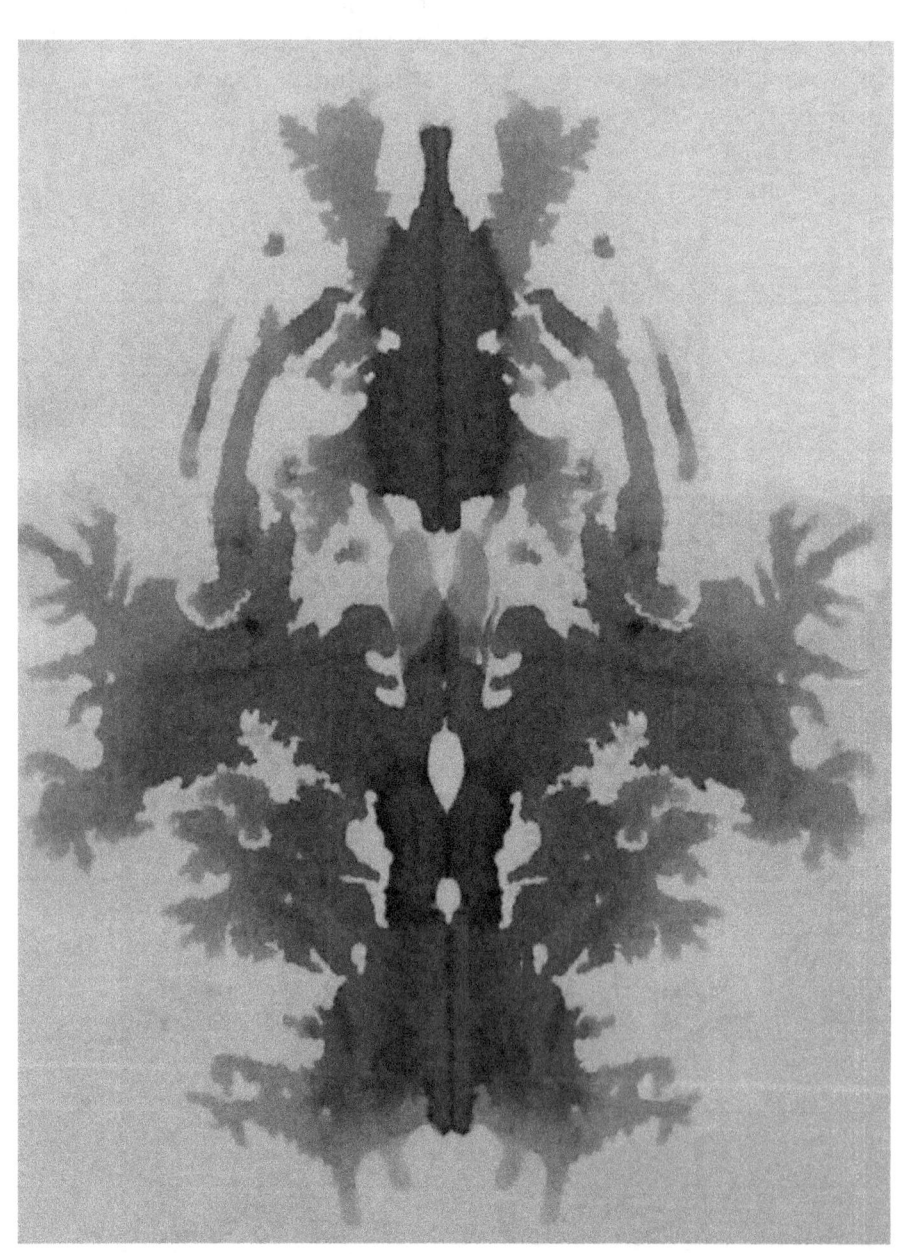

The acrobats were tossing each other all over the stage. There were so many on stage that the audience did not notice when one went missing. I just happened to notice a guy flying higher than the curtains allowed us to see. But, I never saw him return to the stage.

What do you think?

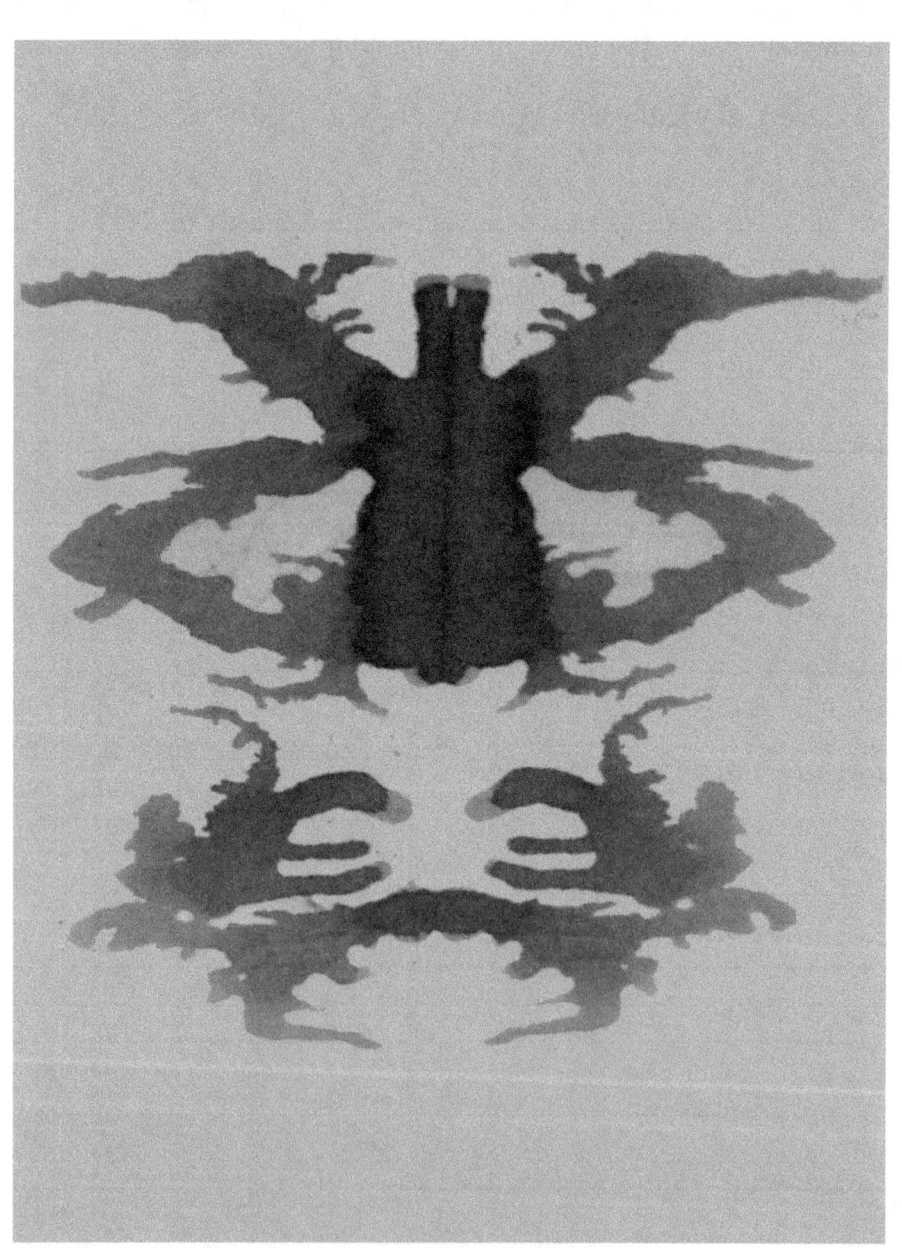

I lived very within walking distance to the company that made Hula Hoops. Two long blocks and over the railroad tracks, passed the Police Department and around the corner, there it was: the maker of plastic toys that fascinated us. The Hula Hoop kept us in shape. We had contests everyday trying to see who could "hula" the hoop the longest. I think Tommy, the boy across the street usually won. Really would make his sister mad. We all figured that Tommy was practicing when we were not around.

What do you think?

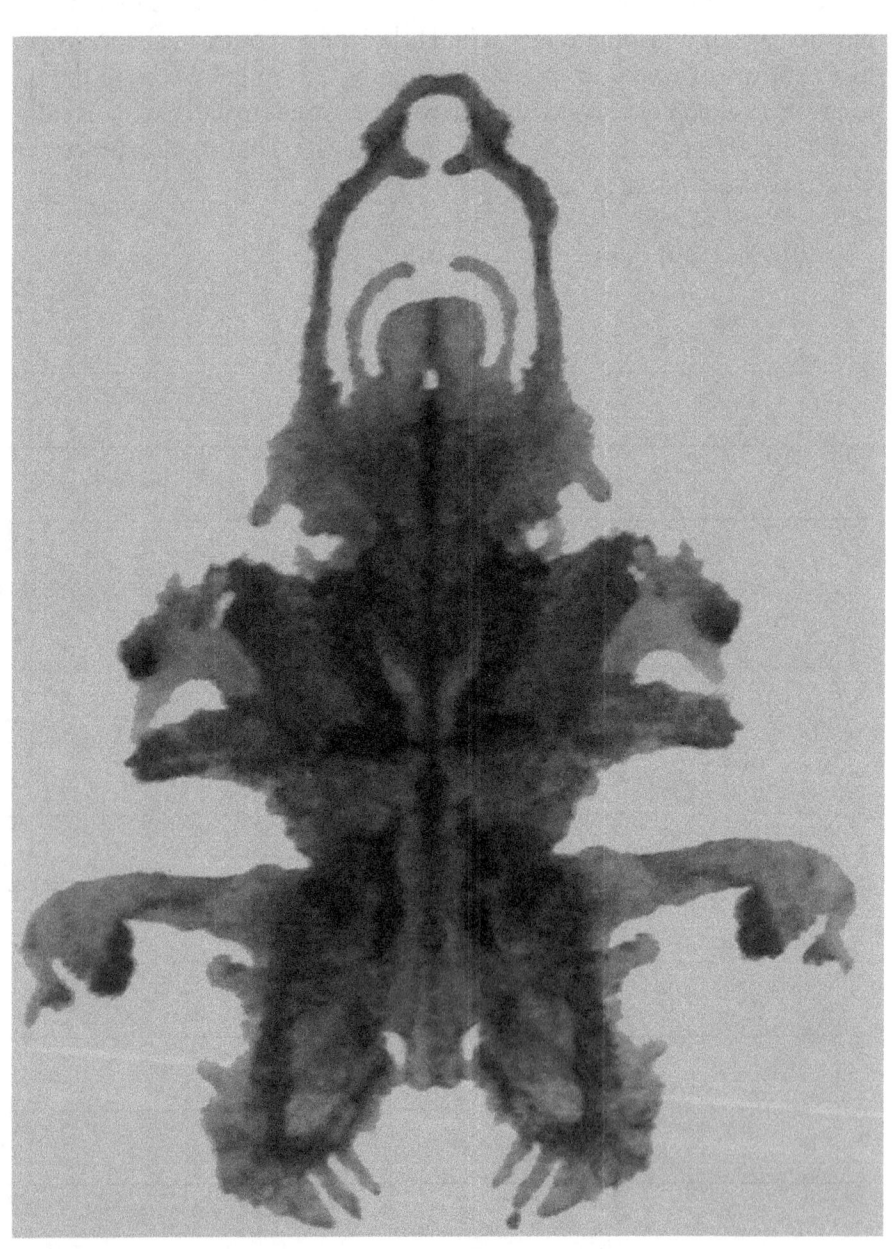

It was a 1938 Chevrolet family car. My daddy had got it practically brand new in 1939. The family car was driven everyday until he traded it in 1956. It took us to church every Sunday and all the way the grandma's house. The car ran good with hardly any problems. Except one, my little five year old cousin Alvin, was looking for a place to hide his rock collection.

They were tiny rocks and they sank to the bottom of the gas tank. Daddy was able to remove the tank and empty out the rocks and a few handfuls of dirt. All would have been okay, except a few small pebbles must have made it to the fuel line. So every other year or so the family car would cough and sputter and refuse to travel. Daddy had to remove the gas tank, get to the fuel line and blow air through it until the pebble moved on out.

The horn on the steering wheel was a bit odd. It looked like another steering wheel only smaller. Daddy could pull it out of the center of the column while we were driving down the road. Grabbing the horn wheel, he would hand it over to my mother. She would freak out as daddy said, "Here, you drive for awhile."

What do you think?

The little boy, Jesse, was out in the field when he saw his pet goat, Beebee. As he ran towards Beebee, he stumbled on a tree stump. About that time, a larger goat that Jesse had not seen before, appeared at the edge of the field. How did he get on this side of the fence? As this large goat approached Beebee, Jesse stood up. What was about to happen was something Jesse never could explain. The goat trotted past Beebee and positioned himself right up against Jesse's right leg. Without hesitating, Jesse jump on the back of the large goat. Talk about a wild ride. Jesse managed to ride the goat for about two minutes before he was bucked off.

What do you think?

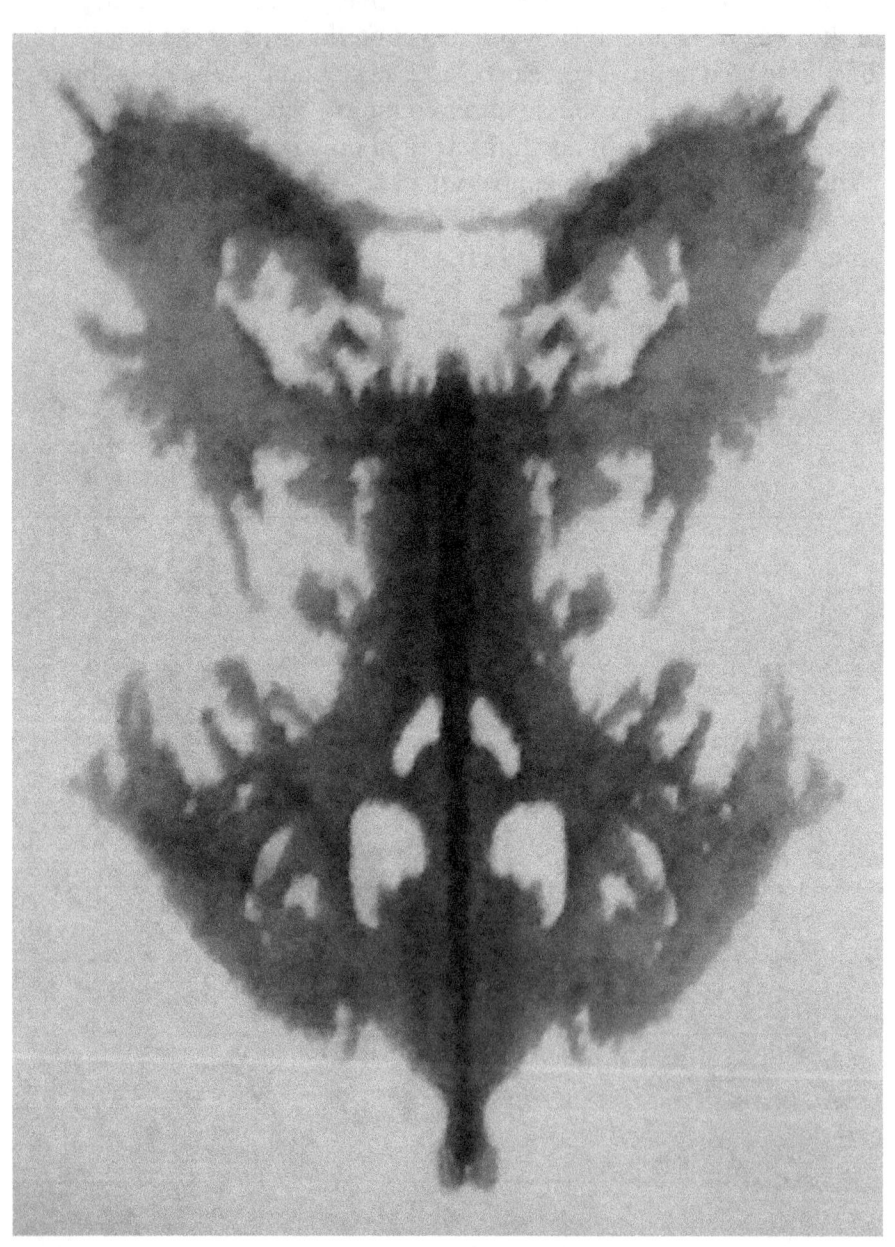

Our cat, Mickey, learned how to open the icebox. We watched him one day as he stared at the handle, studying its position. Mickey walked back and forth with his eyes fixed on the handle. Suddenly he leaped up the door and grabbed at it. He missed. But, Mickey kept at it until he hit the handle just right, and "bingo" the door opened. Mickey now had access to any kind of treat he wanted. Mickey wasn't just satisfied with the bottom shelf, he had to stretch to peek at the top shelf. Guess he wanted a drink of milk.

What do you think?

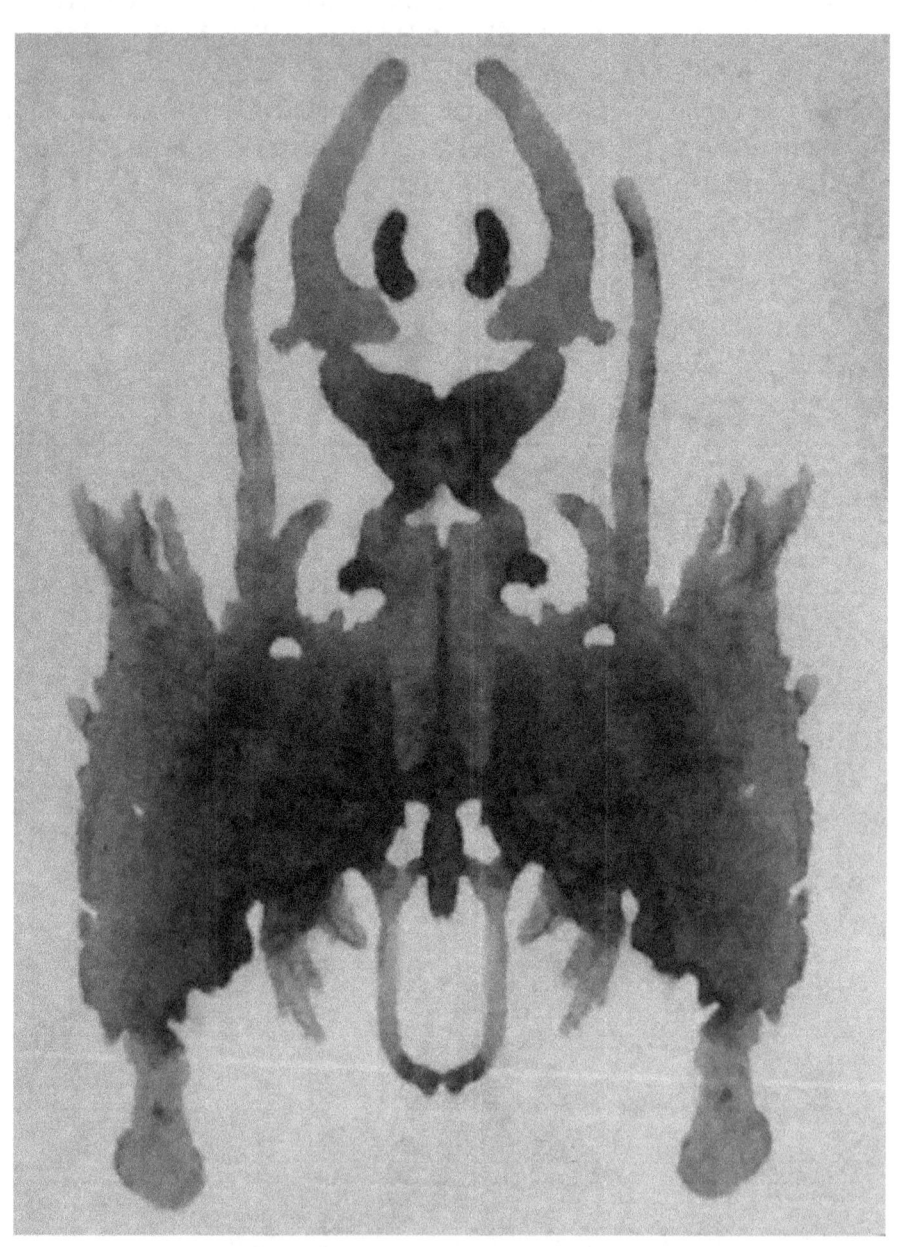

This light fixture is so fancy that it belongs in a very large house. Maybe in the hall entrance way? Or, over the dining room table. I don't know. There is an old fashion Edison bulb hanging right in the center. It kind of spoils the look of this chandelier.

What do you think?

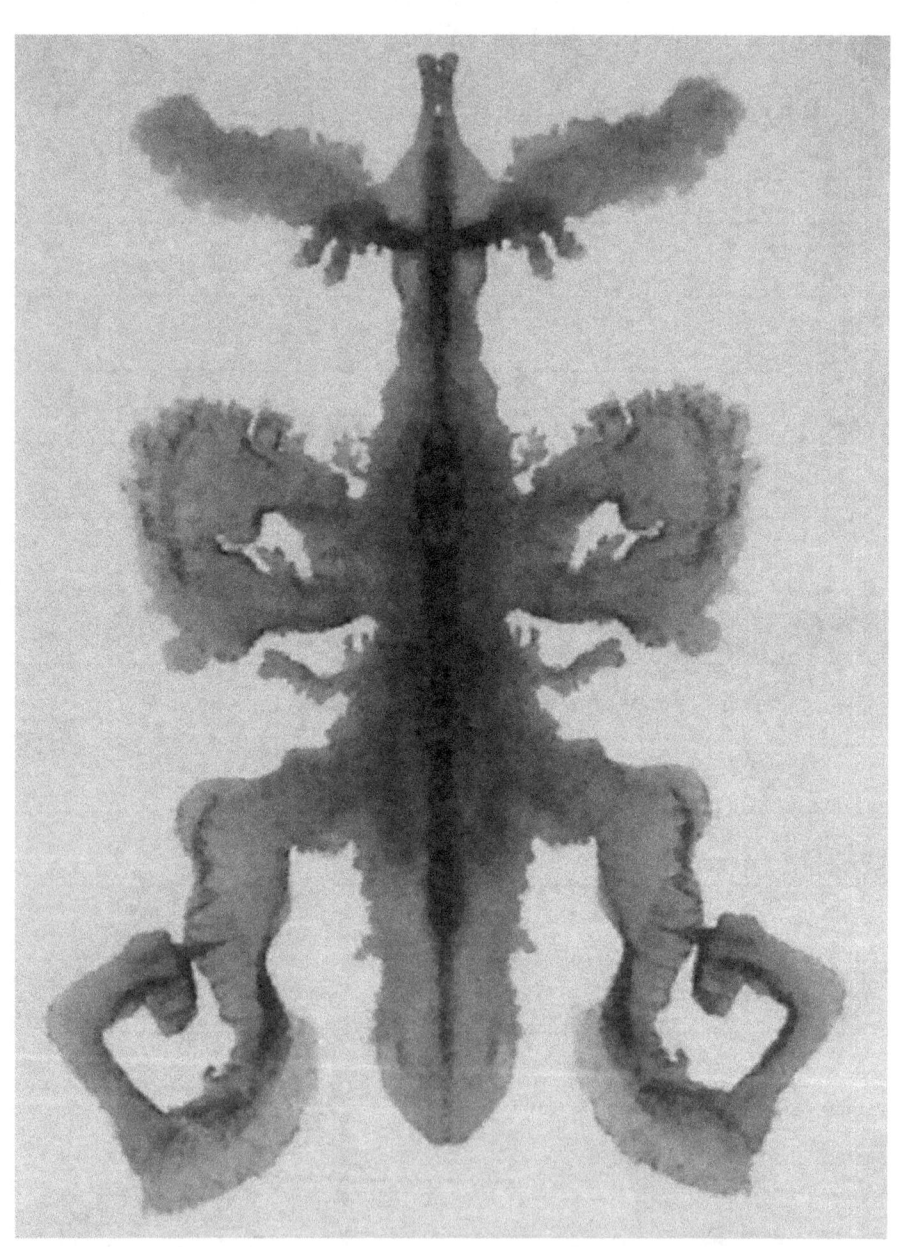

My first "wheels" was a tricycle. Riding a trike was simple to learn. As a young child, the tricycle allow a freedom much more fun than running. When we ran away from mommy, she usually found a way to head us off and catch us. But, the tricycle let us go faster and further away. Of course, I was confined to my backyard. Only in my backyard on the tricycle I could pretend I was traveling to grandma's house.

What do you think?

Mom bought me a membership to a local gym. As the instructor approached me I was amazed at his strong muscles. He was definitely a bodybuilder. He showed me how to work the machines that would improve my breathing and stamina. My favorite is the rowing machine. Even though I don't really travel across a lake, I daydream as I am rowing. Some days I am alone on the ocean during a storm and have to row like mad to get to safety. Other days I am on the lake just casually rowing in circles.

What do you think?

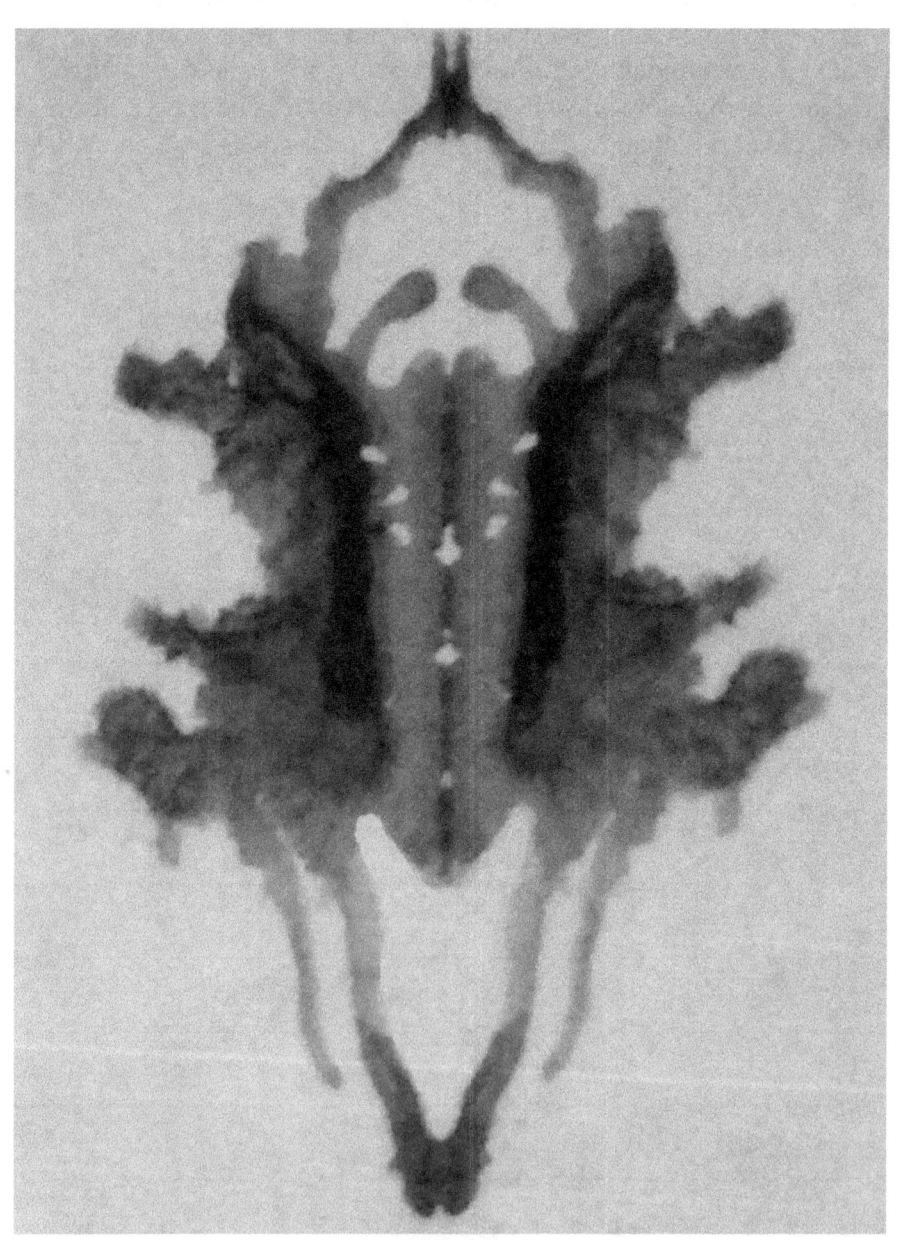

At the ballet when a Ballerina spins fast, I am told that she must fix her eyes on one point, perhaps out in the audience. She does this to keep her balance. Saw this happen in a movie years ago. The Russian Ballerina fixed her eyes on the actor Paul Newman. I totally understood, who wouldn't want to stare at the handsome Paul Newman?

What do you think?

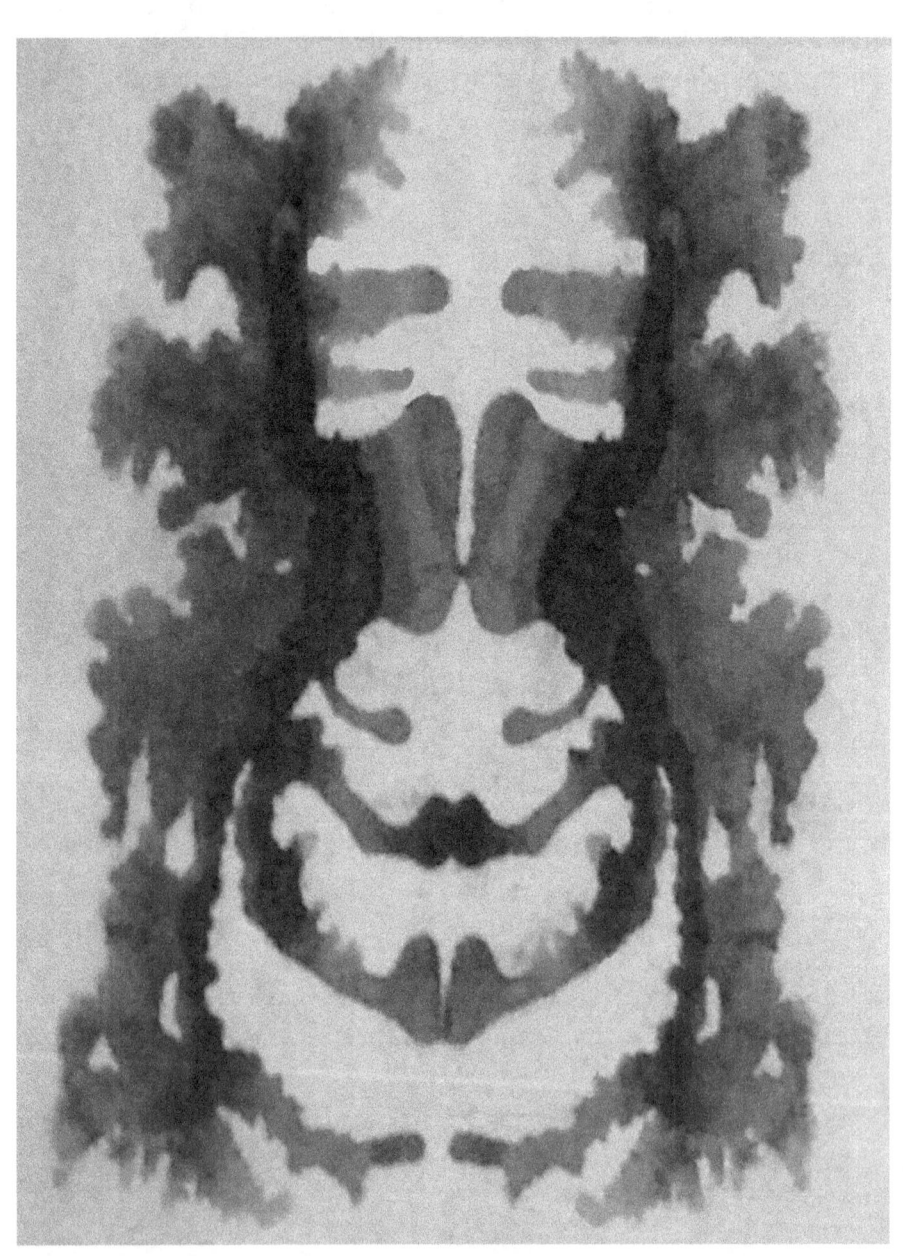

No one every really told me the difference between Gerbils and Hamsters. Actually I always thought they all looked like mice. Anyway, I had a Gerbil that was shy. He hid when a stranger came in the room. Where was he going to go? He was in a cage, protected from most everything, including the cat. At dinnertime, he would wait patiently with his paws clasped together until his food was delivered. I think he was praying.

What do you think?

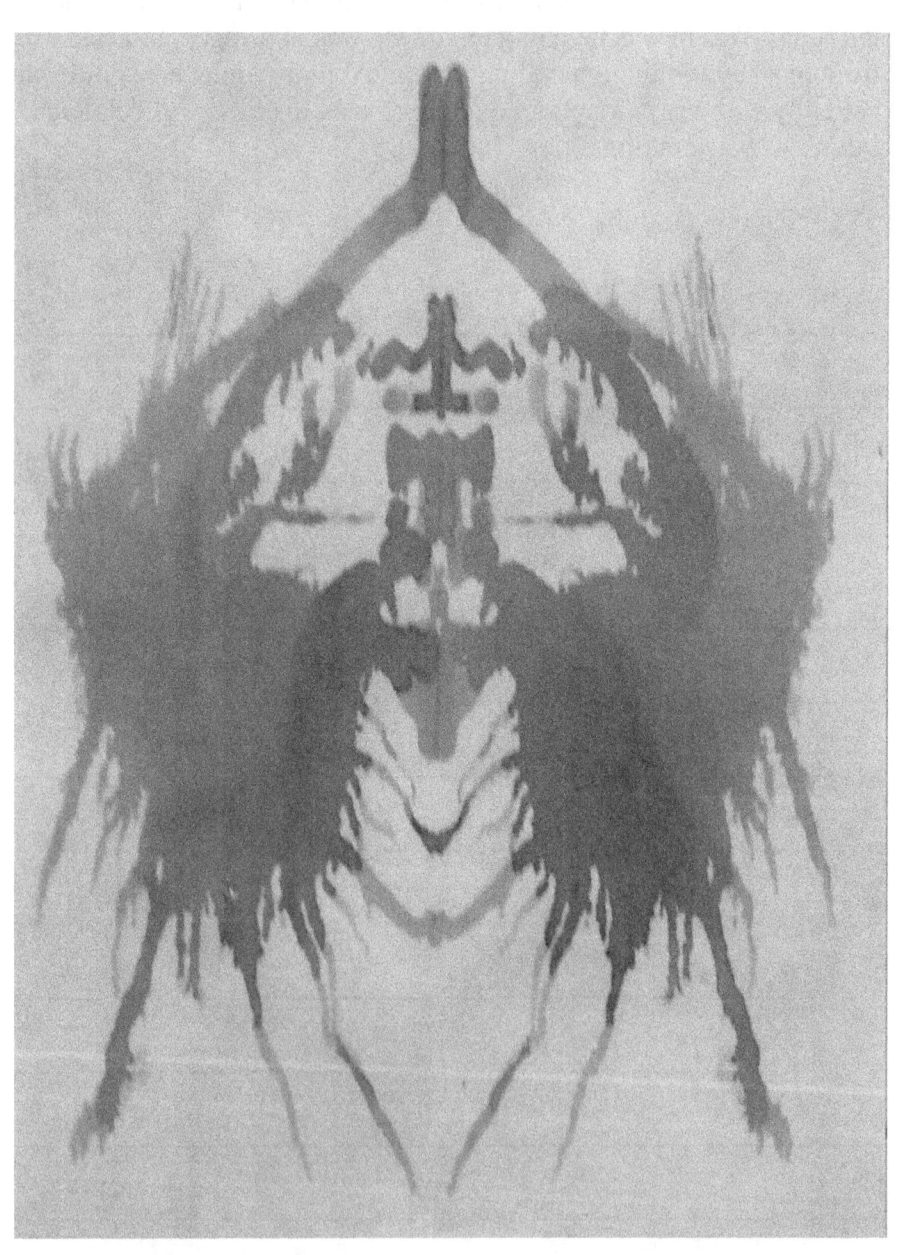

Ink! Ink! What do you think?

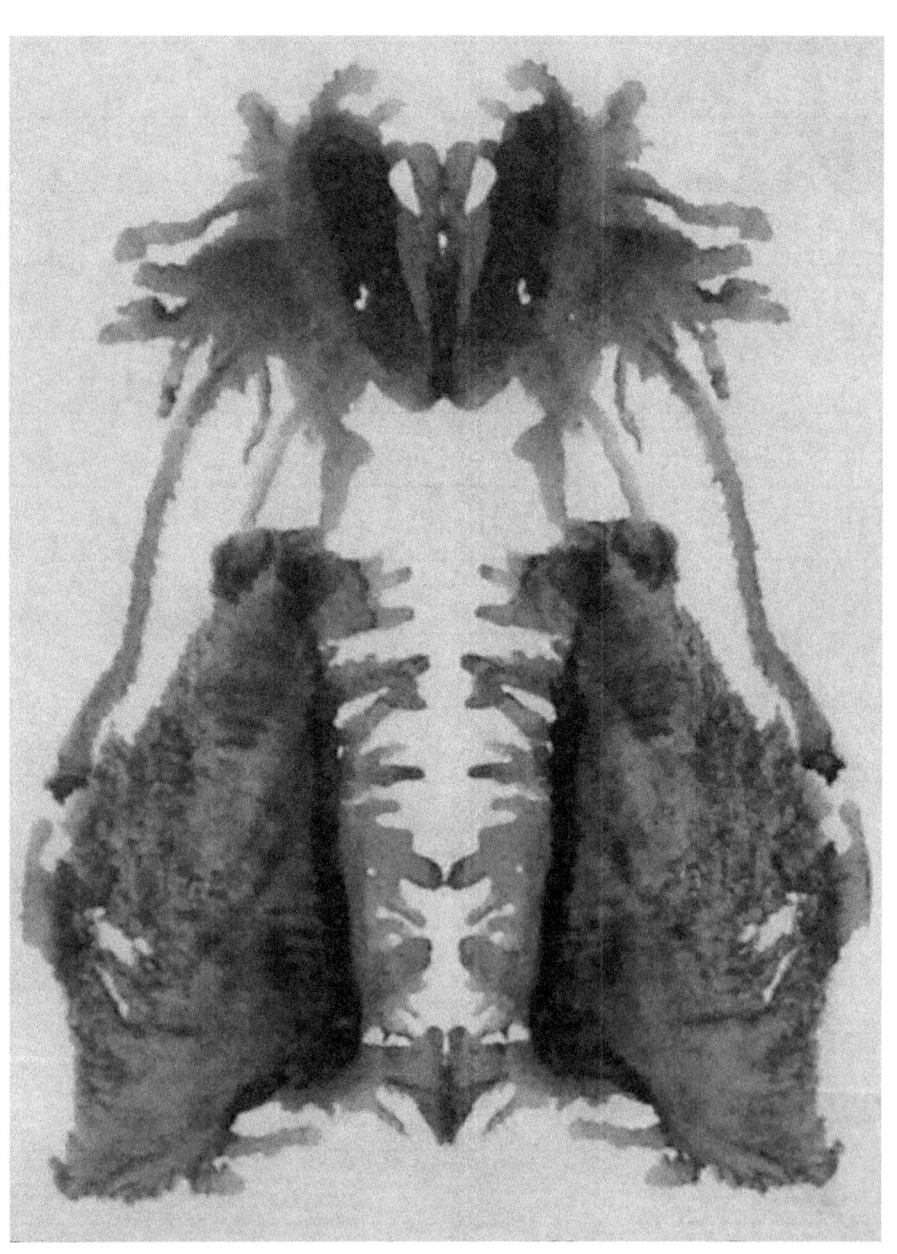

The bullfighter entered the ring. His red cape was draped over his shoulders. There was a sadness felt by the surrounding crowd of spectators. The beloved bullfighter and the spectators all knew that this was his final time in the bullring. The giant bull came charging out into the ring. It was as if the bull and the bullfighter both knew this was a time to grieve. The bull charged, the red cape swirled in front of him. Once, twice, and then it happened. The bull stood still, the fighter stood facing him, they looked into each others eyes and appeared to be nodding in agreement.

The bullfighter put his hand on the bull's head and they left the ring together.

What do you think?

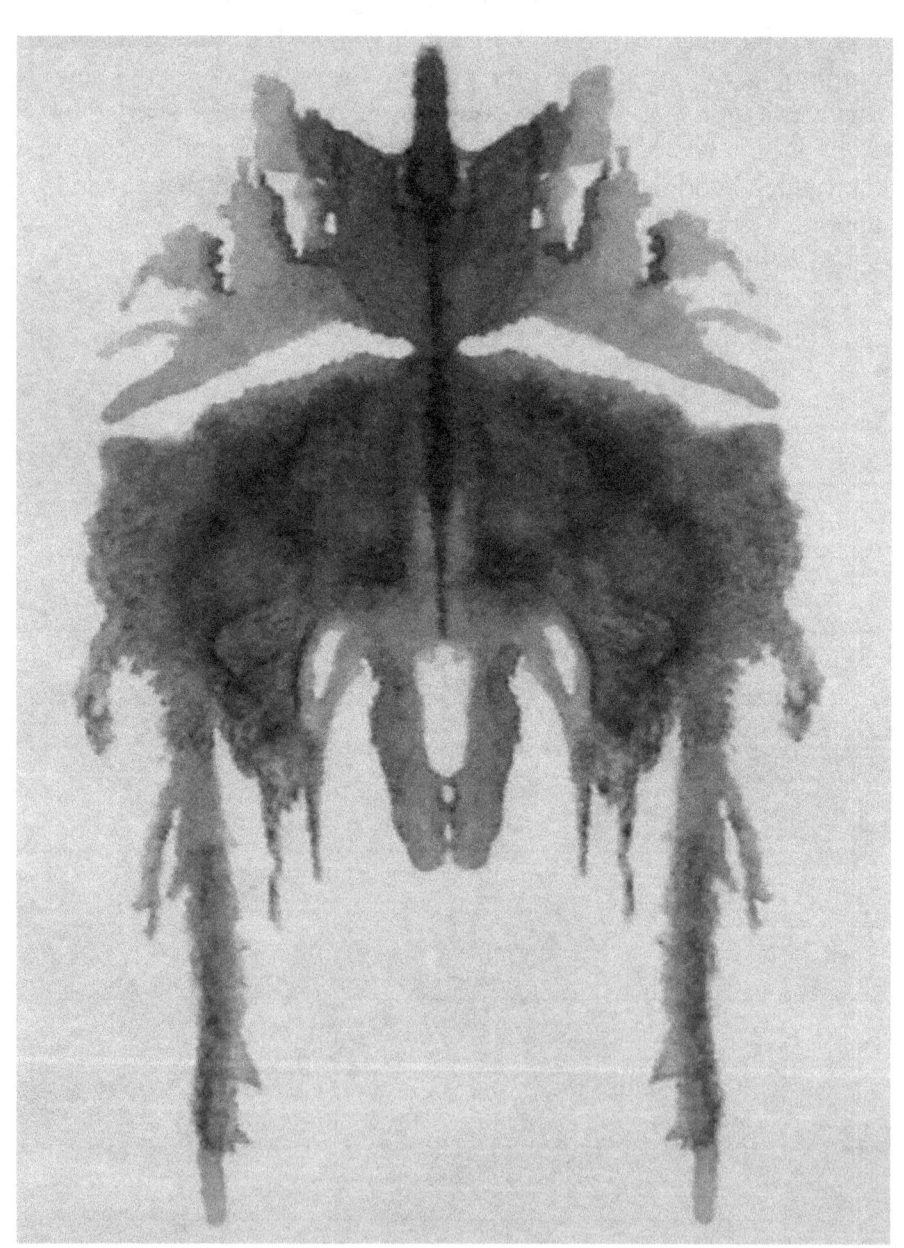

The large ducks were acting strange. They had suddenly started to circle in the center of the pond. It was a perfect circle, each following the duck in front. They got faster and faster. The water in the pond was now splashing all over the place. The ducks were getting lots of green murky stuff all over them. This pond was full of stringy green weeds and mold. As the ducks circled, the green stuff was being flung out of the pond. Soon the fish had a cleaner place to swim about.

What do you think?

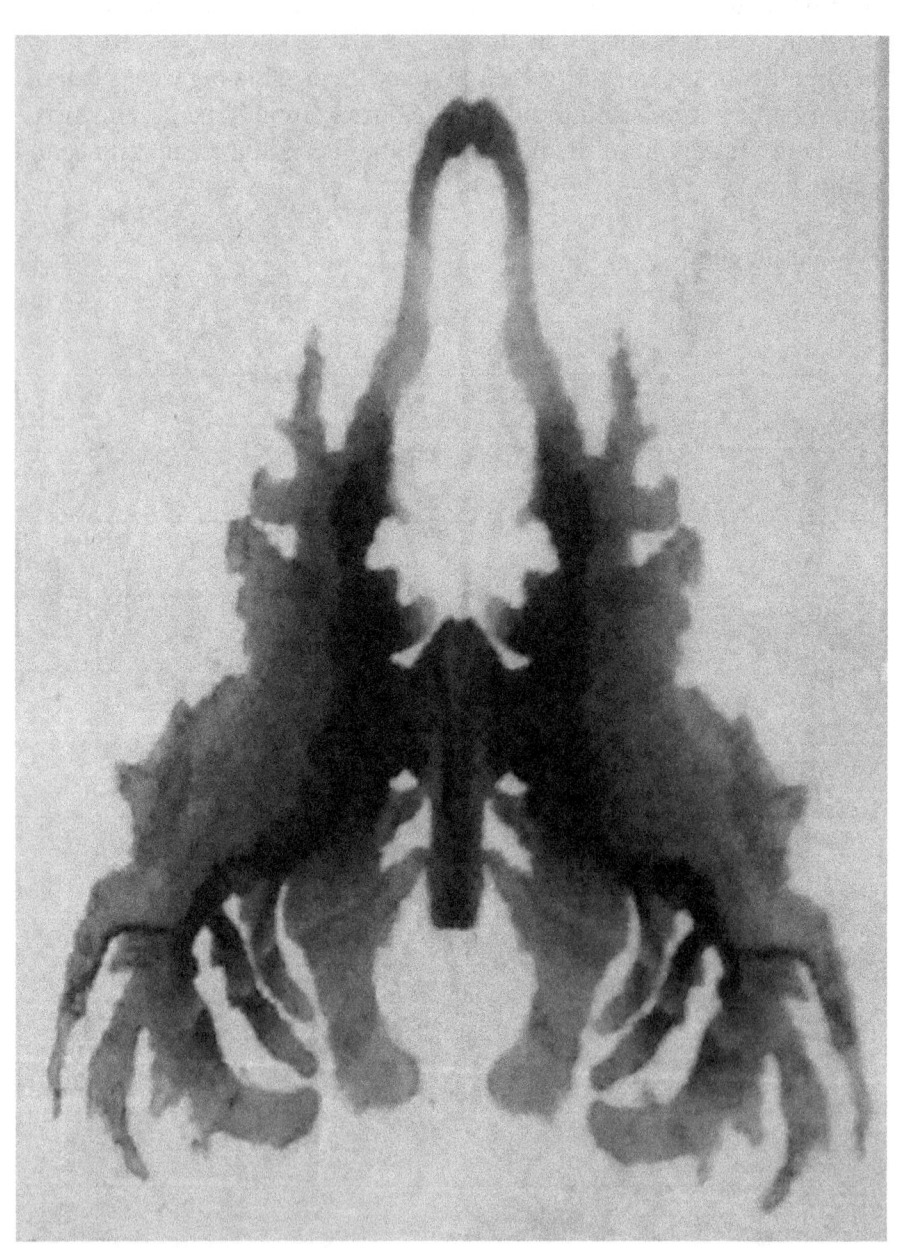

The battle of the two knights was about to begin. The king and his party had finally settled into their seats. Out from opposite sides the knights rode into the arena. Their horses were covered with protection gear that looked very much like decorations. The long jostling poles were polished and shining in the sun. First they met in the middle and touched their poles together high in the air. As the knights returned to their starting points, they were each trying to build up their self confidence. Let the battle begin!

What do you think?

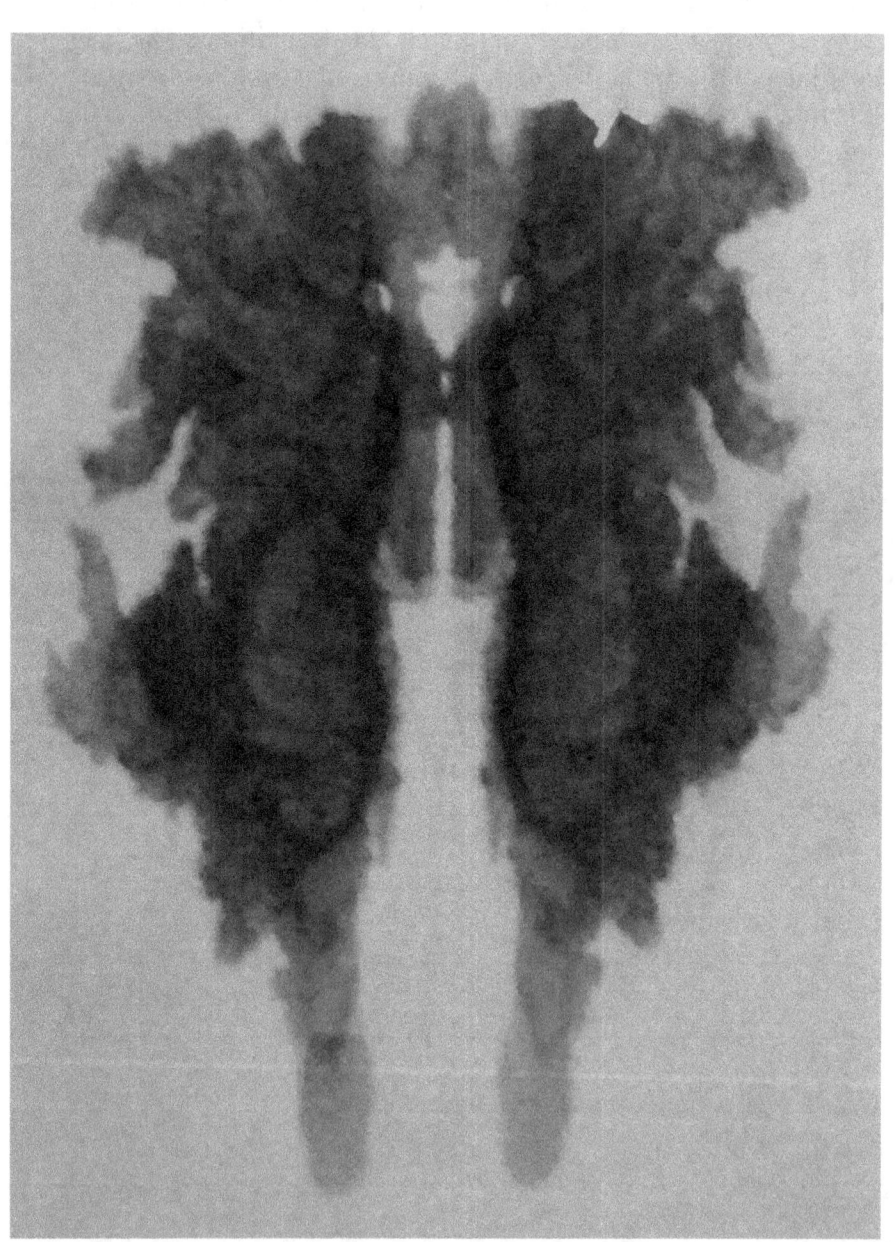

In the 1950's when ladies went shopping, they were really dressed up. Hat, gloves, stockings, and high heels. At the most exclusive department stores there was a machine in the back room that washed all the coins that came through the store. Why? The ladies wore white gloves, and certainly did not want to touch dirty coins.

What do you think?

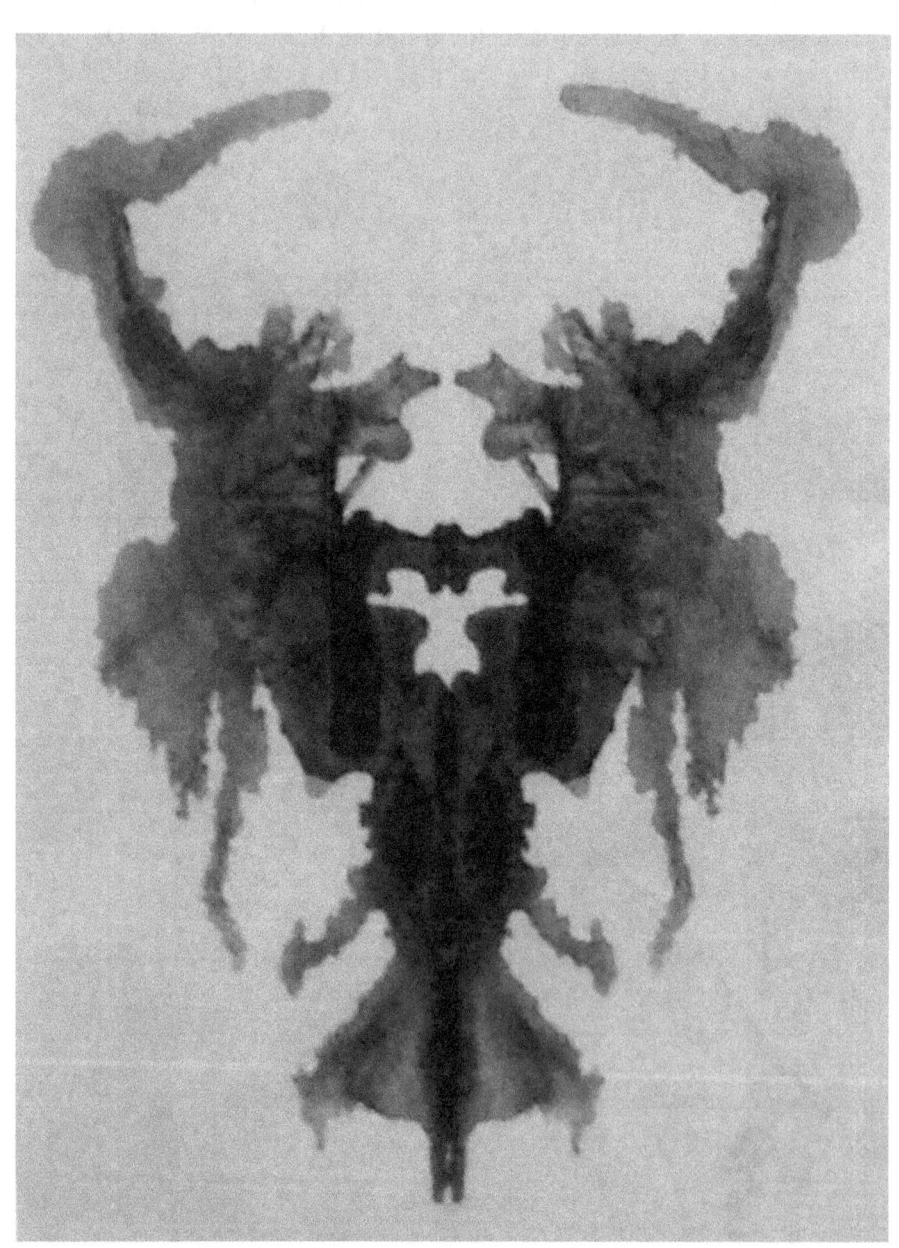

"Boys, I wish you would stop your fighting!" said mom.

What do you think?

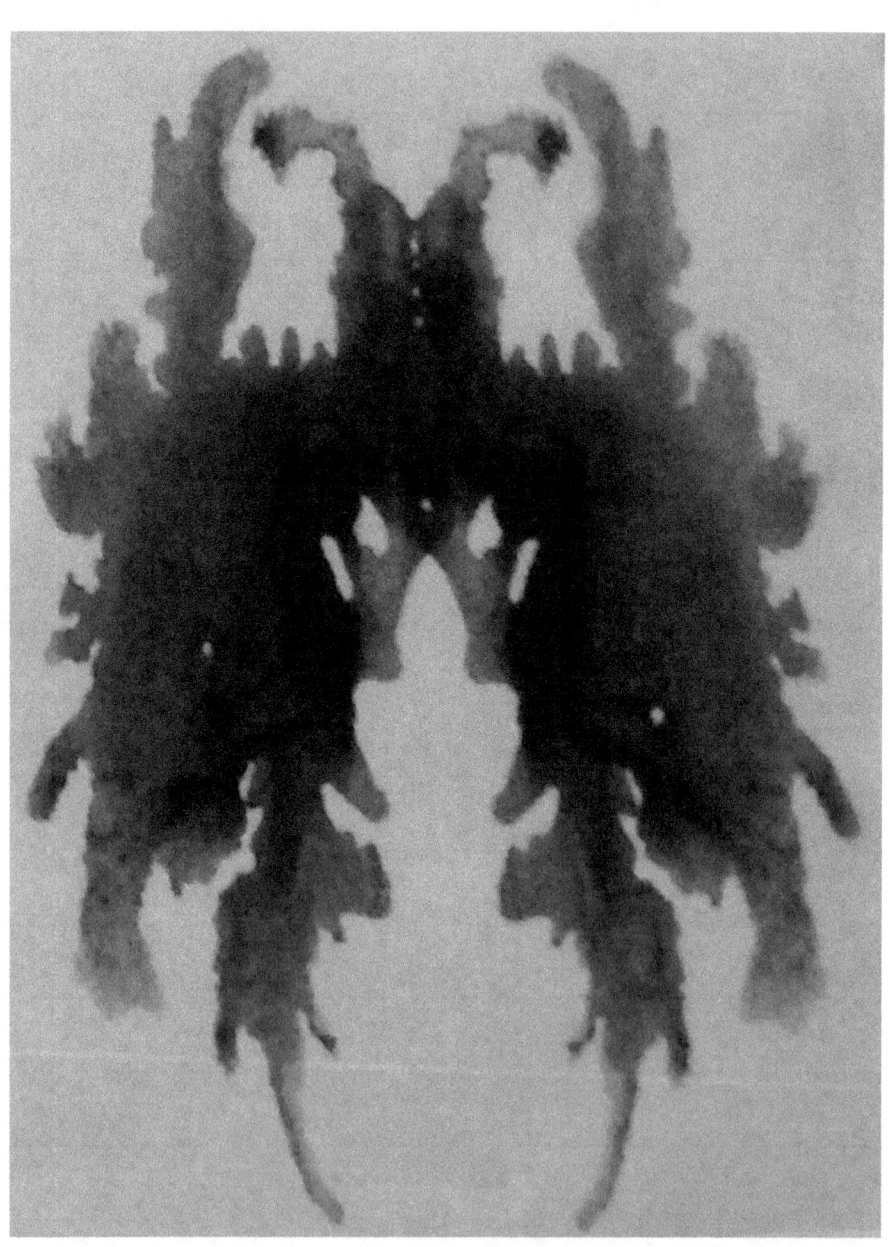

With these eyes I can see all the way to the end of the street. I can also hear very well with these ears. My feelers can tell me how fast the train is traveling.

What do you think?

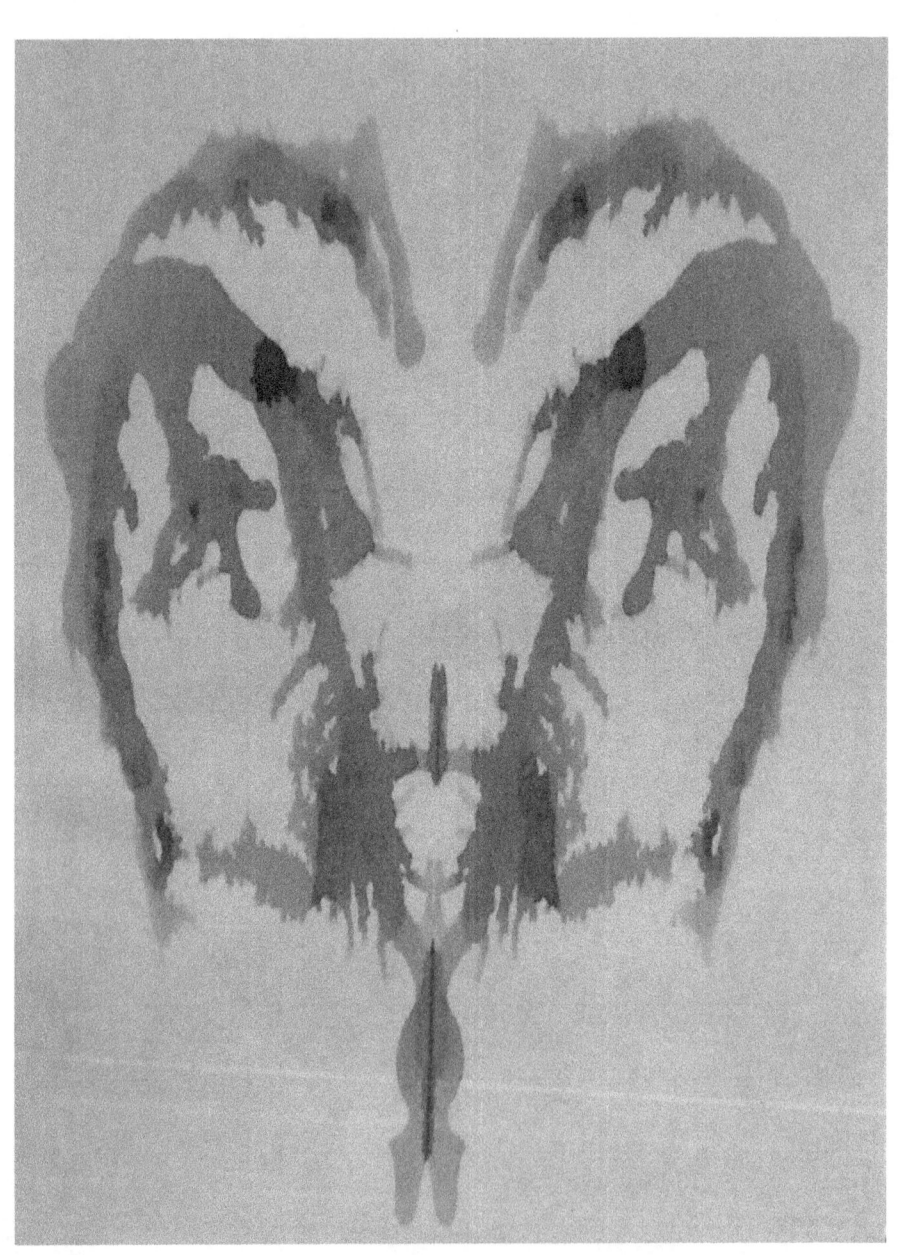

I am going to let you all look at this ink blot and figure it out by yourself. My son and I were going through all the ink blots when he exclaimed with a grin, "Do you see it?" We compared our thoughts and almost agreed on what we saw. For me, his excitement brought back wonderful memories of the times Grandma Ellen and I shared "ink blots."

What do you think?

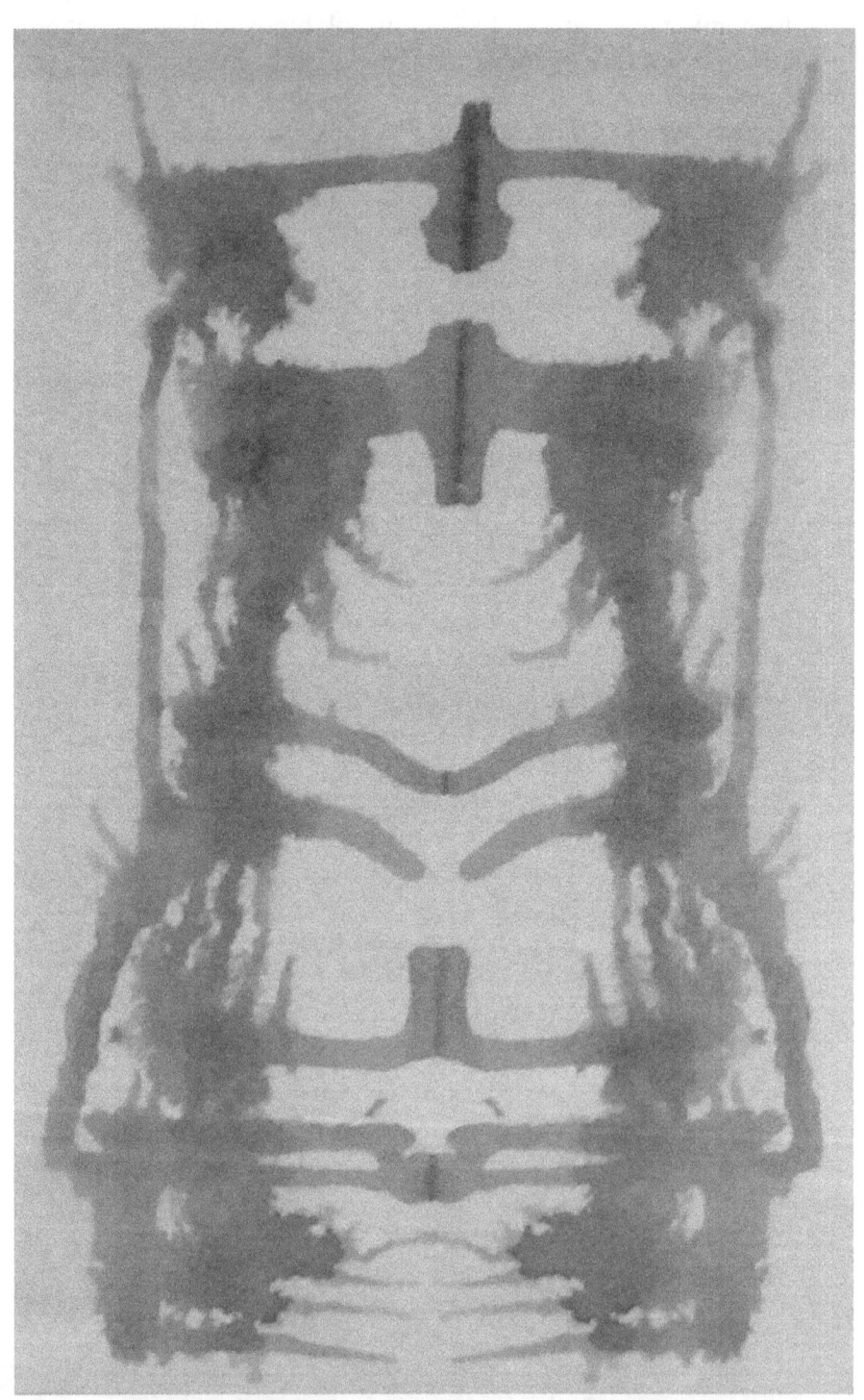

Relax

A summer breeze upon my skin,
The faint, sweet scent of Jasmine;
Soft, green grass beneath my head
The stresses of life soon I will shed.
Sky of blue and clouds of white
Bring fantasy worlds into my sight.
A dragon, a pony, Dad's pickup truck,
I'll see it all with any luck.

Soon fall gives way to winter's chill
My inkblots book will fit that bill.
What will I find when I search today?

Lisa Engel Moore

What do you think?

Grandma and I were walking through the wondrous gardens at the museum. The flowers were blooming and the birds were singing. Grandma was going on and on about how this reminded her of Finland when she was a child. That didn't make too much sense to me as the statues around us looked very oriental. But, I never pointed that out to her, as she was almost in another world as she talked.

What do you think?

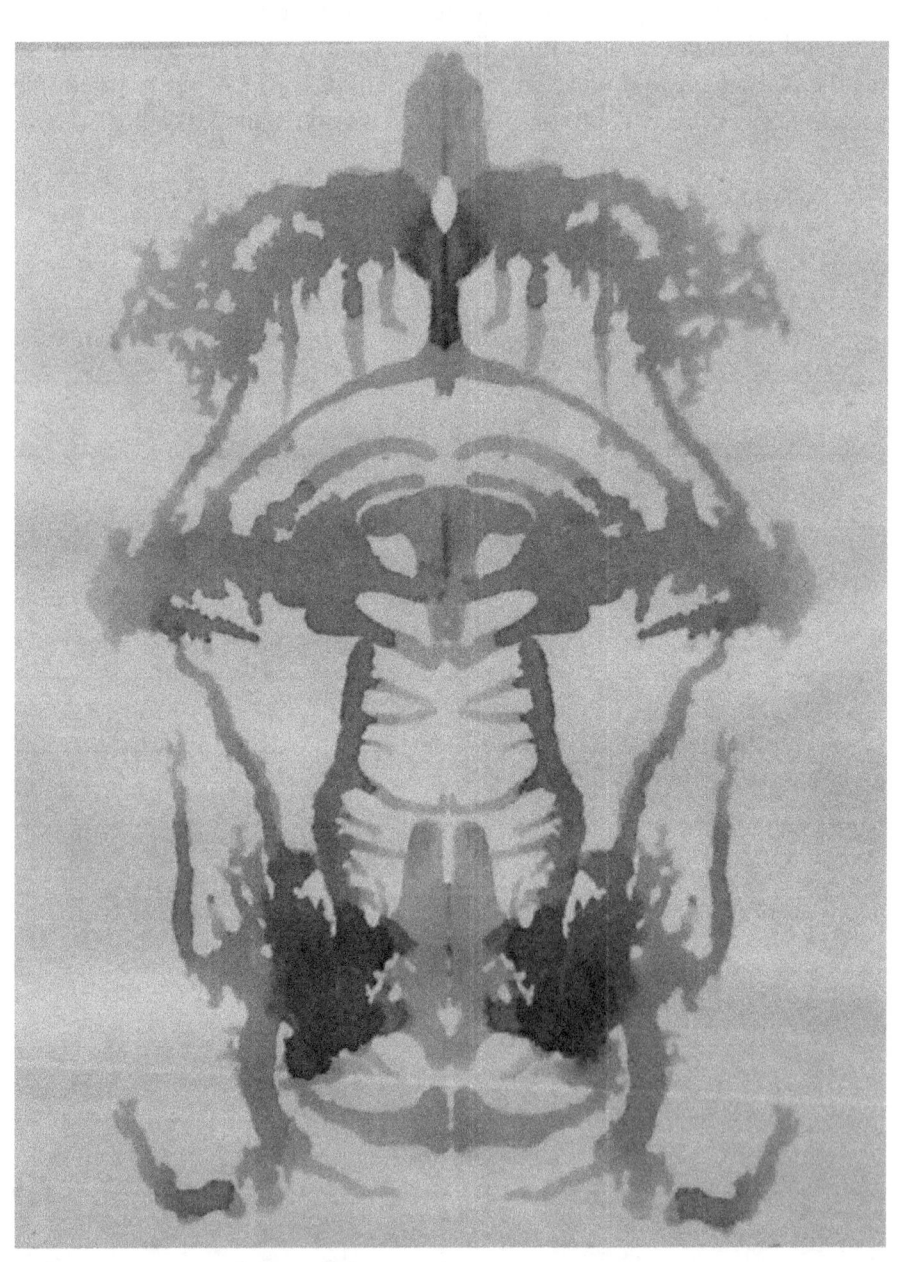

"How are we going to get the football off of the roof?" James was asking. Wade had been fooling around while they were supposed to be playing catch. "I don't know," Wade replied. "Where's the ladder?" he added. James frowned. "There is no ladder. My dad lent it to a friend and they haven't returned it," he answered. Now Wade asked, "How are we going to get the football off of the roof?" The boys sat down on the grass to think about it. Mom brought out some cookies and lemonade. She took one look at the situation and said, "James, you can reach the football if you stand on Wade's shoulders."

What do you think?

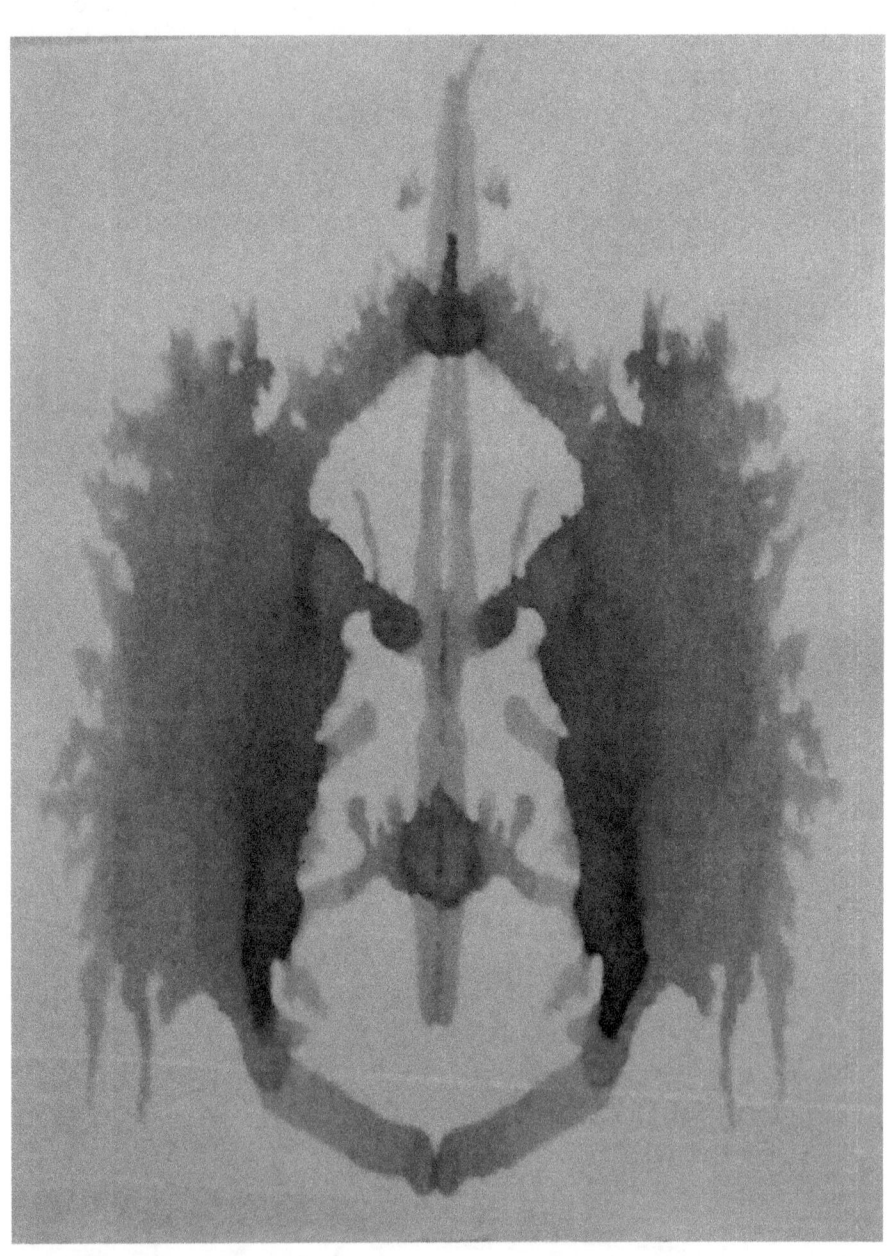

When I had my wisdom teeth taken out, my cheeks swelled up like balloons. But I didn't care; I was so excited about all the ice cream I was going to get. The nurse said, "Sorry, ice cream is for getting your tonsils out. You get Jell-O."

What do you think?

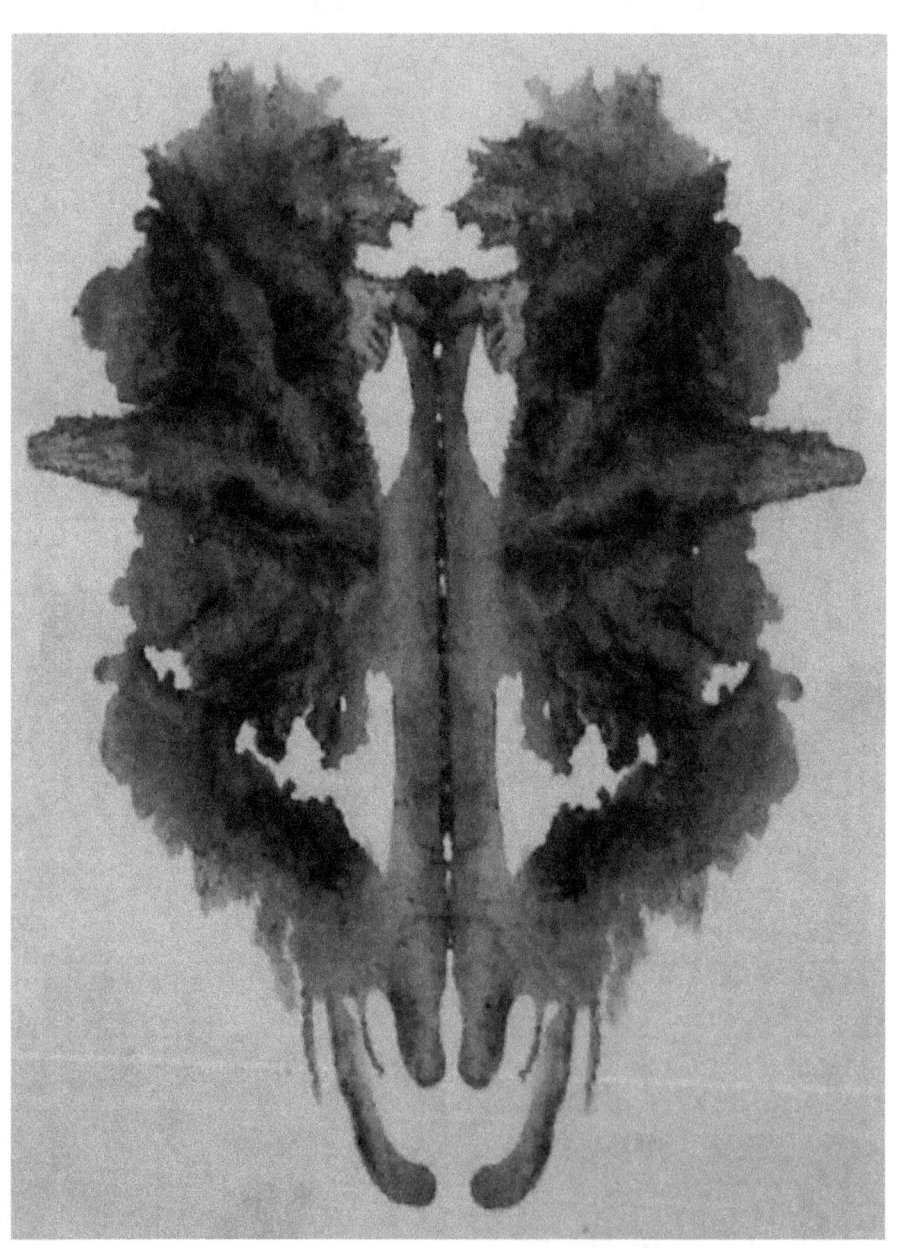

Nice to meet you. Where did you come from? Is that a acorn tree behind you? We were told never to cross over the fence, but that tree is calling me. Should we switch places? Nobody would know, and you could get a fresh drink of water from my pond.

What do you think?

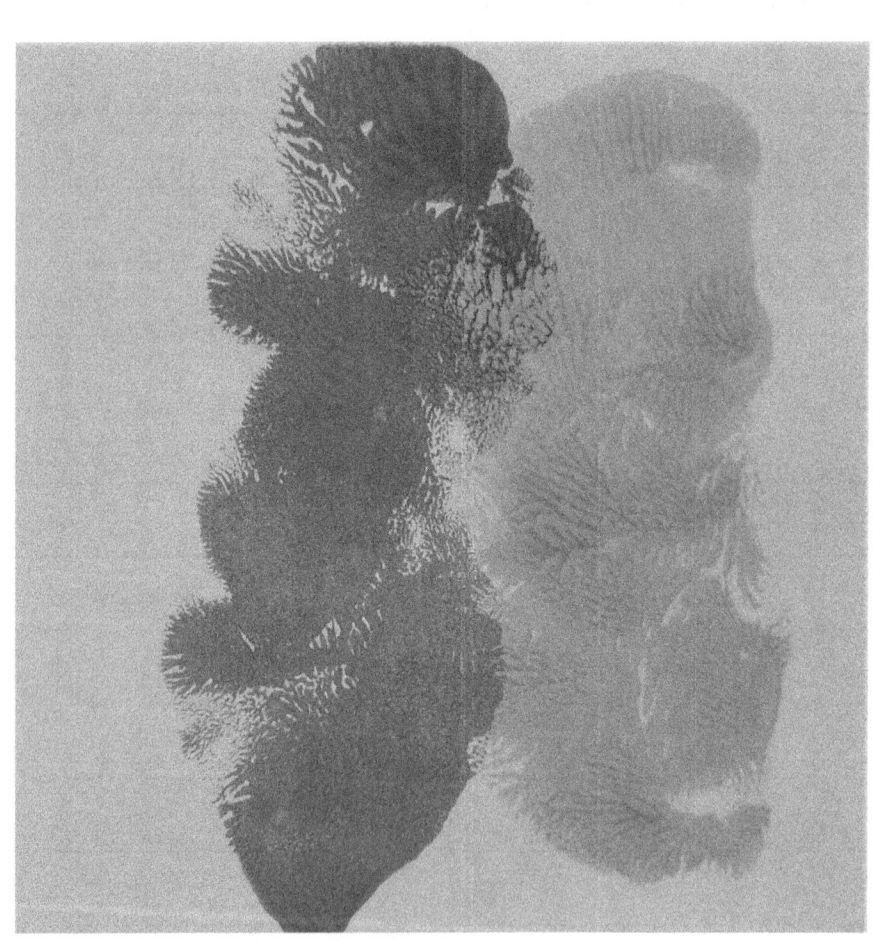

Here is another "inky" treasure created by my great-grandson, Eli. In this masterpiece, he may see a hero and a villain, side-by-side, in one of his comics he enjoys writing. As for me, I see the treasures my little ones used to make for me, whether at school or here at home at play. These were the simple days, the fun days when they would bring out the paint and dab their little hands and feet to make the next artwork that would hang on my refrigerator for the month. Their little fingerprints, all uniquely theirs, created turkeys, Santas, flowers and battle scenes. They had no idea that I treasured these little spontaneous gifts more than any ever bought at a store. Seeing their joy as they handed them to me, and watching their little faces awaiting my excitement was the icing on the cake. Most of those treasures are long since gone, but the memories of little hands showing me love will never fade.

What do you think?

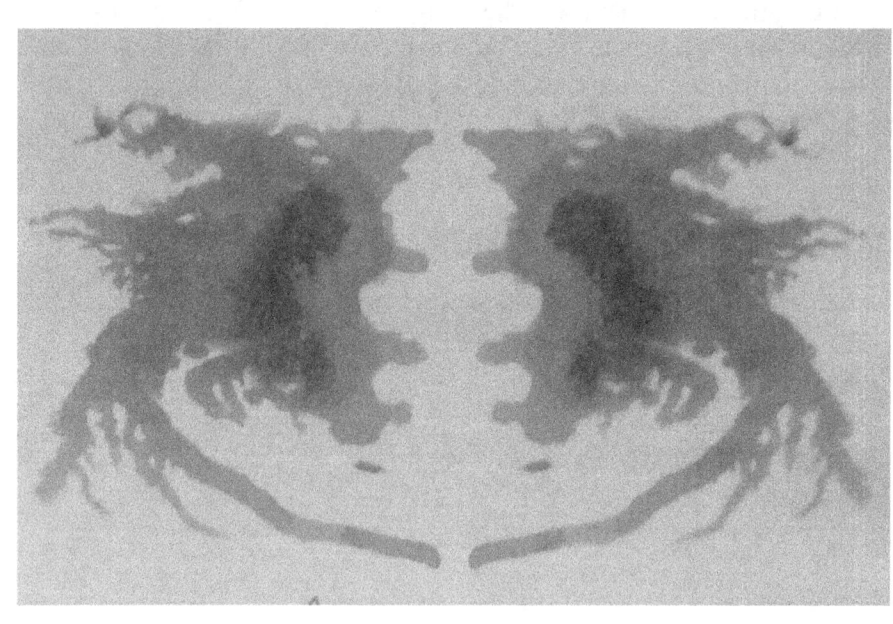

My grandpa used to play chess in the park with all the other grandpas. It was a battle like no other.

What do you think?

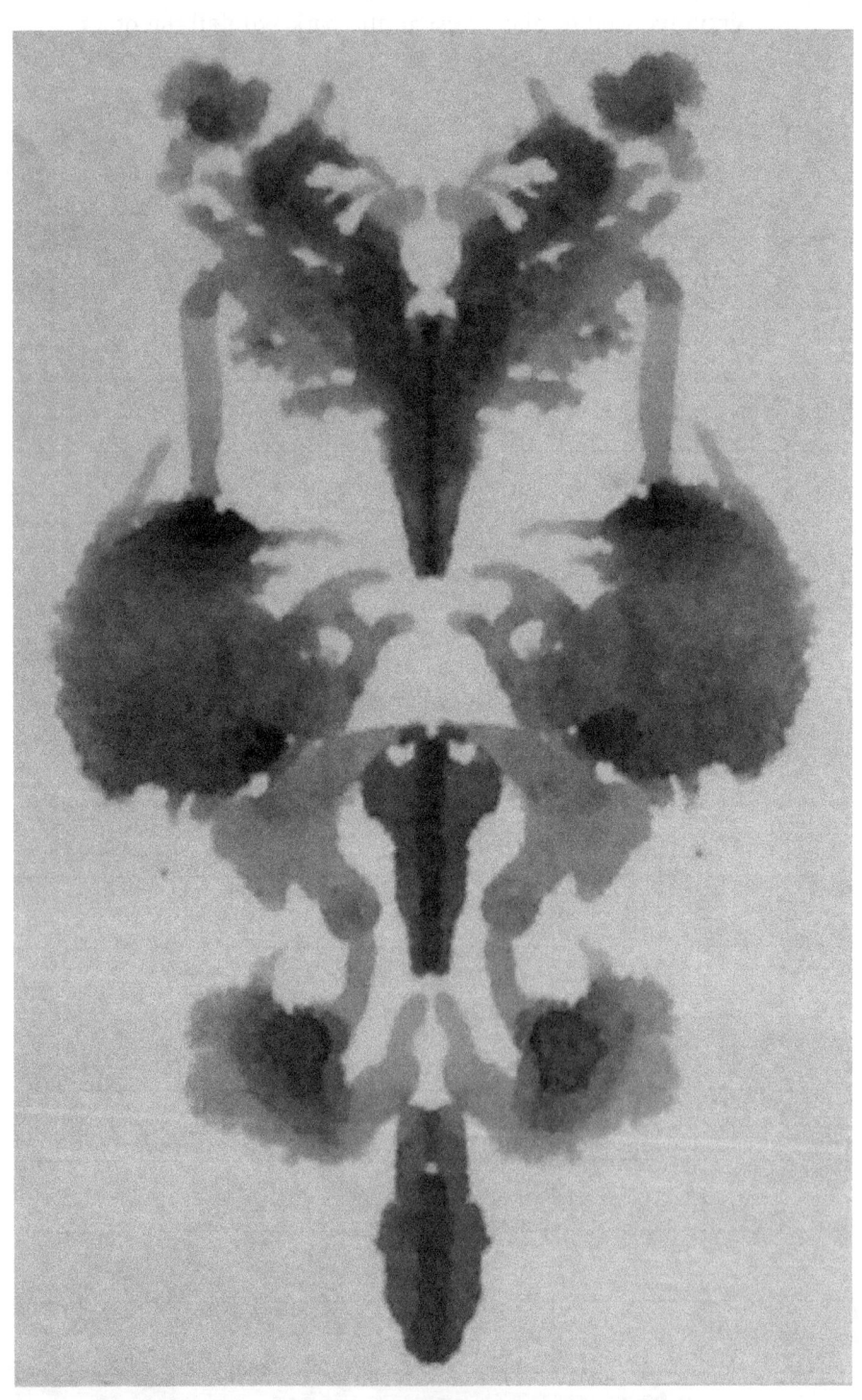

Why do mama birds put worms so deep in the baby's beak?

What do you think?

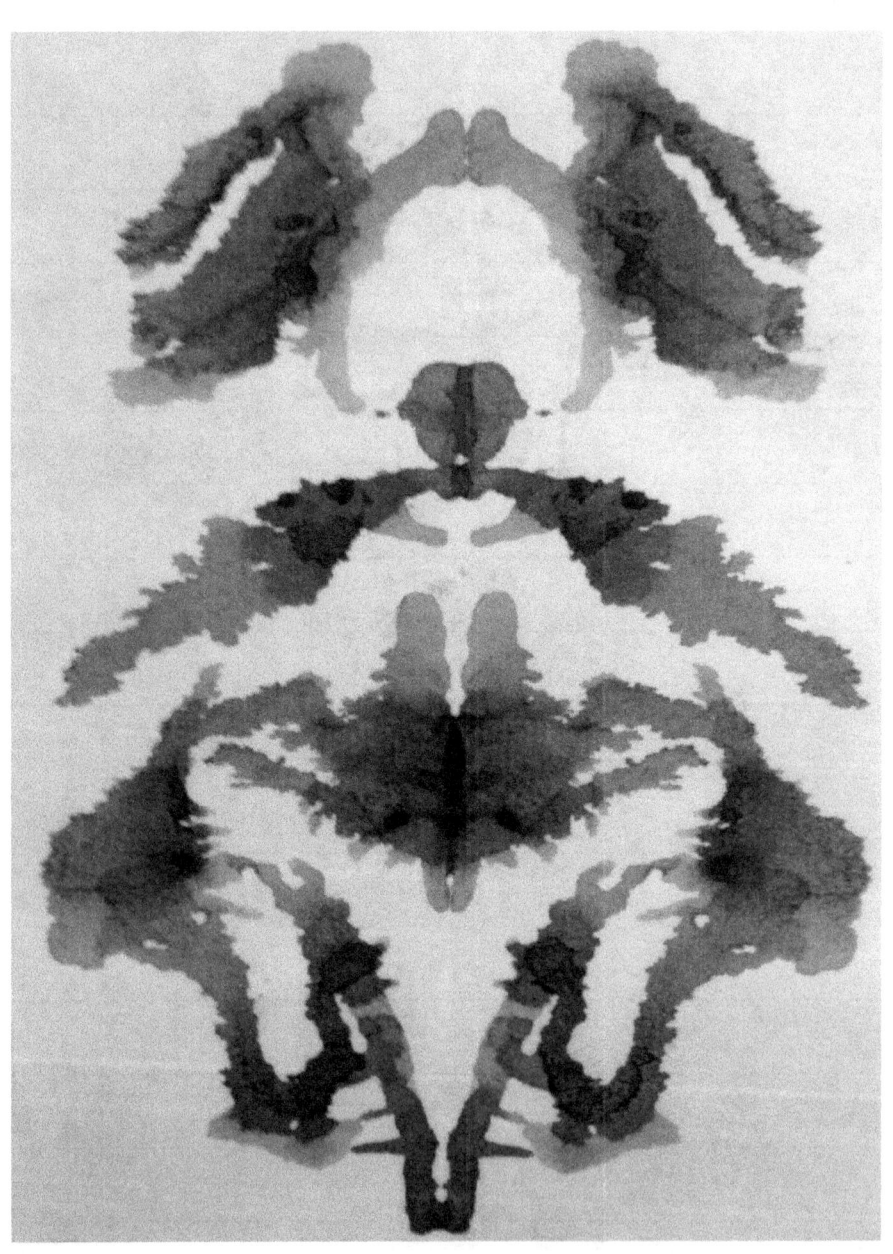

Riding around in the big old orange van was kind of embarrassing for me. It looked like an orange blob coming down the street. To make matters worse mom and dad had installed bright lime-green bucket seats in the front. You definitely could see us coming as we arrived at school each morning.

In our back yard we had two or three dogs at any given time. Exit, the mixed-up breed, Choc Tau, the German Shepherd, and Blue, our Labrador Retriever. Old Blue loved to go for a ride. So every once in awhile mom would show up at school with Blue sitting in the bucket seat observing the world.

Here they came down the road, stopping right in front of me. As I opened the van door, I looked around to see if anyone was watching. I had to beg Blue to get down, take my place in the lime-green bucket seat, and try to look casual. But "old Blue" had a different idea. He needed to see everything that was going on. He climbed into the seat with me, and pushed and leaned, and pushed some more. Soon I was actually standing in the door well, smashed against the window. So much for being casual. "Mom!"

What do you think?

Steam it for two minutes and serve it with butter. Yum Yum.

What do you think?

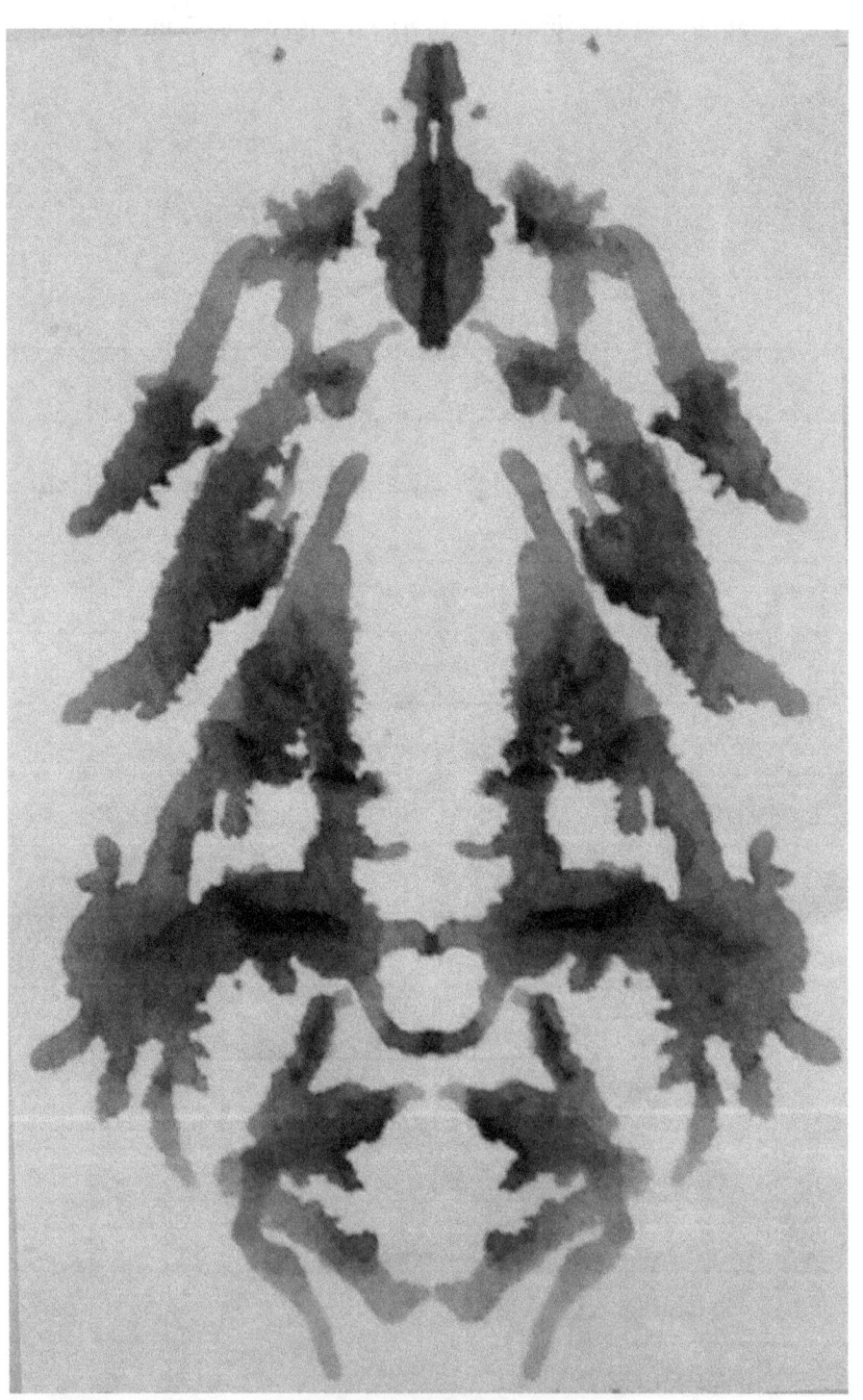

Ink! Ink! What do you think?

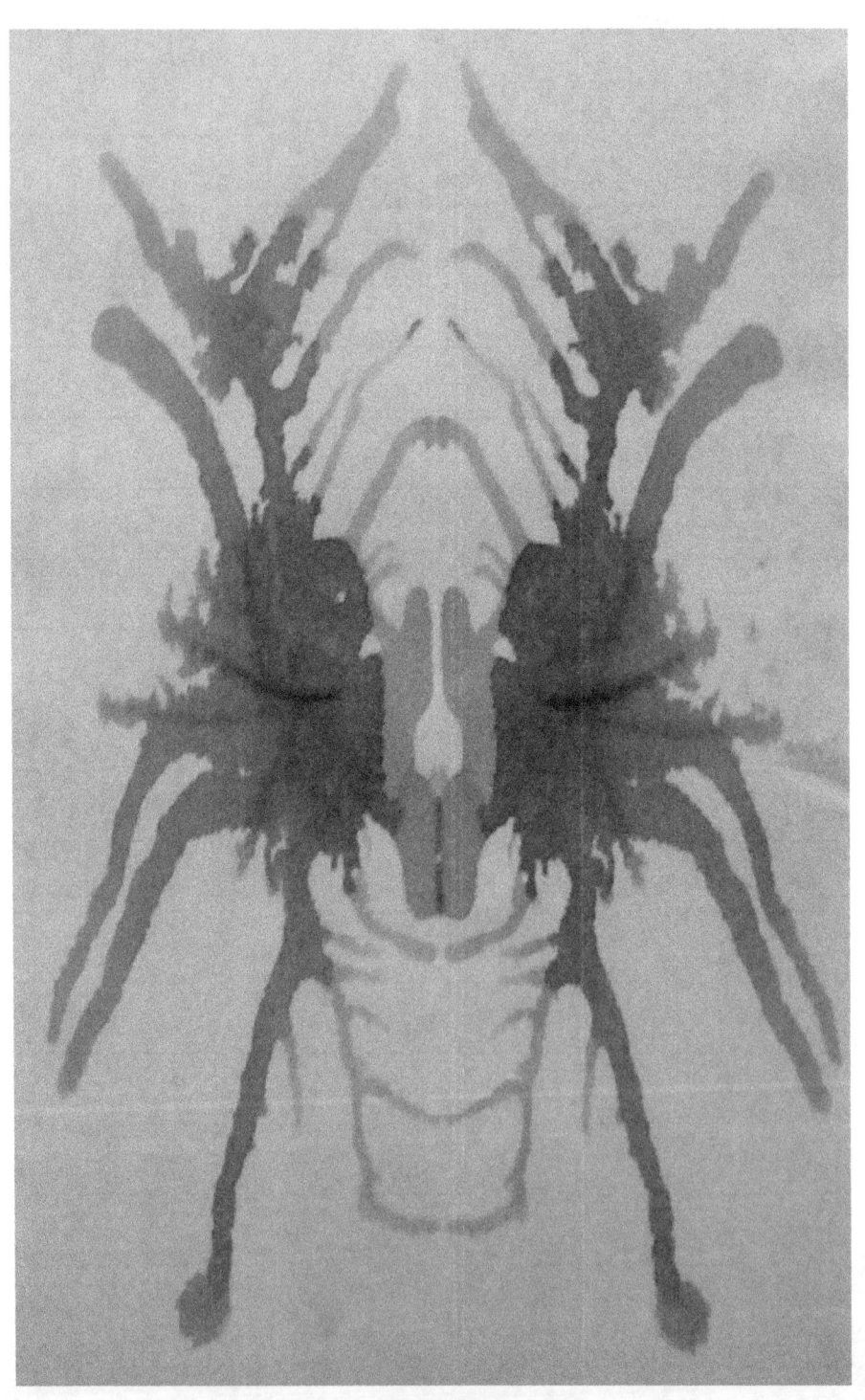

Is there intelligent life on Mars? Is there intelligent life on Earth? What do you think?

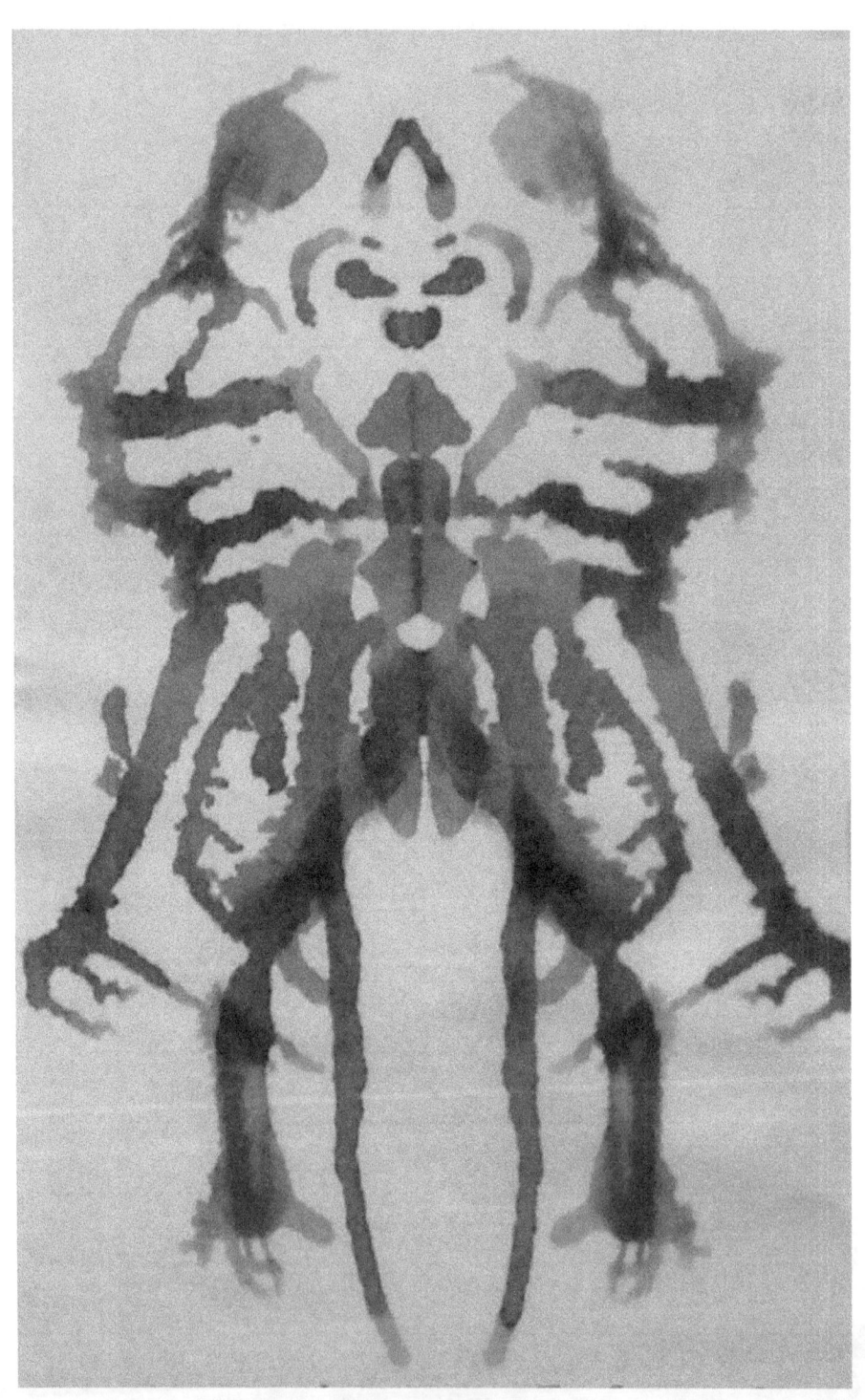

Watch out, this one might reach out and grab you!

What do you think?

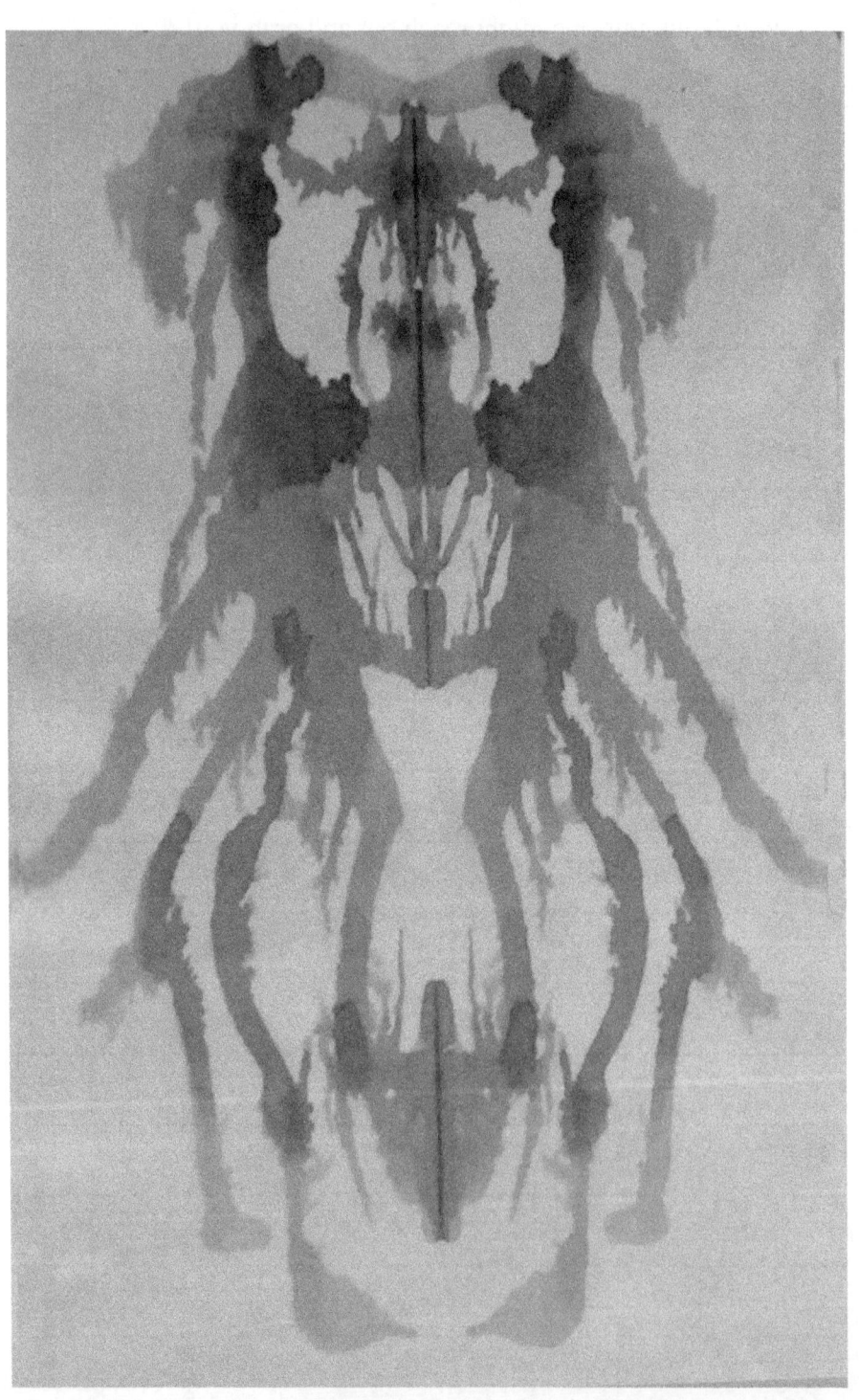

Diving into the beautiful ocean waters is one of her favorite sports. The diving suit and oxygen tank let her sink deeper than she ever had before. She was hoping to find the wreck of the famous ship that sank just off the coast of her homeland. But, she was getting distracted by all the fish wildlife.

What do you think?

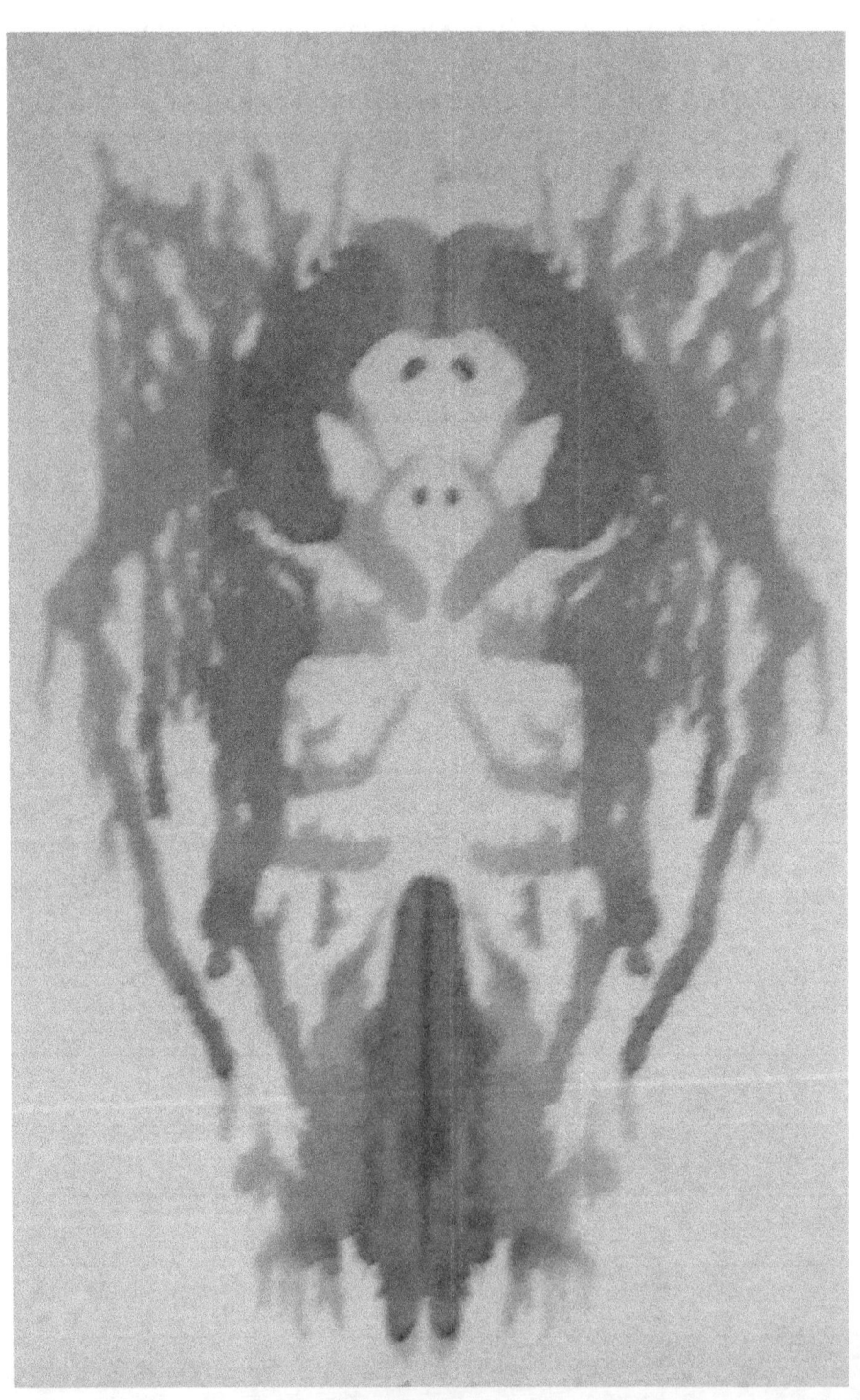

What are you going to dress up for on Halloween? Do you need to wear a wig? I'm thinking about some angel wings.

What do you think?

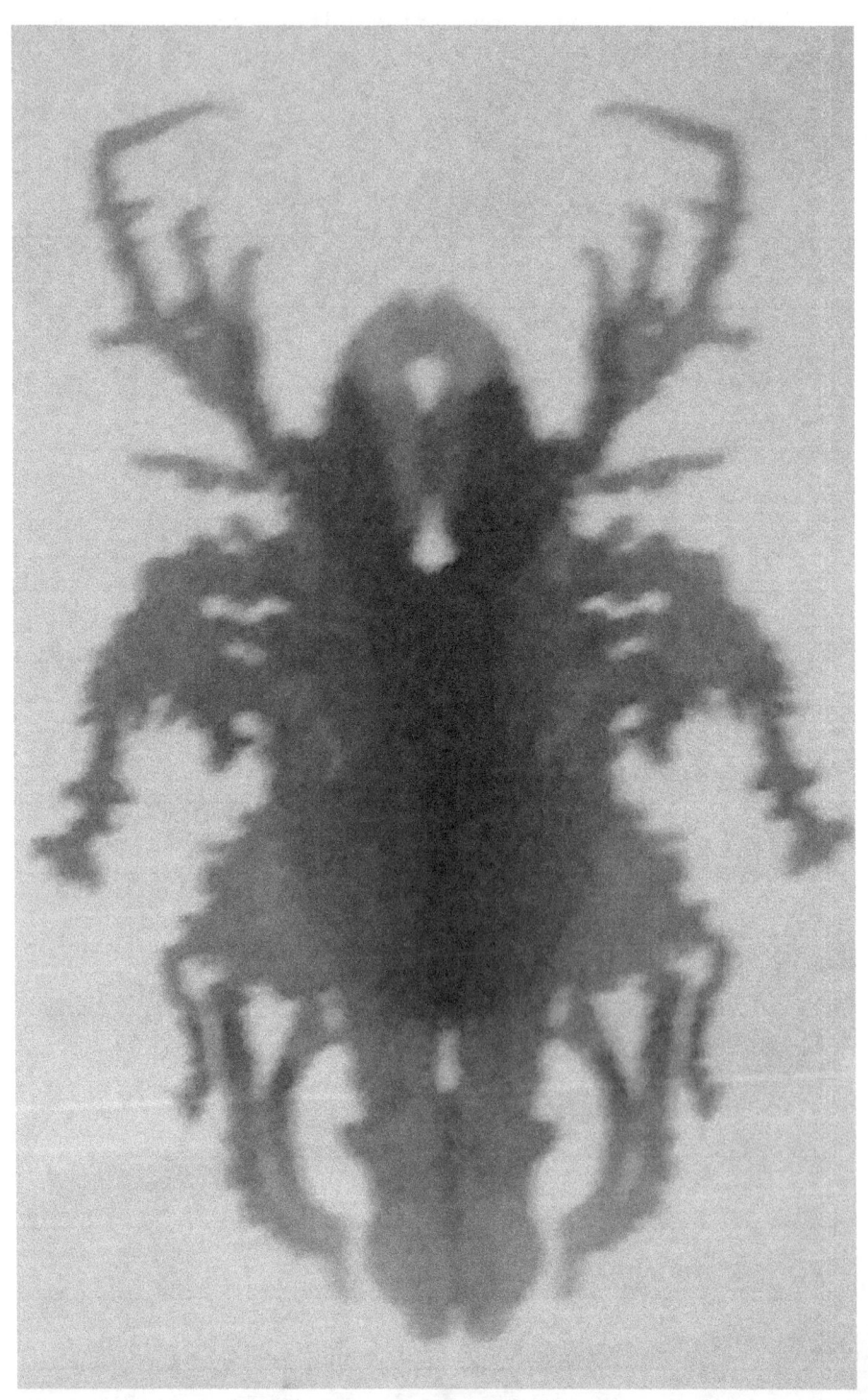

Motorcycle? Moped? or Mo' ideas?

What do you think?

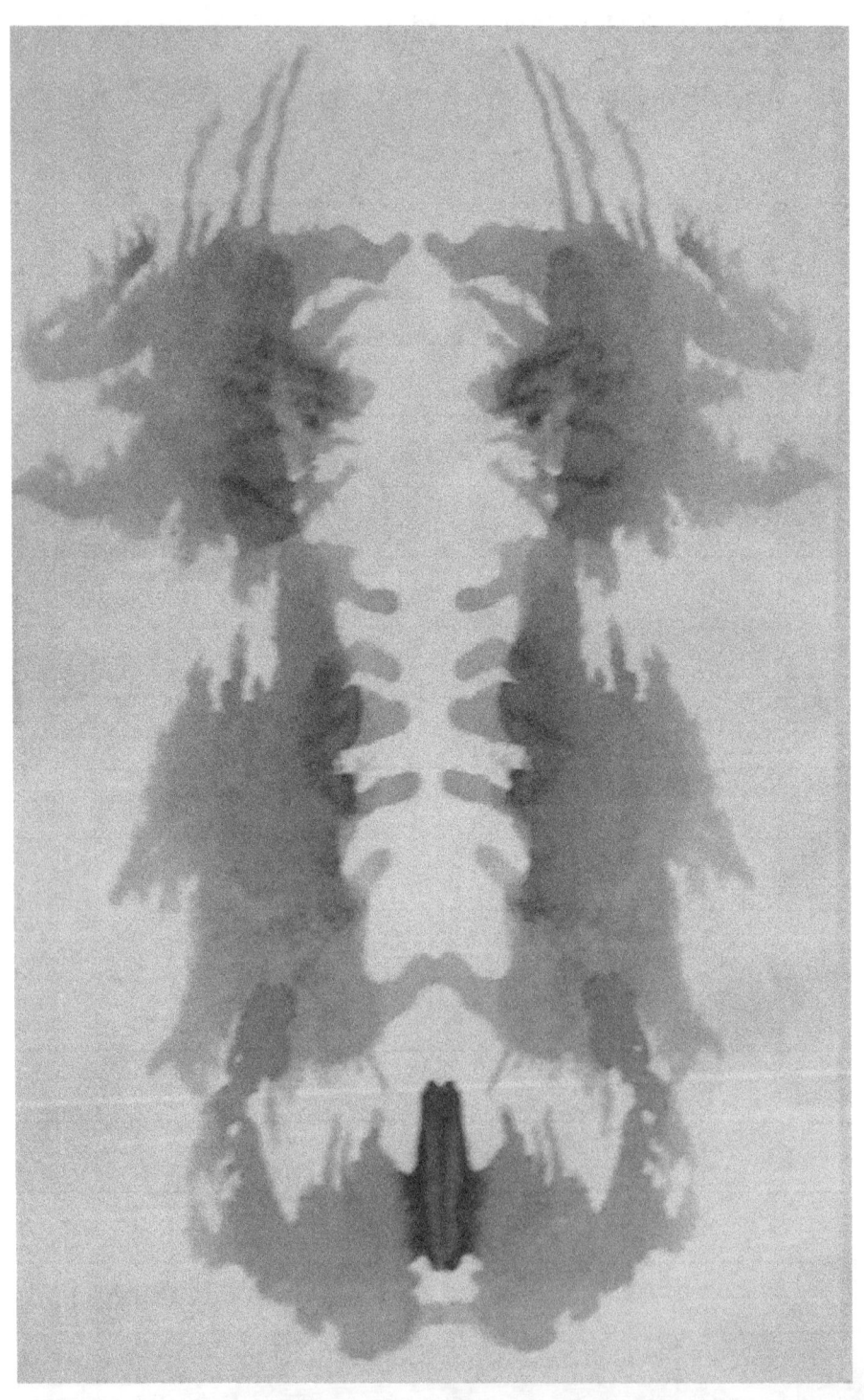

The doctor told him that the X-ray was perfect except for all the chewing gum he swallowed when he were five years old.

What do you think?

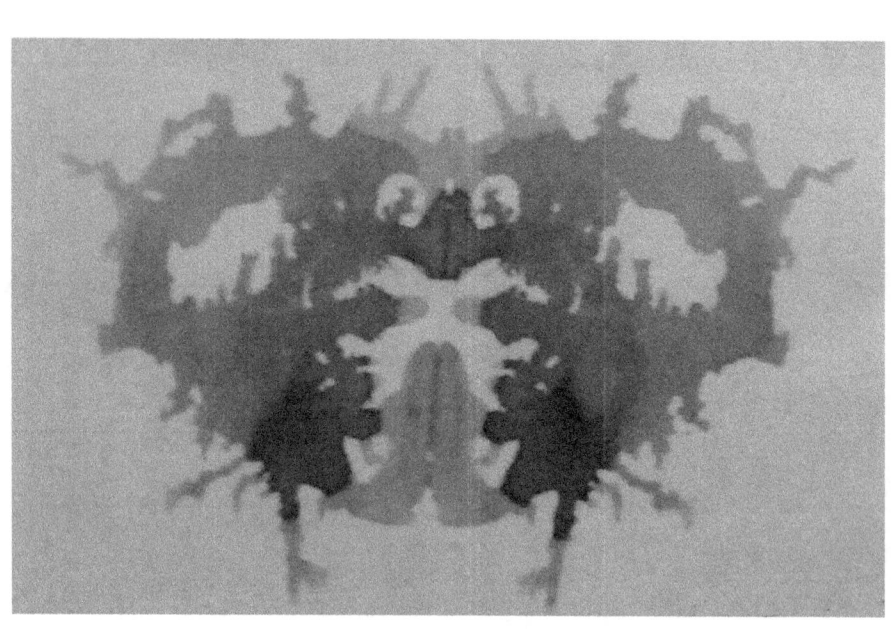

Say your prayers boys, we are jumping out of the plane now!

What do you think?

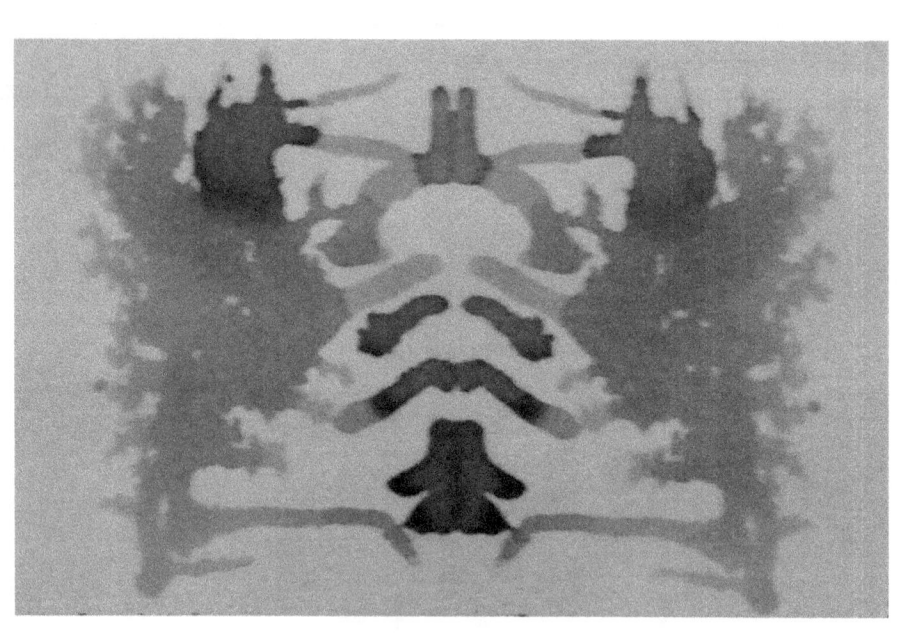

The knights climbed aboard their trusty steeds and entered the arena. They were friends, but they needed to put on a good show for the king. This king liked to see exciting battles. The two knights had to make it look real.

What do you think?

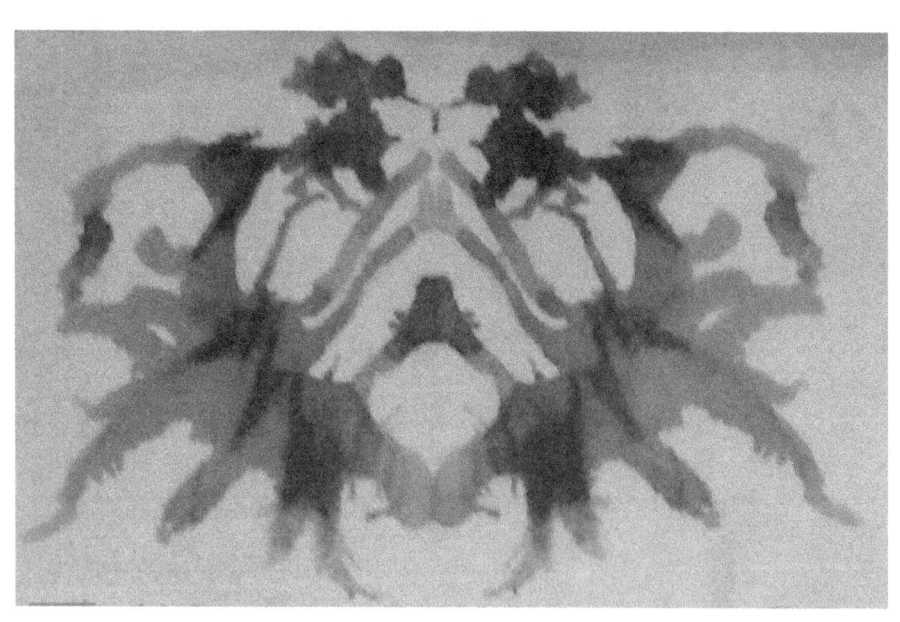

As the music blared in the background, her animal costume was getting heavier and heavier, as the ballerina tried to remember her next move.

What do you think?

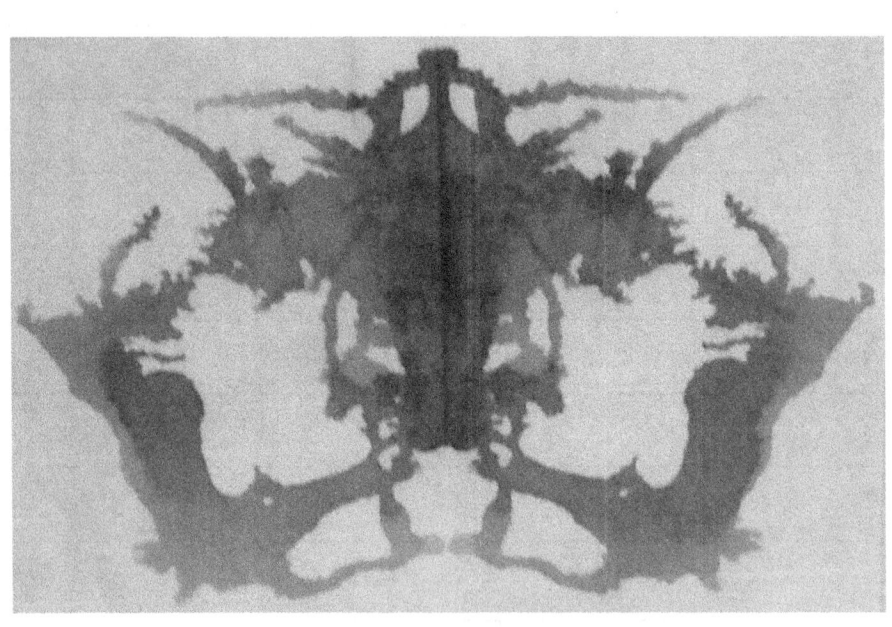

The two seahorses were confused when they tried to follow the fishermen. The fishermen had no idea that they were being followed. If they had known, they might have made it easier for the seahorses. Instead, they were dragging their fishing poles back and forth across the pond.

What do you think?

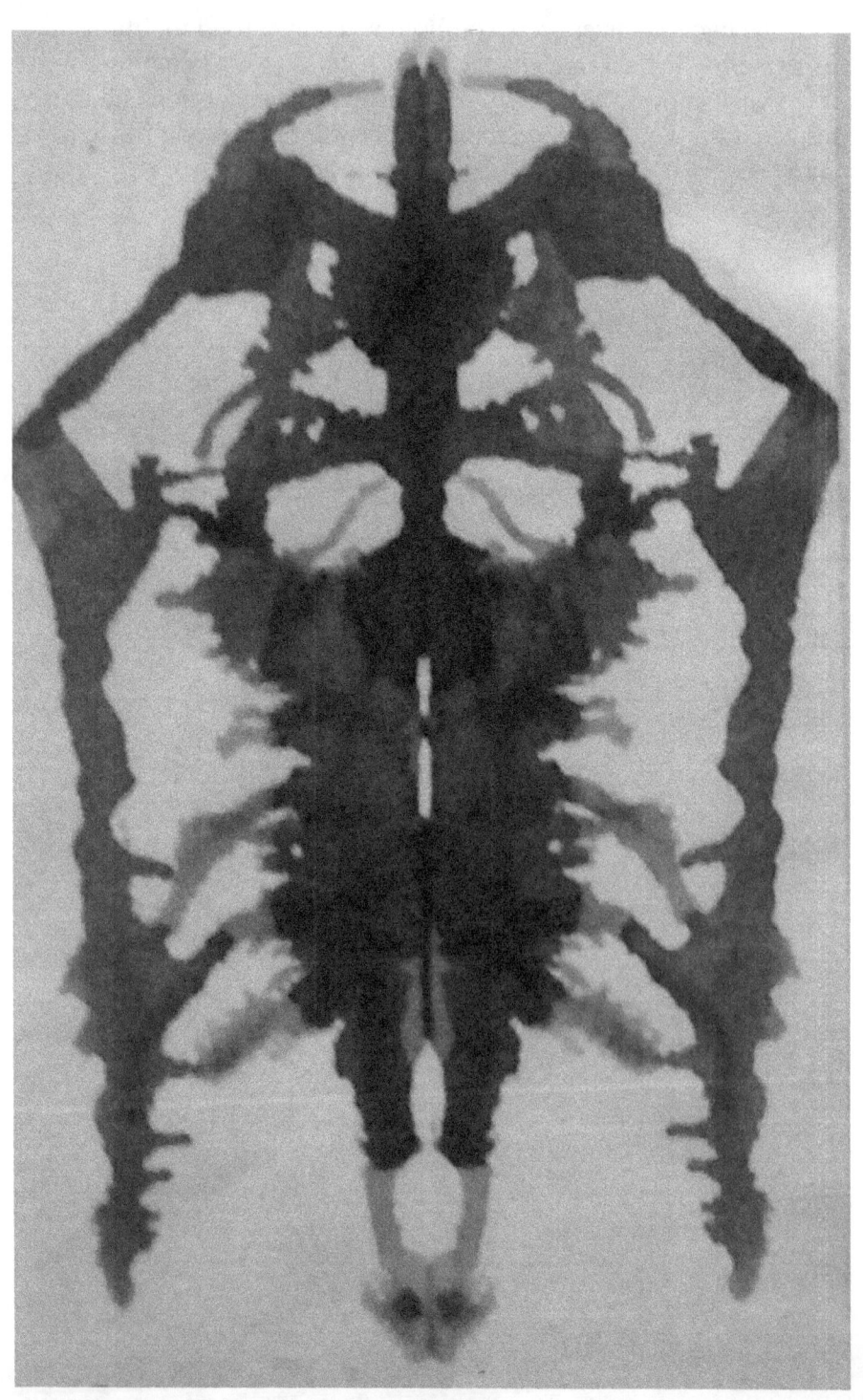

I can get to the bottom of the mountain before you.

What do you think?

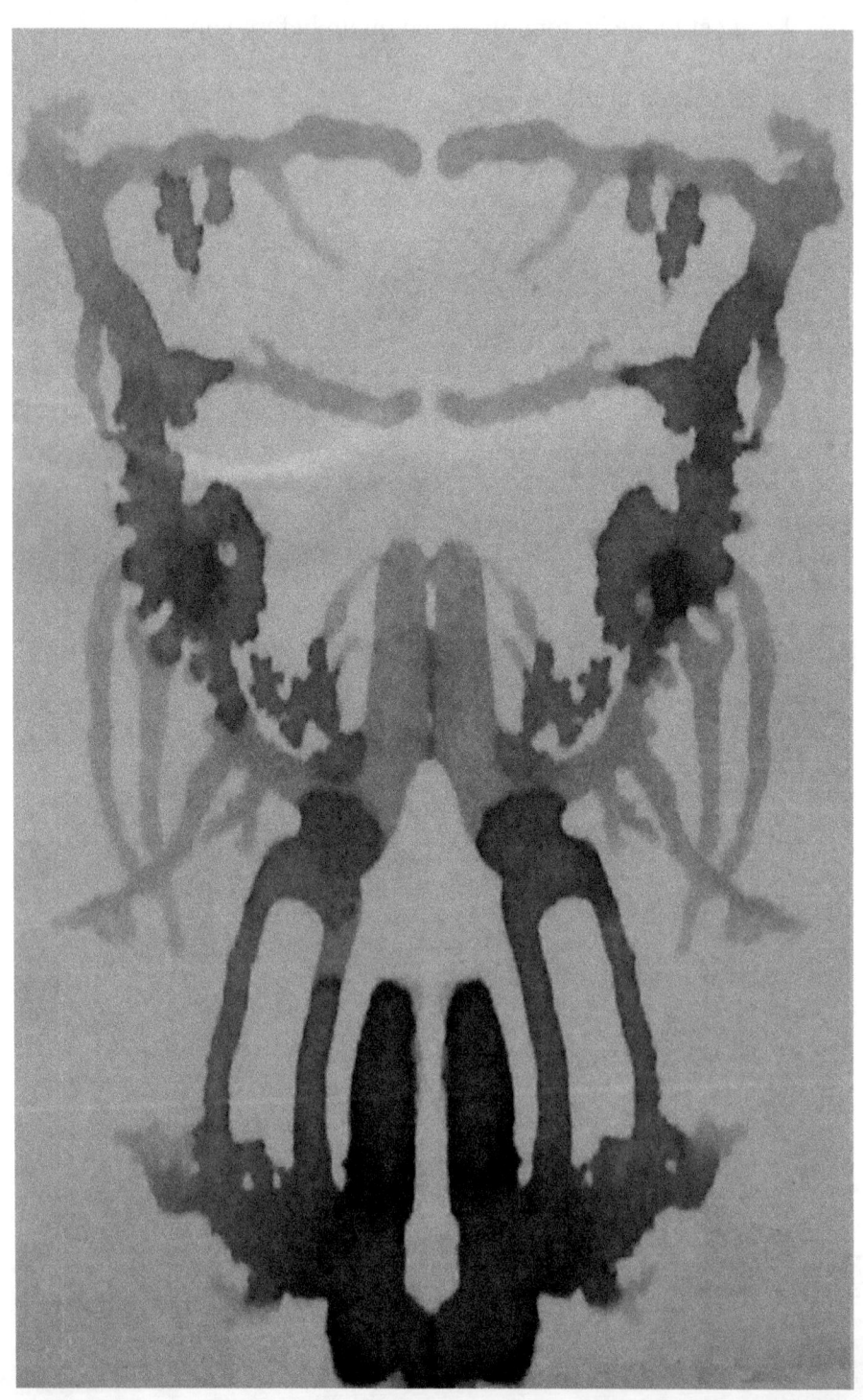

As the two ladies read over their applications, they looked up at each other. Each was wondering if the other would get the job.

What do you think?

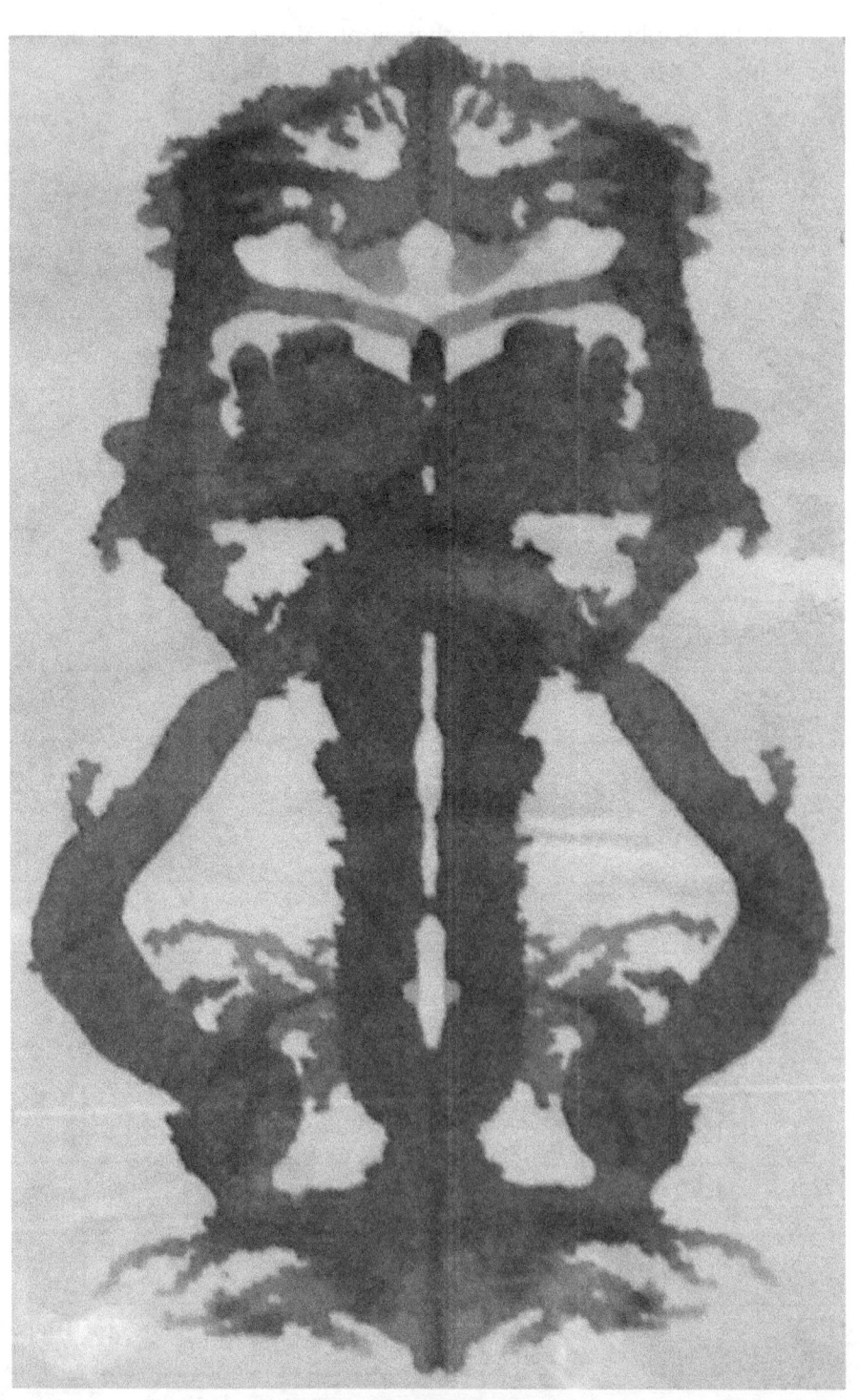

Note from the Author

Well, I hope you enjoyed your trip through this book of inkblots, as much as I enjoyed going through my grandmother's inkblot scrapbooks. Putting this book together was really a joint family operation. First, of course, I am grateful to my grandma Ellen Swedman who faithfully put the inkblots into her scrapbooks for safe keeping; then my daughter, Lisa Engel Moore, whose poetry shows up on a few of these pages and the back cover. She also gets credit for the name INK! INK! WHAT DO YOU THINK? Next there's my great-grandson Eli Webb. At twelve years of age he is an aspiring artist. You will find two of his "style" of inkblots hidden in this book.

I can't forget my publisher, Bethel 1808. They spent many hours making sure my inkblots were set just right. They worked with me patiently, answering questions, pushing me forward when I started lagging, and got me to the finish line. Thank you Bethel 1808.

To schedule a book signing
or speaking engagement,
connect with the author at:

CousinLinnea@gmail.com

For information about this book
contact the publisher at:

Bethel1808.com

www.ingramcontent.com/pod-product-compliance
Lightning Source LLC
LaVergne TN
LVHW051114080426
835510LV00018B/2027